BASIC CHINESE:
A GRAMMAR AND WORKBOOK

'Very well structured and clearly explained'
(Dr Qian Kan, Cambridge University)

Basic Chinese introduces the essentials of Chinese syntax. Each of the 25 units deals with a particular grammatical point and provides associated exercises. Features include:

• clear, accessible format
• many useful language examples
• jargon-free explanations of grammar
• ample drills and exercises
• full key to exercises

All Chinese entries are presented in both *pinyin* romanization and Chinese characters, and are accompanied, in most cases, by English translations to facilitate self-tuition in both spoken and written Chinese.

Basic Chinese is designed for students new to the language. Together with its sister volume, *Intermediate Chinese*, it forms a compendium of the essentials of Chinese syntax.

Yip Po-Ching is Lecturer in Chinese Studies at the University of Leeds and **Don Rimmington** is Emeritus Professor of East Asian Studies and former head of the East Asian Studies Department at the University of Leeds. They are the authors of *Chinese: An Essential Grammar* (1996), and *Intermediate Chinese: A Grammar and Workbook* (1998).

Titles of related interest published by Routledge:

Basic Chinese: A Grammar and Workbook
by Yip Po-Ching and Don Rimmington

Intermediate Chinese: A Grammar and Workbook
by Yip Po-Ching and Don Rimmington

Chinese: An Essential Grammar
by Yip Po-Ching and Don Rimmington

Colloquial Chinese: A Complete Language Course
by Kan Qian

Colloquial Chinese CD-ROM
by Kan Qian

Colloquial Chinese (Reprint of the first edition)
by Ping-Cheng T'ung and David E. Pollard

The Chinese Lexicon
by Yip Po-Ching

Basic Cantonese: A Grammar and Workbook
by Virginia Yip and Stephen Matthews

Intermediate Cantonese: A Grammar and Workbook
by Virginia Yip and Stephen Matthews

Cantonese: A Comprehensive Grammar
by Stephen Matthews and Virginia Yip

Colloquial Cantonese: A Complete Language Course
by Keith S. T. Tong and Gregory James

BASIC CHINESE:
A GRAMMAR AND
WORKBOOK

Yip Po-Ching and Don Rimmington
with Zhang Xiaoming and Rachel Henson

London and New York

First published 1998 by Routledge
11 New Fetter Lane, London EC4P 4EE

Simultaneously published in the USA and Canada
by Routledge
29 West 35th Street, New York, NY 10001

Reprinted in 1999, 2000

Routledge is an imprint of the Taylor & Francis Group

© 1998 Yip Po-Ching and Don Rimmington

Typeset in Times by Graphicraft Limited, Hong Kong
Printed and bound in Great Britain by TJ International Ltd, Padstow, Cornwall

British Library Cataloguing in Publication Data
A catalogue record for this book is available from the British Library

Library of Congress Cataloguing in Publication Data
Yip, Po-Ching, 1935–
    Basic Chinese :   a grammar and workbook   /   Yip Po-Ching and Don
  Rimmington.
        p.   cm.
    Includes bibliographical references and index.
    ISBN 0–415–16036–7 (alk. paper). — ISBN 0–415–16037–5 (pbk. :
  alk. paper)
    1. Chinese language—Grammar.   2. Chinese language—Syntax.
  3. Chinese language—Textbooks for foreign speakers—English.
  I. Rimmington, Don.   II. Title.
  PL1111.Y56   1998
  495.1′82421—dc21   97–46475
                                                           CIP

ISBN 0–415–16036–7 (hbk)
ISBN 0–415–16037–5 (pbk)

CONTENTS

INTRODUCTION

This book is designed to assist learners of Mandarin or Modern Standard Chinese, which is the language spoken by close on 70 per cent of the people of China. It presents the essential features of Chinese syntax in an easily accessible reference-and-practice format. We hope that it will be helpful both to beginners and to more advanced students of the language and we envisage that it will be suitable for classroom and for self-tuition use, as well as reference purposes.

The book sets forth most of the basic elements of Chinese syntax, dealing with simple sentences and the main grammatical categories. The material is laid out over 25 units, and is introduced on a graded basis with more elementary items in the early units and more complex patterns in the later sections.

Each unit deals with an individual language category or structure, and provides follow-up exercises for immediate reinforcement. A key to the exercises is given at the end of the book. Readers may wish to consult the units separately or work progressively through the book, but we suggest that, when going through a particular unit, they attempt all the exercises in it, before consulting the key.

Practical, functional vocabulary is used in the grammatical explanations and the exercises and is introduced as far as possible on a cumulative basis. All illustrative examples throughout the book are given in Chinese script and *pinyin* romanization, with English translations.

Students interested in pursuing their practical study of the Chinese language to a higher level should consult the companion volume to this book, *Intermediate Chinese: A Grammar and Workbook*.

The preparation of the book received financial assistance from the University of Leeds Academic Development Fund. Two Research Assistants, Ms Zhang Xiaoming and Ms Rachel Henson carried out much of the important work of assembling the illustrative material. The project could also not have been completed without the painstaking efforts of Ms Li Quzhen, who closely monitored the vocabulary progression and proof-read the text. Any errors or omissions are, of course, the fault of the authors.

Note: We have used 'a' rather than 'ɑ', which is the standard form in *pinyin* romanisation.

UNIT ONE
Nouns: singular and plural

A   In Chinese, as in other languages, nouns may be differentiated into a number of categories. The largest category is the common noun, which covers tangible, discrete entities, e.g. 大人 **dàrén** adult, 树 **shù** tree, etc. The common noun is the main focus of this unit, but other noun categories are:

  (i) proper noun (for one individual entity):
      e.g. 中国 **zhōngguó** China, 李明 **lǐ míng** Li Ming (name of a person)
 (ii) material noun (for non-discrete entities):
      e.g. 铁 **tiě** iron, 茶 **chá** tea
(iii) abstract noun (for non-tangible entities):
      e.g. 文化 **wénhuà** culture, 经济 **jīngjì** economy

B   Chinese common nouns, unlike English ones, make no distinction in form between singular and plural:

苹果	**píngguǒ**	apple/apples
孩子	**háizi**	child/children
一个苹果	**yī gè píngguǒ**	an/one apple
两个苹果	**liǎng gè píngguǒ**	two apples
一个孩子	**yī gè háizi**	a/one child
两个孩子	**liǎng gè háizi**	two children

C   Another important feature of the common noun in Chinese is that when it is used with a numeral, the numeral has to have a measure word between it and the noun (see also Unit 6). 个 **gè** is by far the most common measure word and it can occur with a wide range of nouns:

一个人	**yī gè rén**	a/one person
两个学生	**liǎng gè xuésheng**	two students
三个面包	**sān gè miànbāo**	three loaves of bread
四个橙子	**sì gè chéngzi**	four oranges
五个鸡蛋	**wǔ gè jīdàn**	five eggs

六个城市	**liù gè chéngshì**	six cities
七个国家	**qī gè guójiā**	seven countries
八个商店	**bā gè shāngdiàn**	eight shops
九个男孩子	**jiǔ gè nán háizi**	nine boys
十个女孩子	**shí gè nǚ háizi**	ten girls

A considerable number of nouns or sets of nouns are linked with particular measure words:

一本书	**yī běn shū**	a/one book
一支笔	**yī zhī bǐ**	a/one pen
一把牙刷	**yī bǎ yáshuā**	a/one toothbrush

Some measure words are similar to English measures:

| 两片面包 | **liǎng piàn miànbāo** | two slices of bread |
| 一块蛋糕 | **yī kuài dàngāo** | a piece of cake |

Measure words are also used with abstract and material nouns:

一个建议	**yī gè jiànyì**	a suggestion	(abstract)
一个借口	**yī gè jièkǒu**	an excuse	(abstract)
一个理想	**yī gè lǐxiǎng**	an ambition/ideal	(abstract)
一杯咖啡	**yī bēi kāfēi**	a cup of coffee	(material)
一张纸	**yī zhāng zhǐ**	a piece of paper	(material)
一块布	**yī kuài bù**	a piece of cloth	(material)

Note 1: Notice that with 一 **yī** you distinguish between 'a/an' and 'one' in speech by the degree of emphasis given to it. The phrase 一个杯子 **yī gè bēizi**, for example, may mean 'one mug' if 一 **yī** is stressed and 'a mug' if 一 **yī** is not stressed. In the latter meaning 一 **yī** can be omitted altogether if it comes after a verb. The distinction is illustrated in the following exchanges:

你去哪儿？ **nǐ qù nǎr**
Where are you going?

我想去商店买(一)个杯子。 **wǒ xiǎng qù shāngdiàn mǎi (yī) gè bēizi** (一 **yī** is unstressed)
I'm going to the shop to buy a mug.

你要买几个杯子？ **nǐ yào mǎi jǐ gè bēizi**
How many mugs do you want to buy?

我只要买一个杯子。 **wǒ zhǐ yào mǎi yī gè bēizi** (一 **yī** is stressed)
I only want to buy one mug.

Note 2: In Chinese 杯子 **bēizi** may mean 'cup' or even 'glass' as well as 'mug'.

Note 3: 想 **xiǎng** and 要 **yào** are both modal verbs, i.e. verbs which precede main verbs to indicate the mood or attitude of the subject (see Unit 17). While 想 **xiǎng** emphasizes 'plan' or 'inclination', 要 **yào** indicates 'wish' or 'will'. They may generally be used interchangeably.

D   It is possible to pluralize human nouns by adding the suffix 们 **men**. The suffixed noun undergoes two changes:

(i) A noun with 们 **men** suffix becomes definite in reference:

学生们进来了	**xuéshengmen jìn lái le**	*The* students came in.
朋友们 . . .	**péngyoumen . . .**	Friends . . . (as in addressing a particular audience)

One cannot say:

*谁是学生们？	**shéi shì xuéshengmen**	(*lit.* Which of you are students?)
*我想交朋友们	**wǒ xiǎng jiāo péngyoumen**	(*lit.* I want to make friends.)

Note: 人们 **rénmen** is an exception. It means 'people' in an indefinite sense:

人们说 . . .   **rénmen shuō** . . .   people say . . . / they say . . .

(ii) A noun with 们 **men** suffix is incompatible with a 'numeral + measure word' phrase:

One cannot say:

*三个工程师们	**sān gè gōngchéngshīmen**	(*lit.* three engineers)
*九个孩子们	**jiǔ gè háizimen**	(*lit.* nine children)

Note: 们 **men** is an in-built element in plural personal pronouns (see also Unit 3):

我们	**wǒmen**	we/us		你们	**nǐmen**	you (plural)
他们	**tāmen**	they/them (masculine or common)		她们	**tāmen**	they/them (feminine)

It is not possible to pluralize non-human nouns with the suffix 们 **men**:

*狗们	**gǒumen**	(*lit.* dogs)
*杯子们	**bēizimen**	(*lit.* cups/glasses/mugs)

E   Nouns or noun phrases (e.g. 'numeral + measure word + noun') may be linked together by the conjunction 和 **hé** 'and':

笔和纸 **bǐ hé zhǐ**
pens and paper

男孩子和女孩子 **nán háizi hé nǚ háizi**
boys and girls

三个蛋糕和四个面包 **sān gè dàngāo hé sì gè miànbāo**
three cakes and four loaves of bread

他有两本书和一支笔。 **tā yǒu liǎng běn shū hé yī zhī bǐ**
He has two books and one pen.

我要吃两片面包、一个鸡蛋和一块蛋糕。
wǒ yào chī liǎng piàn miànbāo | yī gè jīdàn hé yī kuài dàngāo
I want to eat two slices of bread, an egg and a piece of cake.

Note: The ' 、 ' dun-comma, seen in this last example, is peculiar to Chinese punctuation and is used for listing items in a series:

她想买四个苹果、三个橙子、两个面包和一打鸡蛋。
tā xiǎng mǎi sì gè píngguǒ | sān gè chéngzi | liǎng gè miànbāo hé yī dá jīdàn
She would like to buy four apples, three oranges, two loaves of bread and a dozen eggs.

Exercise 1.1

Translate the following phrases into Chinese:

1 a child	9 two suggestions	17 two pens
2 one child	10 six countries	18 ten cups
3 two children	11 eight shops	19 two cups of tea
4 three oranges	12 nine students	20 three books
5 a dozen eggs	13 seven engineers	21 four adults
6 four loaves of bread	14 a friend	22 six pieces of paper
7 five slices of bread	15 a person	23 a cake
8 a city	16 one mug	24 a piece of cake

Exercise 1.2

Decide on the emphasis given to 一 **yī** in the sentences below by putting brackets round the 一 where it may be omitted:

1 我们交一个朋友吧！	**wǒmen jiāo yī gè péngyou ba**	Let's be friends!
2 我想买一打鸡蛋。	**wǒ xiǎng mǎi yī dá jīdàn**	I want to buy a dozen eggs.
3 他只是一个学生。	**tā zhǐ shì yī gè xuésheng**	He is only a student.
4 我想吃一个橙子。	**wǒ xiǎng chī yī gè chéngzi**	I want to eat an orange.

5 我们有一个建议。	**wǒmen yǒu yī gè jiànyì**	We have a suggestion.
6 我只想去一个国家。	**wǒ zhǐ xiǎng qù yī gè guójiā**	I only want to go to one country.
7 我要去买一把牙刷。	**wǒ yào qù mǎi yī bǎ yáshuā**	I want to go and buy a toothbrush.
8 她只有一个孩子。	**tā zhǐ yǒu yī gè háizi**	She only has one child.

Note: 吧 **ba** is a sentence particle for a tentative request (see Unit 20).

Exercise 1.3

Decide which of the following sentences are incorrect and make the necessary corrections:

1 我碰见两个朋友们。 **wǒ pèng jiàn liǎng gè péngyoumen**
   (碰见 **pèng jiàn** 'to bump into')
   I bumped into two friends.
2 他想找一借口。 **tā xiǎng zhǎo yī jièkǒu** (找 **zhǎo** 'to find')
   He wanted to find an excuse.
3 孩子们要吃苹果们。 **háizimen yào chī píngguǒmen**
   The children wanted to eat apples.
4 他们想去三国家。 **tāmen xiǎng qù sān guójiā**
   They would like to visit three countries.
5 我想喝杯茶。 **wǒ xiǎng hē bēi chá** (喝 **hē** 'to drink')
   I would like to have a cup of tea.
6 她有中国朋友们。 **tā yǒu zhōngguó péngyoumen**
   She has Chinese friends.
7 你要吃几面包？ **nǐ yào chī jǐ miànbāo**
   How many slices of bread would you like to eat?
8 谁要买鸡蛋？ **shuí/shéi yào mǎi jīdàn**
   Who wants to buy eggs?

Exercise 1.4

Translate the sentences below into English:

1 你要买几个面包？	**nǐ yào mǎi jǐ gè miànbāo**
2 她想吃两块蛋糕。	**tā xiǎng chī liǎng kuài dàngāo**
3 我碰见三个中国人。	**wǒ pèng jiàn sān gè zhōngguó rén**
4 我要喝杯咖啡。	**wǒ yào hē bēi kāfēi**
5 我想去五个国家。	**wǒ xiǎng qù wǔ gè guójiā**
6 她是一个工程师。	**tā shì yī gè gōngchéngshī**
7 我有两个孩子。	**wǒ yǒu liǎng gè háizi**

8　我只想去一个城市。　　**wǒ zhǐ xiǎng qù yī gè chéngshì**
9　谁想买书？　　　　　　**shuí/shéi xiǎng mǎi shū**
10　我有个建议。　　　　　**wǒ yǒu gè jiànyì**

Exercise 1.5

Translate the following phrases and sentences into Chinese. Don't forget to use the dun-comma where necessary.

1　apples and oranges
2　adults and children
3　three slices of bread, a cup of coffee and a piece of cake
4　four books and six pens
5　I would like to visit three countries.
6　I would like to have a cup of tea.
7　She only wants to go to two shops.
8　She wants to buy a loaf of bread, two cakes, five apples and a dozen eggs.
9　The child has only one ambition.
10　I bumped into three Chinese friends.

UNIT TWO
Definite and indefinite reference and demonstratives

A   There are no definite or indefinite articles 'the/a(n)' in Chinese. Definite or indefinite reference is commonly indicated by the positioning of the noun in the sentence. Generally speaking, a noun placed before the verb will be of definite reference, while a noun placed after the verb will be of indefinite reference.

Definite reference:

> 笔在那儿。 **bǐ zài nàr** *The* pen(s) are there.
> (笔 **bǐ** 'pen' is positioned before the verb 在 **zài** 'be in/at'.)

Indefinite reference:

> 哪儿有笔？ **nǎr yǒu bǐ** Where is there *a* pen?/Where are there *some* pens?
> (笔 **bǐ** 'pen' is positioned after the verb 有 **yǒu** 'exist'.)

If a noun is moved from after the verb to the beginning of the sentence, thereby becoming the topic of the sentence, it will take on definite reference. Consider the meaning of 花儿 **huār** in the following sentences:

> 你买了花儿没有？ **nǐ mǎi le huār méiyǒu**
> Have you bought *any* flowers? (*lit.* you have bought flowers or not)

> 花儿你买了没有？ **huār nǐ mǎi le méiyǒu**
> Have you bought *the* flowers? (*lit.* flowers you have bought or not)

Note: 了 **le** in the above examples is an aspect marker which is used as a suffix to a verb to indicate completed action (see Unit 15) and 没有 **méiyǒu** negates completed action (see Unit 16). They occur here in the affirmative-negative form of question (See Unit 18).

B   A noun at the beginning of a sentence may, however, be of indefinite reference if the speaker is making a general comment rather than narrating an event or incident. The comment in a topic-comment sentence, as we shall see, usually consists of an adjective, the verb 是 **shì** 'to be', a modal verb or a verb that indicates a habitual action:

香蕉很好吃。	**xiāngjiāo hěn hǎochī**	Bananas are delicious.	(adjective)
橙子不是蔬菜。	**chéngzi bù shì shūcài**	Oranges are not vegetables.	(verb 是 **shì** 'to be')
猫会抓老鼠。	**māo huì zhuā lǎoshǔ**	Cats can catch mice.	(modal verb)
马吃草。	**mǎ chī cǎo**	Horses eat grass.	(verb that indicates a habitual action)

In the above examples, 香蕉 **xiāngjiāo** 'bananas', 橙子 **chéngzi** 'oranges', 猫 **māo** 'cats' and 马 **mǎ** 'horses', as topics to be commented on, are of indefinite reference, in spite of the fact they are placed before the verb.

On the other hand, if the noun before the verb is modified by a 'numeral (other than 一 **yī** "one") + measure word' phrase, it may still be regarded as of definite reference, particularly when 都 **dōu** is present to refer to the plurality of the subject:

三个孩子都上学。 **sān gè háizi dōu shàngxué**
All the three children go to school. (*lit.* three children all go to school)

两件毛衣都在柜子里。 **liǎng jiàn máoyī dōu zài guìzi li**
Both of the jumpers are in the wardrobe.
(*lit.* two jumpers are both in the wardrobe)

Note: 柜子 **guìzi** is a general term in Chinese which may mean 'wardrobe', 'cabinet', 'cupboard', etc. depending on the context.

C   A noun before the verb may also take on indefinite reference if it is preceded by 有 **yǒu** 'exist':

有人找你。 **yǒu rén zhǎo nǐ**
There is someone looking for you.

有毛衣在柜子里。 **yǒu máoyī zài guìzi li**
There is a sweater/there are (some) sweaters in the wardrobe.

In these sentences with 有 **yǒu** a numeral or an expression such as (一)些 **(yī)xiē** 'some' or 几 **jǐ** + measure 'a few' may be used with the noun:

有两个鸡蛋在碗里。 **yǒu liǎng gè jīdàn zài wǎn li**
There are two eggs in the bowl.

有(一)些花儿在花瓶里。 **yǒu (yī)xiē huār zài huāpíng li**
There are some flowers in the vase.

有几本书在书架上。 **yǒu jǐ běn shū zài shūjià shang**
There are a few/several books on the (book)shelf.

A more common way of phrasing sentences expressing location in Chinese is to begin with a location phrase (e.g. 花瓶里 **huāpíng li** 'in the vase', 书架上 **shūjià shang** 'on the bookshelf'), since the location phrase is likely to be of definite reference and a pre-verbal position is more natural for it (see Units 11 & 13):

花瓶里有(一)些花儿。 **huāpíng li yǒu (yī)xiē huār**
There are some flowers in the vase. (*lit*. In the vase there are some flowers.)

书架上有几本书。 **shūjià shang yǒu jǐ běn shū**
There are a few books on the (book)shelf. (*lit*. On the bookshelf there are a few books.)

碗里有两个鸡蛋。 **wǎn li yǒu liǎng gè jīdàn**
There are two eggs in the bowl. (*lit*. In the bowl there are two eggs.)

屋子里有一张桌子和四把椅子。 **wūzi li yǒu yī zhāng zhuōzi hé sì bǎ yǐzi**
There are a table and four chairs in the room.
(*lit*. In the room there are a table and four chairs.)

桌子上有(一)个花瓶。 **zhuōzi shang yǒu (yī) gè huāpíng**
There is a vase on the table. (*lit*. On the table there is a vase.)

柜子里有毛衣。 **guìzi li yǒu maóyī**
There is a sweater/are sweaters in the wardrobe.
(*lit*. In the wardrobe there is a sweater/are sweaters.)

那儿有笔，这儿有纸。 **nàr yǒu bǐ | zhèr yǒu zhǐ**
There is a pen/are pens over there and (there is) some paper here.
(*lit*. There there is a pen/are pens, here there is some paper.)

D   A noun which comes after the verb will always be of indefinite reference unless a demonstrative 这 **zhè/zhèi** 'this' or 那 **nà/nèi** 'that' + measure word is used:

我朋友喜欢这张照片。 **wǒ péngyou xǐhuan zhè/zhèi zhāng zhàopiàn**
My friend likes this photograph.

我不喜欢那幅画儿。 **wǒ bù xǐhuan nà/nèi fú huàr**
I don't like that painting.

Note: 这 **zhè** may also be pronounced 'zhèi' and 那 **nà**, 'nèi' when followed by a measure word. The probable explanation for this is that 'zhèi' and 'nèi' are fusions of 'zhè + yī' and 'nà + yī':

这只狗	**zhèi zhī gǒu**	this dog
那只猫	**nèi zhī māo**	that cat

In the plural, these demonstratives are followed by 些 **xiē** or a 几 **jǐ** + measure word phrase to mean 'these' or 'those':

她要这些毛衣。 **tā yào zhè/zhèi xiē máoyī**
She wants these sweaters.

她要这几件毛衣。 **tā yào zhè/zhèi jǐ jiàn máoyī**
She wants these (few) sweaters.

我买那些碗。 **wǒ mǎi nà/nèi xiē wǎn**
I'll buy those bowls.

我买那几只碗。 **wǒ mǎi nà/nèi jǐ zhī wǎn**
I'll buy those (few) bowls.

这 **zhè/zhèi** and 那 **nà/nèi** may, of course, be used with numbers. In these cases the word order is demonstrative + number + measure:

你喜欢这两张照片吗？ **nǐ xǐhuan zhè/zhèi liǎng zhāng zhàopiàn ma**
Do you like these two photo(graph)s?

你找到了那三把钥匙没有？ **nǐ zhǎo dào le nà/nèi sān bǎ yàoshi méiyǒu**
Have you found those three keys?

Exercise 2.1

Complete the translations below by filling in the blanks:

1 this pen ——— ——— 笔 **bǐ**
2 these pens ——— ——— 笔 **bǐ**
3 that orange ——— ——— 橙子 **chéngzi**
4 those oranges ——— ——— 橙子 **chéngzi**
5 those (few) children ——— ——— ——— 孩子 **háizi**
6 these (few) tables ——— ——— ——— 桌子 **zhuōzi**
7 that cup/glass/mug ——— ——— 杯子 **bēizi**
8 this book ——— ———书 **shū**
9 those schoolbags ——— ———书包 **shūbāo**
10 those (few) bookshelves ——— ——— ——— 书架 **shūjià**

11 this vase   _____ _____花瓶 **huāpíng**
12 these (few) vases   _____ _____ __ 花瓶 **huāpíng**
13 that kitchen   _____ _____ 厨房 **chúfáng**
14 these flowers   _____ _____ 花儿 **huār**
15 those trees   _____ _____ 树 **shù**
16 that piece of cake   _____ _____ 蛋糕 **dàngāo**
17 that school   _____ _____ 学校 **xuéxiào**
18 this toothbrush   _____ _____ 牙刷 **yáshuā**
19 that slice of bread   _____ _____ 面包 **miànbāo**
20 these keys   _____ _____ 钥匙 **yàoshi**
21 those umbrellas   _____ _____ 雨伞 **yǔsǎn**
22 that shop   _____ _____ 商店 **shāngdiàn**
23 those (few) chairs   _____ _____ _____ 椅子 **yǐzi**
24 these (few) paintings   _____ _____ _____ 画儿 **huàr**

Exercise 2.2

Indicate which of the two English translations below is the correct version of the Chinese in each case:

1 她喜欢狗。 **tā xǐhuan gǒu**
  She likes the dogs./She likes dogs.
2 我买这顶帽子。 **wǒ mǎi zhè/zhèi dǐng màozi**
  (顶 **dǐng** measure word for hats/caps)
  I'll buy this hat./I'll buy that hat.
3 你带了雨伞没有？ **nǐ dài le yǔsǎn méiyǒu**
  (带 **dài** 'to bring along; to take with')
  Have you brought an umbrella?/Have you brought the umbrella?
4 钥匙在哪儿？ **yàoshi zài nǎr**
  Where are the keys?/Where can I find some keys?
5 毛衣你带了没有？ **máoyī nǐ dài le méiyǒu**
  Have you brought a jumper?/Have you brought the jumper?
6 她有孩子没有？ **tā yǒu háizi méi yǒu**
  Has she got any children?/Has she got the children with her?
7 桌子上有只碗。 **zhuōzi shang yǒu zhī wǎn**
  There is a bowl on the table./The bowl is on the table.
8 有件毛衣在柜子里。 **yǒu jiàn máoyī zài guìzi li**
  The jumper is in the wardrobe./There is a jumper in the wardrobe.
9 筷子在桌子上。 **kuàizi zài zhuōzi shang**
  The chopsticks are on the table./There are some chopsticks on the table.
10 你会用筷子吗？ **nǐ huì yòng kuàizi ma** (用 **yòng** 'to use')
  Do you know how to use chopsticks?/Do you know how to use the chopsticks?

Note: 吗 **ma** is a sentence particle which is used at the end of a statement to convert it into a general question asking for either confirmation or denial (see Unit 18).

Exercise 2.3

Translate the following sentences into English paying attention to whether the nouns involved are of definite or indefinite reference:

1 哪儿有书？ **nǎr yǒu shū**
2 书在哪儿？ **shū zài nǎr**
3 厨房里有一个蛋糕。 **chúfáng li yǒu yī gè dàngāo**
4 猫在屋子里。 **māo zài wūzi li**
5 钥匙你带了没有？ **yàoshi nǐ dài le méiyǒu**
6 你带了雨伞没有？ **nǐ dài le yǔsǎn méiyǒu**
7 香蕉你吃了没有？ **xiāngjiāo nǐ chī le méiyǒu**
8 我们想买花儿。 **wǒmen xiǎng mǎi huār**
9 孩子们在学校里。 **háizimen zài xuéxiào li**
10 我喜欢吃苹果。 **wǒ xǐhuan chī píngguǒ**
11 四件毛衣和三顶帽子都在柜子里。
　　 sì jiàn máoyī hé sān dǐng máozi dōu zài guìzi li
12 十个学生都想去中国。 **shí gè xuésheng dōu xiǎng qù zhōngguó**
13 你有筷子没有？ **nǐ yǒu kuàizi méi yǒu**
14 苹果、橙子、蛋糕和面包都在厨房里。
　　 píngguǒ | chéngzi | dàngāo hé miànbāo dōu zài chúfáng li

Exercise 2.4

Translate the following sentences into Chinese:

1 Where are there any shops?
2 Oranges are good to eat.
3 There are a few mugs on the table.
4 There are some books on the bookshelf.
5 Do you have a pen on you?
6 The bowls are in the cupboard.
7 Where is the key?
8 There are some flowers in the vase.
9 Where are the boys?
10 Do you have a jumper?
11 Do you like these photo(graph)s?
12 Have you found the books?
13 These two books are very interesting.
14 I like those three pictures.
15 Where are those five students?

UNIT THREE
Personal pronouns

A Chinese personal pronouns

	Singular	*Plural*
1st person	我 **wǒ** I/me	我们 **wǒmen** we/us
		咱们 **zánmen** we/us (including the listener)
2nd person	你 **nǐ** you	你们 **nǐmen** you
	您 **nín** you (polite form)	
3rd person	他 **tā** he/him	他们 **tāmen** they/them (masculine)
	她 **tā** she/her	她们 **tāmen** they/them (feminine)
	它 **ta** it	它们 **tāmen** they/them (neuter)

As can be seen the personal pronouns have no case distinctions:

我是中国人。	**wǒ shì zhōngguó rén**	I am Chinese.
她来看我。	**tā lái kàn wǒ**	She came to see me.
你好!	**nǐ hǎo**	Hello!/ How are you?
你们住在哪儿?	**nǐmen zhù zài nǎr**	Where do you (plural) live?
我们不认识他们。	**wǒmen bù rènshi tāmen**	We don't know them.
她们不喜欢她。	**tāmen bù xǐhuan tā**	They don't like her.

Note: As 他 and 她 are both pronounced **tā**, gender differentiation in speech (rather than in writing) is only possible through context.

B 咱们 **zánmen** 'we, us' is employed only when the speaker wants consciously to include the listener(s):

咱们走吧。	**zánmen zǒu ba**	Let's go.
再见! 我们走了。	**zàijiàn | wǒmen zǒu le**	Goodbye. We're off now.

Note: 了 **le** in the second example above is a sentence particle (see *Intermediate Chinese*, Unit 8), which comes at the end of a statement to indicate some suggestion of a change, etc.

C   它 **tā**/它们 **tāmen** is mostly used to refer to animals:

你今天见过我的那只猫没有？
nǐ jīntiān jiàn guo wǒ de nà/nèi zhī māo méiyǒu
Have you seen my cat today?

我刚才见过它。 **wǒ gāngcái jiàn guo tā**
I saw it just now.

水池里有很多金鱼。 它们都很好看。
shuǐchí li yǒu hěn duō jīnyú | tāmen dōu hěn hǎokàn
There are a lot of goldfish in the pool. They are all very beautiful.

In spoken Chinese, 它 **tā**/它们 **tāmen** is rarely used to refer to inanimate objects since the reference is clear without it:

自行车修好了没有？ **zìxíngchē xiū haǒ le méiyǒu**
Has the bike been repaired?
昨天修好了。 **zuótiān xiū hǎo le**
It was repaired yesterday.

你看过那个电影没有？ **nǐ kàn guo nà/nèi gè diànyǐng méiyǒu**
Have you seen that film?
看过了，可是不喜欢。 **kàn guo le | kěshì bù xǐhuan**
I have seen it, but I don't like it.

One does not usually say:

*它修好了。 **tā xiū hǎo le**
*看过它了，可是不喜欢它。 **kàn guo tā le | kěshì bù xǐhuan tā**

It occurs only occasionally in expressions where without it ambiguity might arise:

别动它!	**bié dòng tā**	Don't touch it!
vs		
别动!	**bié dòng**	Don't you move!
别管它吧!	**bié guǎn tā ba**	Don't bother about it.
vs		
你别管!	**nǐ bié guǎn**	None of your business.

Note 1: A time expression in Chinese (e.g. 今天 **jīntiān** 'today', 昨天 **zuótiān** 'yesterday', 刚才 **gāngcái** 'just now', etc.) is usually placed immediately before the verb. As Chinese verbs do not inflect for tense, these time expressions provide a time reference for the verbs (see Unit 14).

Note 2: In the above examples, 见过 **jiàn guo** implies a chance occurrence, whereas 看过 **kàn guo** suggests deliberate purpose. In both cases 过 **guo** is an aspect marker indicating past experience (see Unit 15).

D 您 **nín** is the polite form of 你 **nǐ**. It is a fusion of 你 **nǐ** and 们 **men** and therefore has no plural form. (One cannot say *您们 **nínmen**.) To express a plural for 您 **nín**, one uses an appositional phrase:

您三位是中国人吗？ **nín sān wèi shì zhōngguó rén ma**
Are the three of you Chinese?
您几位是哪国人？ **nín jǐ wèi shì nǎ guó rén**
Where are you (people) from?

Note: 位 **wèi** is a polite measure word for 'people'.

E Possession, whether as an adjective or a pronoun, is indicated by the addition of the particle 的 **de** to the personal pronoun:

我的	**wǒ de**	my/mine	
我们的	**wǒmen de**	our/ours	
你的	**nǐ de**	your/yours	
你们的	**nǐmen de**	your/yours	
他的	**tā de**	his	
他们的	**tāmen de**	their/theirs	(masculine)
她的	**tā de**	her/hers	
她们的	**tāmen de**	their/theirs	(feminine)
它的	**tā de**	its	
它们的	**tāmen de**	their/theirs	(neuter)

你的教室在哪儿？	**nǐ de jiàoshì zài nǎr**	Where is your classroom?
这是他们的车。	**zhè shì tāmen de chē**	This is their car.
那把雨伞是我的。	**nà/nèi bǎ yǔsǎn shì wǒ de**	That umbrella is mine.

的 **de** may be omitted before nouns where the possessor has a close relationship with the person or object:

我妈妈想跟你妈妈谈谈。 **wǒ māma xiǎng gēn nǐ māma tántan**
My mother would like to talk to your mother.

我哥哥想认识你弟弟。 **wǒ gēge xiǎng rènshi nǐ dìdi**
My older brother would like to meet/get to know your younger brother.

你父母好吗？ **nǐ fùmǔ hǎo ma**
How are your parents?

你家在哪儿？ **nǐ jiā zài nǎr**
Where is your home?

Note 1: 的 **de** also follows nouns to indicate possession:

我妹妹喜欢骑我姐姐的自行车。 **wǒ mèimei xǐhuan qí wǒ jiějie de zìxíngchē**
My younger sister likes to ride my elder sister's bicycle.

我弟弟喜欢邻居的那只小猫。 **wǒ dìdi xǐhuan línjū de nà/nèi zhī xiǎo māo**
My younger brother likes that kitten of our neighbours'.

我姐姐喜欢开爸爸的车。 **wǒ jiějie xǐhuan kāi bàba de chē**
My elder sister likes driving father's car.

Note 2: The possessive phrase always comes before the demonstrative:

邻居的那只小猫	**línjū de nà/nèi zhī xiǎo māo**	that kitten of our neighbours'
我的那件毛衣	**wǒ de nà/nèi jiàn máoyī**	that jumper of mine
你的这些书	**nǐ de zhè/zhèi xiē shū**	these books of yours
他的这几幅画儿	**tā de zhè/zhèi jǐ fú huàr**	these few paintings of his

F   自己 **zìjǐ** 'oneself':

(i) It is used immediately after the subject in apposition to it:

我们自己没有电视(机)。	**wǒmen zìjǐ méi yǒu diànshì(jī)**	We don't have a television (set) ourselves.
他自己走了。	**tā zìjǐ zǒu le**	He left by himself.
我自己来。	**wǒ zìjǐ lái**	I'll do it (by) myself./I'll help myself. (e.g. at a meal)

Note: 来 **lái** which basically means 'to come' is used here in an idiomatic sense to indicate personal involvement.

(ii) It may also be used as a reflexive object:

别骂自己。   **bié mà zìjǐ**   Don't blame yourself.

(iii) With the addition of the particle 的 **de**, it means 'one's own':

这是我自己的事儿。 **zhè shì wǒ zìjǐ de shìr**
This is my (own) business.

那辆车不是我们自己的，是别人的。
nà/nèi liàng chē bù shì wǒmen zìjǐ de | shì biéren de
That car is not our own; it is somebody else's.

Exercise 3.1

Complete the Chinese translations of the English sentences below by adding the correct personal pronouns where necessary. (Bear in mind that it may not be necessary to fill in the blanks in all cases.)

1 I like him, and he likes me, too.
   _____ 喜欢 _____ ，_____ 也喜欢 _____。(也 **yě** 'also')
   _____ **xǐhuan** _____ | _____ **yě xǐhuan** _____
2 We want to see them, but they don't want to see us.
   _____ _____ 想去见 _____ _____ ，但是 _____ _____ 不想见 _____
   _____。(但是 **dànshì** 'but')
   _____ **xiǎng qù jiàn** _____ _____ | **dànshì** _____ **bù xiǎng jiàn** _____
3 You don't know her, but she knows you.
   _____ 不认识 _____ ，但是 _____ 认识 _____。
   _____ **bù rènshi** _____ | **dànshì** _____ **rènshi** _____
4 Dad, Mum, would you like some coffee?
   爸爸、妈妈，_____ _____ 要喝咖啡吗？
   bàba | māma | _____ **yào hē kāfēi ma**
5 Where's she? I want to talk to her.
   _____ 在哪儿？_____ 想跟 _____ 谈谈。
   _____ **zài nǎr |** _____ **xiǎng gēn** _____ **tántan**
6 We have two dogs. They live in his room.
   _____ _____ 有两条狗。_____ _____ 都住在 _____ _____ 房间里。
   (条 **tiáo** measure word for dogs)
   _____ **yǒu liǎng tiáo gǒu |** _____ **dōu zhù zài** _____ _____ **fángjiān li**
7 I don't like those flowers. Do you like them?
   _____ 不喜欢那些花儿。_____ 喜欢 _____ 吗？
   _____ **bù xǐhuan nà/nèi xiē huār |** _____ **xǐhuan** _____ **ma**
8 Do you want to see that film? Let's go and see it.
   你想看那个电影吗？咱们去看 _____ 吧。
   nǐ xiǎng kàn nà/nèi gè diànyǐng ma | zánmen qù kàn _____ **ba**

Exercise 3.2

Complete the Chinese translations of the following by filling in the blanks:

1 I like my work.
   我喜欢 _____ _____ 工作。 **wǒ xǐhuan** _____ _____ **gōngzuò**
2 Is Li Ming a good friend of yours?
   李明是 _____ (_____) 好朋友吗？
   lǐ míng shì _____ (_____) **hǎo péngyou ma**

3 My family live in the country.

———— 家住在乡村。

—— **jiā zhù zài xiāngcūn** (乡村 **xiāngcūn** 'the countryside')

4 This bike is my older brother's.

这辆自行车是 ——— ——— ———。

zhè/zhèi liàng zìxíngchē shì ——— ——— ———

5 That hat is hers.

那顶帽子是 ——— ———。 **nà/nèi dǐng màozi shì** ——— ———

6 Those three children are all our neighbours'.

那三个孩子都是 ——— ——— ——— ——— ———。

nà/nèi sān gè háizi dōu shì ——— ——— ———

7 Their parents don't live in London.

——— ——— (———) 父母不住在伦敦。

——— (———) **fùmǔ bù zhù zài lúndūn** (父母 **fùmǔ** 'parents')

8 This is her daughter and that is my son.

这是 ——— (———) 女儿；那是 ——— (———) 儿子。

zhè shì ——— (———) **nǚ'ér | nà shì** ——— (———) **érzi**

9 The kitten is sleeping on Father's chair.

小猫睡在 ——— ——— 椅子上。

xiǎo māo shuì zài ——— ——— **yǐzi shang**

10 This is our classroom.

这是 ——— ——— ——— 教室。

zhè shì ——— ——— **jiàoshì** (教室 **jiàoshì** 'classroom')

11 He often repairs his car himself.

他常常 ——— ——— 修汽车。

tā chángcháng ——— **xiū qìchē**

12 That child doesn't have a bicycle of his own.

那个孩子没有 ——— ——— ——— 自行车。

nà/nèi gè háizi méi yǒu ——— ——— **zìxíngchē**

Exercise 3.3

Complete the Chinese translations below with nouns or personal pronouns in their possessive forms:

1 This car is my elder brother's; that car is my own.

这辆车是 ——— ——— ——— ———，那辆是 ——— ——— ———。

zhè/zhèi liàng chē shì ——— ——— ——— **| nà/nèi liàng shì** ——— ———

2 This umbrella is his. Where is mine?

这把(雨)伞是 ——— ———，——— ——— 在哪儿？

zhè/zhèi bǎ (yǔ)sǎn shì ——— ——— **|** ——— ——— **zài nǎr**

3 This cat is from his house. Where is our cat?

这只猫是 ＿＿＿ ＿＿＿ ＿＿＿，我家的猫在哪儿？

zhè/zhèi zhī māo shì ＿＿＿ ＿＿＿ ＿＿＿ | wǒ jiā de māo zài nǎr

4 This jumper is mine. Yours is in the wardrobe.

这件毛衣是 ＿＿＿，＿＿＿ ＿＿＿ 在柜子里。

zhè/zhèi jiàn máoyī shì ＿＿＿ ＿＿＿ | ＿＿＿ ＿＿＿ zài guìzi li

5 Have you ever met my parents?

你见过 ＿＿＿ 父母吗？

nǐ jiàn guo ＿＿＿ fùmǔ ma

6 Do you know his father?

你认识 ＿＿＿ 爸爸吗？

nǐ rènshi ＿＿＿ bàba ma

7 Your apples taste nice; mine are awful.

＿＿＿ ＿＿＿ 苹果很好吃，＿＿＿ ＿＿＿ 不好吃。

＿＿＿ ＿＿＿ píngguǒ hěn hǎochī | ＿＿＿ ＿＿＿ bù hǎochī

8 These three pictures are yours; those two are hers.

这三幅画儿是 ＿＿＿ ＿＿＿，那两幅是 ＿＿＿ ＿＿＿。

zhè/zhèi sān fú huàr shì ＿＿＿ ＿＿＿ | nà/nèi liǎng fú shì ＿＿＿ ＿＿＿

9 My elder sister likes driving Father's car, but doesn't like riding her own bicycle.

我姐姐喜欢开 ＿＿＿ ＿＿＿ ＿＿＿ 车，但是不喜欢骑（＿＿＿）＿＿＿ ＿＿＿ ＿＿＿ 自行车。

wǒ jiějie xǐhuan kāi ＿＿＿ ＿＿＿ chē | dànshì bù xǐhuan qí (＿＿＿) ＿＿＿ ＿＿＿ zìxíngchē

10 The garden at your home is very pretty.

＿＿＿ ＿＿＿ ＿＿＿ 花园很好看。

＿＿＿ ＿＿＿ ＿＿＿ huāyuán hěn hǎokàn

11 I like those goldfish of our neighbour's.

我喜欢 ＿＿＿ ＿＿＿ ＿＿＿ ＿＿＿ ＿＿＿ ＿＿＿ 金鱼。

wǒ xǐhuan ＿＿＿ ＿＿＿ ＿＿＿ ＿＿＿ ＿＿＿ jīnyú

12 My younger brother does not like wearing that jumper of his.

我弟弟不喜欢穿（＿＿＿）＿＿＿ ＿＿＿ ＿＿＿ ＿＿＿ 毛衣。

wǒ dìdi bù xǐhuan chuān (＿＿＿) ＿＿＿ ＿＿＿ ＿＿＿ ＿＿＿ máoyī

Exercise 3.4

Replace 你 **nǐ** and 你们 **nǐmen** in the following sentences with their polite forms:

1 你想喝杯茶吗？ **nǐ xiǎng hē bēi chá ma**
   Would you like some tea?
2 你们是哪国人？ **nǐmen shì nǎ guó rén**
   Which country are you all from?
3 你们请坐。 **nǐmen qǐng zuò** (请 **qǐng** 'please'; 坐 **zuò** 'to sit')
   Please take a seat. (addressing a few visitors)

4 你是英国人吗？ **nǐ shì yīngguó rén ma**
  Are you from Britain?
5 你们要吃点儿蛋糕吗？
  nǐmen yào chī diǎnr dàngāo ma (点儿 **diǎnr** 'a bit (of)')
  Would you like some cake?
6 我够了，谢谢你。 **wǒ gòu le | xièxie nǐ** (够 **gòu** 'enough')
  I'm fine/I've had enough, thanks.

Exercise 3.5

Decide whether 我们 **wǒmen** or 咱们 **zánmen** should strictly be used in the following situations:

1 We must be off now. Goodbye.
  ＿＿＿＿ ＿＿＿＿ 走了。再见！＿＿＿＿ **zǒu le | zàijiàn**
2 Let's be friends.
  ＿＿＿＿ ＿＿＿＿ 交个朋友吧！＿＿＿＿ **jiāo gè péngyou ba**
3 We would like some beer. Thank you.
  ＿＿＿＿ ＿＿＿＿ 想喝点儿啤酒。谢谢您！
  ＿＿＿＿ **xiǎng hē diǎnr píjiǔ | xièxie nín** (啤酒 **píjiǔ** 'beer')
4 I am Li. What's your name? Do let us introduce ourselves.
  我姓李。您贵姓？ ＿＿＿＿ ＿＿＿＿ 认识一下吧！
  wǒ xìng lǐ | nín guìxìng | ＿＿＿＿ **rènshi yīxià ba** (一下 **yīxià** 'briefly')
5 Let's go together.
  ＿＿＿＿ ＿＿＿＿ 一起走吧！＿＿＿＿ **yīqǐ zǒu ba** (一起 **yīqǐ** 'together')
6 We live in London. Where do you live?
  ＿＿＿＿ ＿＿＿＿ 住在伦敦。你们住在哪儿？
  ＿＿＿＿ **zhù zài lúndūn | nǐmen zhù zài nǎr**

UNIT FOUR
Interrogative pronouns

A The main interrogative pronouns in Chinese are:

谁 **shéi (shuí** – less colloquial)	who/whom
谁的 **shéi de**	whose
什么 **shénme**	what
哪 **nǎ/něi** + measure word	which
哪儿 **nǎr**/什么地方 **shénme dìfang**	where/what place

B The most important feature about Chinese interrogative pronouns is that, unlike English practice which shifts all interrogative pronouns to the beginning of the question, Chinese keeps them in the position in the sentence where the answers would be expected:

他是谁？	**tā shì *shéi***	Who is he?
他是我的老师。	**tā shì *wǒ de lǎoshī***	He is my teacher.
谁走了？	***shéi* zǒu le**	Who has left?
李先生走了。	***lǐ xiānsheng* zǒu le**	Mr Li has left.
你去见谁？	**nǐ qù jiàn *shéi***	Who did you go to see?
我去见张经理。	**wǒ qù jiàn *zhāng jīnglǐ***	I went to see Mr/Mrs Zhang, the manager.
这是谁的书包？	**zhè shì *shéi de* shūbāo**	Whose is this satchel?
这是我同学的书包。	**zhè shì *wǒ tóngxué de* shūbāo**	This is my coursemate's satchel.
你想喝点儿什么？	**nǐ xiǎng hē diǎnr *shénme***	What would you like to drink?
我想喝点儿啤酒。	**wǒ xiǎng hē diǎnr *píjiǔ***	I would like to have some beer.

你找什么？	**nǐ zhǎo *shénme***	What are you looking for?
我找我的手表。	**wǒ zhǎo *wǒ de shǒubiǎo***	I'm looking for my watch.
我的大衣在哪儿？	**wǒ de dàyī zài *nǎr***	Where is my coat?
你的大衣在这儿。	**nǐ de dàyī zài *zhèr***	Your coat is here.

C   In addition to 谁 **shéi/shuí**, 哪位 **nǎ/něi wèi** (*lit.* 'which person') may be used to express a more respectful personal enquiry:

哪位是你爸爸？	**nǎ/něi wèi shì nǐ bàba**	Which person is your father?
您要见哪位？	**nín yào jiàn nǎ/něi wèi**	Who do you want to see?

Note: 什么人 **shénme rén** (*lit.* 'what person') on the other hand has a tone of rudeness or contempt:

她是什么人？	**tā shì shénme rén**	Who's she (anyway)?
你碰见了什么人？	**nǐ pèngjiàn le shénme rén**	Who were those people you met?

D   谁的 **shéi de** 'whose' may be used as an interrogative adjective to qualify a noun, or as an interrogative pronoun:

这是谁的钱包？ **zhè shì *shéi de* qiánbāo** (adjective)
Whose purse/wallet is this?
这是我的钱包。 **zhè shì *wǒ de* qiánbāo**
This is my purse/wallet.

这把钥匙是谁的？ **zhè/zhèi bǎ yàoshi shì *shéi de*** (pronoun)
Whose is this key?
这把钥匙是我的。 **zhè/zhèi bǎ yàoshi shì *wǒ de***
This key is mine.

你喜欢谁的画儿？ **nǐ xǐhuan *shéi* de huàr** (adjective)
Whose picture do you like?
我喜欢那个画家的画儿。 **wǒ xǐhuan *nà/nèi gè huàjiā* de huàr**
I like pictures by that artist.

E   什么 **shénme** 'what' likewise may be used as an adjective or a pronoun:

这些是什么蔬菜？ **zhè/zhèi xiē shì *shénme* shūcài** (adjective)
What kind of vegetables are these?
这些是白菜。 **zhè/zhèi xiē shì *báicài***
These are Chinese cabbages.

这些是什么？ **zhè/zhèi xiē shì *shénme*** (pronoun)
What are these?

这些是梨。 **zhè/zhèi xiē shì** *lí*
These are pears.

你想吃(一)点儿什么？ **nǐ xiǎng chī (yī)diǎnr** *shénme* (pronoun)
What would you like (to eat)?
我想吃(一)点儿蛋糕。 **wǒ xiǎng chī (yī)diǎnr** *dàngāo*
I'd like (to eat) some cake.

你买了(一)些什么东西？ **nǐ mǎi le (yī)xiē** *shénme* **dōngxi** (adjective)
What things did you buy?
我买了一瓶咖啡、一包茶叶和一束鲜花。
wǒ mǎi le *yī píng kāfēi | yī bāo cháyè* **hé** *yī shù xiānhuā*
I bought a bottle of coffee, a packet of tea and a bunch of flowers.

你明天想做什么？ **nǐ míngtiān xiǎng** *zuò shénme* (pronoun)
What do you want to do tomorrow?
我明天想去游泳。 **wǒ míngtiān xiǎng** *qù yóuyǒng*
I want to go swimming tomorrow.

F   哪 **nǎ/něi** meaning 'which' (not to be confused with 哪儿 **nǎr** 'where') can only be used in conjunction with a measure word or 'numeral + measure word' phrase:

哪张？	*nǎ/něi* **zhāng**	Which one? (e.g. newspaper, sheet of paper, table, etc.)
这张。	*zhè/zhèi* **zhāng**	This one.
你要哪三个？	**nǐ yào** *nǎ/něi* **sān gè**	Which three do you want?
我要那三个。	**wǒ yào** *nà/nèi* **sān gè**	I want those three.
哪些便宜点儿？	*nǎ/něi* **xiē piányi diǎnr**	Which ones are cheaper?
这些便宜点儿。	*zhè/zhèi* **xiē piányi diǎnr**	These ones are cheaper.
你买哪两本书？	**nǐ mǎi** *nǎ/něi* **liǎng běn shū**	Which two books are you going to buy?
我买那两本书。	**wǒ mǎi** *nà/nèi* **liǎng běn shū**	I'm buying those two books.
哪把伞是你的？	*nǎ/něi* **bǎ sǎn shì nǐ de**	Which umbrella is yours?
这把伞是我的。	*zhè/zhèi* **bǎ sǎn shì wǒ de**	This umbrella is mine.

G   哪儿 **nǎr** 'where' and 什么地方 **shénme dìfang** 'what place' naturally ask about location.

(i) They may occur at the object position, particularly after 去 **qù** 'to go (to)' and 在 **zài** 'to be at/in/on':

你去哪儿/什么地方？ **nǐ qù** *nǎr/shénme dìfang*
Where are you going?
我去朋友家。 **wǒ qù** *péngyou jiā*
I'm going to my friend's place.

你的自行车在哪儿/什么地方？ **nǐ de zìxíngchē zài** *nǎr/shénme dìfang*
Where is your bike?
我的自行车在家里。 **wǒ de zìxíngchē** *zài jiā li*
My bicycle is at home.

(ii) They are also regularly used at the beginning of the sentence followed by the verb 有 **yǒu** 'to exist':

哪儿/什么地方有邮筒？ *nǎr/shénme dìfang* **yǒu yóutǒng**
Where is there/can I find a pillar-box?
马路对面有邮筒。 *mǎlù duìmiàn* **yǒu yóutǒng**
There's a pillar-box across the road.

哪儿/什么地方有东西吃？ *nǎr/shénme dìfang* **yǒu dōngxi chī**
Where can I find something to eat?
(*lit.* Where is there something to eat?)
冰箱里有东西吃。 *bīngxiāng li* **yǒu dōngxi chī**
There are things to eat in the fridge.

The second example above illustrates the common pattern: 'location + 有 **yǒu** + noun object + verb' in which 有 **yǒu** and the verb in fact share the same object. The verb which comes last in the sentence is similar to an English infinitive qualifying the noun object which precedes it.
Here are some more examples:

哪儿有好电影看？ *nǎr* **yǒu hǎo diànyǐng kàn**
Where can we go to see a good film?
(*lit.* Where is there a good film (to) see?)
那家电影院有好电影看。 *nà/nèi jiā diànyǐngyuàn* **yǒu hǎo diànyǐng kàn**
There is a good film on show in that cinema.
(*lit.* At that cinema there is a good film (to) see.)

哪儿有冰激凌卖？ *nǎr* **yǒu bīngjilíng mài**
Where can (we) buy ice-cream?
(*lit.* Where is there ice-cream to be sold/for sale?)
马路对面有。那儿有一辆冰激凌车。
mǎlù duìmiàn **yǒu** | *nàr* **yǒu yī liàng bīngjilíng chē**

Across the road. There's an ice-cream van there.
(*lit.* Across the road there is (some). There there is an ice-cream van.)

哪儿有车租? ***nǎr* yǒu chē zū**
Where are there cars for/to hire?
对不起，这儿没有车租。 **duìbuqǐ | *zhèr* méiyǒu chē zū**
I'm sorry, there aren't any cars for hire here.
(*lit.* Here there are not cars (to) hire.)

(iii) 哪儿 **nǎr** and 什么地方 **shénme dìfang** are also commonly used after a coverb (see Unit 24) such as 在 **zài** 'in, at, on', 到 **dào** 'to', etc., to create a coverbal phrase. These coverbal phrases come before the verb:

你孩子在哪儿学习? **nǐ háizi zài *nǎr* xuéxí**
Where is/are your child(ren) studying?
我孩子在大学学习。 **wǒ háizi zài *dàxué* xuéxí**
My child(ren) is/are studying at the university.

你爸爸在什么地方工作? **nǐ bàba zài *shénme dìfang* gōngzuò**
Where does your father work?
我爸爸在一家银行工作。 **wǒ bàba zài *yī jiā yínháng* gōngzuò**
My father works at a bank.

他到哪儿/什么地方去? **tā dào *nǎr*/*shénme dìfang* qù**
Where is he going?
他到办公室去。 **tā dào *bàngōngshì* qù**
He's going to his office.

Note: 家 **jiā**, as you may have noticed, is the measure word for 电影院 **diànyǐngyuàn** 'cinema', 银行 **yínháng** 'bank', 商店 **shāngdiàn** 'shop', etc. The noun 家 **jiā** also means 'home; house; family'.

Exercise 4.1

Formulate questions based on the sentences below focusing on the words in bold italics. Use interrogative pronouns and switch the first-person and second-person pronouns as necessary.

EXAMPLE:
我去商店买东西。   **wǒ qù shāngdiàn mǎi dōngxi**
I'm going to the shops to buy something.

(a) ***wǒ* qù shāngdiàn mǎi dōngxi**
谁去商店买东西? ***shéi* qù shāngdiàn mǎi dōngxi**

(b) **wǒ qù *shāngdiàn* mǎi dōngxi**
你去哪儿买东西? **nǐ qù *nǎr* mǎi dōngxi**

(c) **wǒ qù shāngdiàn mǎi** *dōngxi*
你去商店买什么？ **nǐ qù shāngdiàn mǎi** *shénme*

(d) **wǒ qù shāngdiàn** *mǎi dōngxi*
你去商店做什么？ **nǐ qù shāngdiàn** *zuò shénme*

1 妈妈去市场买鸡蛋。 **māma qù shìchǎng mǎi jīdàn**
Mother is going to the market to buy eggs.
   (a) *māma* **qù shìchǎng mǎi jīdàn**
   (b) **māma qù** *shìchǎng* **mǎi jīdàn**
   (c) **māma qù shìchǎng mǎi** *jīdàn*
   (d) **māma qù shìchǎng** *mǎi jīdàn*

2 爸爸在办公室写推荐信。 **bàba zài bàngōngshì xiě tuījiànxìn**
Father is writing a reference/a letter of recommendation in the office.
   (a) **bàba zài** *bàngōngshì* **xiě tuījiànxìn**
   (b) **bàba zài bàngōngshì** *xiě tuījiànxìn*
   (c) **bàba zài bàngōngshì xiě** *tuījiànxìn*
   (d) *bàba* **zài bàngōngshì xiě tuījiànxìn**

3 姐姐在厨房里喂猫。 **jiějie zài chúfáng li wèi māo**
(My) elder sister is feeding the cat in the kitchen.
   (a) **jiějie zài** *chúfáng li* **wèi māo**
   (b) **jiějie zài chúfáng li** *wèi māo*
   (c) *jiějie* **zài chúfáng li wèi māo**

4 哥哥在外面修车。 **gēge zài wàimian xiū chē**
(My) elder brother is repairing the car outside.
   (a) **gēge zài wàimian** *xiū chē*
   (b) **gēge zài wàimian xiū** *chē*
   (c) **gēge zài** *wàimian* **xiū chē**
   (d) *gēge* **zài wàimian xiū chē**

5 弟弟去游泳池学游泳。 **dìdi qù yóuyǒngchí xué yóuyǒng**
(My) younger brother is going to the swimming-pool to learn to swim.
   (a) **dìdi qù yóuyǒngchí** *xué yóuyǒng*
   (b) *dìdi* **qù yóuyǒngchí xué yóuyǒng**
   (c) **dìdi qù** *yóuyǒngchí* **xué yóuyǒng**

6 弟弟想请姐姐帮他的忙。 **dìdi xiǎng qǐng jiějie bāng tā de máng**
(My) younger brother would like to ask his elder sister to lend him a hand.
(i.e. give him some help)
   (a) **dìdi xiǎng qǐng** *jiějie* **bāng tā de máng**
   (b) **dìdi xiǎng qǐng jiějie** *bāng tā de máng*
   (c) *dìdi* **xiǎng qǐng jiějie bāngmáng**

7 邻居的孩子在街上骑自行车。 **línjū de háizi zài jiē shang qí zìxíngchē**
(Our) neighbour's child is riding a bicycle in the street.
(a) *línjū de* háizi zài jiē shang qí zìxíngchē
(b) *línjū de háizi zài jiē* shang qí zìxíngchē
(c) línjū de háizi zài jiē shang *qí zìxíngchē*
(d) línjū de háizi zài jiē shang qí *zìxíngchē*
(e) línjū de háizi zài *jiē shang* qí zìxíngchē

8 妹妹明年想跟爷爷去中国旅行。
mèimei míngnián xiǎng gēn yéye qù zhōngguó lǚxíng
(My) younger sister wants to go travelling in China with Grandpa next year.
(a) *mèimei* míngnián xiǎng gēn yéye qù zhōngguó lǚxíng
(b) mèimei míngnián xiǎng *gēn yéye qù zhōngguó lǚxíng*
(c) mèimei míngnián xiǎng gēn *yéye* qù zhōngguó lǚxíng
(d) mèimei míngnián xiǎng gēn yéye qù *zhōngguó* lǚxíng
(e) mèimei míngnián xiǎng gēn yéye qù zhōngguó *lǚxíng*

Exercise 4.2

Translate the following sentences into Chinese using the pattern:

'哪儿 + 有 + noun + verb'

EXAMPLE:
Where can we buy pears? (Where are there pears to be sold/for sale?)
哪儿有梨卖？ **nǎr yǒu lí mài**

1 Where can we hire bicycles?
2 Where can we have coffee?
3 Where can we buy flowers?
4 Where is there any beer to drink?
5 Where can I find something to eat?
6 Where can I see a film?
7 Where can you buy a newspaper? (报纸 **bàozhǐ** 'newspaper')
8 Where can you borrow books? (借 **jiè** 'borrow')
9 Where can you buy fresh vegetables? (新鲜 **xīnxiān** 'fresh')
10 Where can we hire a good car?

Exercise 4.3

Translate these sentences into Chinese:

1 Who would like some tea?
2 Who would like some cake?

  3 Whose is this mug?
  4 What would you like to eat?
  5 Which picture do you prefer?
  6 Who can speak Chinese? (会 **huì** 'can; be skilful with')
  7 Which child is yours?
  8 Whose teacher is Mr Zhang?
  9 Which oranges are you going to buy?
10 What kind of vegetables do you like?
11 Who can repair cars?
12 Who can help me? (能 **néng** 'can; be able to')
13 Who do you want to see?
14 Which two books have you brought with you?
15 What place did you go to?
16 Which countries are you going to?
17 Where is my purse/wallet?
18 Where do you go for coffee?
19 Who are you going to China with?
20 Where did you get acquainted with her?

UNIT FIVE
Numbers

A Numbers in Chinese follow a system based on tens, hundreds, etc.:

一	**yī**	one	十一	**shí yī**	eleven
二	**èr**	two	十二	**shí èr**	twelve
三	**sān**	three	十三	**shí sān**	thirteen
四	**sì**	four	十七	**shí qī**	seventeen
五	**wǔ**	five	十九	**shí jiǔ**	nineteen
六	**liù**	six	二十	**èr shí**	twenty
七	**qī**	seven	三十一	**sān shí yī**	thirty-one
八	**bā**	eight	五十四	**wǔ shí sì**	fifty-four
九	**jiǔ**	nine	八十六	**bā shí liù**	eighty-six
十	**shí**	ten	九十九	**jiǔ shí jiǔ**	ninety-nine
零	**líng**	zero			

Note 1: 幺 **yāo** is sometimes used instead of 一 **yī** in speech (e.g. on the telephone) to avoid the confusion between 一 **yī** 'one' and 七 **qī** 'seven'.

Note 2: The numeral 2 before a measure word is 两 **liǎng** and not 二 **èr**:

两个梨	**liǎng gè lí**	two pears
两个星期/礼拜	**liǎng gè xīngqī/lǐbài**	two weeks

B While in English you count up to a thousand and then repeat up to a million, Chinese counts up to ten thousand (万 **wàn**) and then repeats up to a hundred million (亿 **yì**). The higher numbers are:

一百	**yī bǎi**	100	one hundred
一千	**yī qiān**	1,000	one thousand
一万	**yī wàn**	10,000	ten thousand
一亿	**yī yì**	100,000,000	one hundred million

Figures are expressed from higher to lower units:

一百二十五 **yī bǎi èr shí wǔ**
125 one hundred and twenty-five

一千二百三十五 **yī qiān èr bǎi sān shí wǔ**
1,235 one thousand two hundred and thirty-five

一万二千三百四十五 **yī wàn èr qiān sān bǎi sì shí wǔ**
12,345 twelve thousand three hundred and forty-five

十二万三千四百五十六 **shí èr wàn sān qiān sì bǎi wǔ shí liù**
123,456 one hundred and twenty-three thousand four hundred and fifty-six

一百二十三万四千五百六十七 **yī bǎi èr shí sān wàn sì qiān wǔ bǎi liù shí qī**
1,234,567
one million two hundred and thirty-four thousand five hundred and sixty-seven

一千二百三十四万五千六百七十八。
yī qiān èr bǎi sān shí sì wàn wǔ qiān liù bǎi qī shí bā
12,345,678
twelve million three hundred and forty-five thousand six hundred and seventy-eight

一亿二千三百四十五万六千七百八十九。
yī yì èr qiān sān bǎi sì shí wǔ wàn liù qiān qī bǎi bā shí jiǔ
123,456,789
one hundred and twenty-three million four hundred and fifty-six thousand seven hundred and eighty-nine

It is useful to remember that a million in Chinese is 一百万 **yī bǎi wàn** (= 100 × 10,000).

Note: 零 **líng** 'zero' is used as a filler for any missing unit or units within a figure:

一百零五	**yī bǎi líng wǔ**	105	one hundred and five
一千零四	**yī qiān líng sì**	1004	one thousand and four
一千一百零二	**yī qiān yī bǎi líng èr**	1102	one thousand one hundred and two

C   A fraction is expressed by the pattern: 'denominator 分之 **fēn zhī** numerator'. (分 **fēn** means 'part; component' and 之 **zhī** means 'of'):

三分之一	**sān fēn zhī yī**	1/3	one third
四分之一	**sì fēn zhī yī**	1/4	one quarter
四分之三	**sì fēn zhī sān**	3/4	three quarters
八分之七	**bā fēn zhī qī**	7/8	seven eighths

D   半 **bàn** 'half' followed by a noun functions like a numeral and requires a measure word:

半杯酒	**bàn bēi jiǔ**	half a glass of wine (or any alcoholic drink)
半个西瓜	**bàn gè xīguā**	half a watermelon
半年	**bàn nián**	six months (*lit.* half a year)
半(个)小时/半个钟头	**bàn (gè) xiǎoshí/bàn gè zhōngtóu**	half an hour
半个月	**bàn gè yuè**	two weeks (*lit.* half a month)

半 **bàn** is used *after* a 'number + measure word' phrase to mean 'and a half':

一杯半酒	**yī bēi bàn jiǔ**	a glass and a half of wine (or any alcoholic drink)
两个半西瓜	**liǎng gè bàn xīguā**	two and a half water-melons
三年半	**sān nián bàn**	three and a half years
五个半小时	**wǔ gè bàn xiǎoshí**	five and a half hours
一个半月	**yī gè bàn yuè**	a month and a half

E   Percentages take the form of fractions of 100:

| 百分之四十 | **bǎi fēn zhī sì shí** | 40% |
| 百分之一百零七 | **bǎi fēn zhī yī bǎi líng qī** | 107% |

F   The decimal point is expressed as 点 **diǎn**:

三点六九	**sān diǎn liù jiǔ**	3.69
三十三点三三	**sān shí sān diǎn sān sān**	33.33
六点一七	**liù diǎn yī qī**	6.17

Note: When 零 **líng** 'nought; zero' occurs after the decimal point, it is not a 'filler' but functions as a separate unit and is therefore repeated as necessary. See for instance the following:

| 一千零二点零零二 | **yī qiān líng èr diǎn líng líng èr** |
| 1,002.002 | one thousand and two point zero zero two |

G   Ordinal numbers in Chinese are formed by placing 第 **dì** before the numeral:

| 第一 | **dì yī** | (the) first |
| 第十 | **dì shí** | (the) tenth |

Ordinal numbers, like cardinals, require a measure with a noun:

第一个学生	**dì yī gè xuésheng**	the first student
第十次会议	**dì shí cì huìyì**	the tenth meeting
第三本书	**dì sān běn shū**	the third book

They also regularly occur with frequency, time, etc. measures:

第一次	**dì yī cì**	the first time
第二周	**dì èr zhōu**	the second week
第五课	**dì wǔ kè**	Lesson Five

Note 1: The numeral 2 in an ordinal is 二 **èr** and not 两 **liǎng** even before a measure word:

第二场足球比赛   **dì èr chǎng zúqiú bǐsài**   the second soccer match

One cannot say:

*第两场   **dì liǎng chǎng**   the second match

Note 2: In some cases Chinese does not use ordinal numbers where the equivalent phrase in English would:

一年级 **yī niánjí** the first year/the first form (in school, etc.)
二楼 **èr lóu** the first floor ('ground floor' in English is counted as 一楼 **yī lóu** or 地下 **dì xià** and 'first floor' therefore becomes 二楼 **èr lóu**.)

H   Approximate numbers in Chinese can be expressed by placing 左右 **zuǒyòu** or 上下 **shàngxià** 'approximately' after the 'numeral + measure word' phrase or 大约 **dàyuē** 'about' or 差不多 **chàbuduō** 'almost' before it:

三公斤左右	**sān gōngjīn zuǒyòu**	about three kilograms
五米上下	**wǔ mǐ shàngxià**	about five metres
大约两点钟	**dàyuē liǎng diǎn zhōng**	about two o'clock
大约两(个)小时/钟头	**dàyuē liǎng (gè) xiǎoshí/ zhōngtóu**	about two hours
差不多三十英里	**chàbuduō sān shí yīnglǐ**	almost thirty miles

Note: Observe the difference between 两点钟 **liǎng diǎn zhōng** 'two o'clock' and 两个钟头/小时 **liǎng gè zhōngtóu/xiǎoshí** 'two hours' (see Unit 8).

Approximation with the number 10 and its multiples, up to and including 100, may also be expressed using 来 **lái**:

十来年	**shí lái nián**	around ten years
四十来岁	**sì shí lái suì**	about forty years old
(一)百来个	**(yī) bǎi lái gè**	a little over a hundred

However, with 千 **qiān** 'thousand' and 万 **wàn** 'ten thousand', 多 **duō** is used instead for a similar purpose:

两千多年	**liǎng qiān duō nián**	over two thousand years
三万多人	**sān wàn duō rén**	over thirty thousand people

Note: Observe the difference between 年 **nián** 'year' (period of time) and 岁 **suì** 'year (of age)'.

Any two consecutive numbers from one to nine may also be used to express approximation:

一、两年	**yī | liǎng nián**	one or two years
两、三天	**liǎng | sān tiān**	two or three days
十七、八个人	**shí qī | bā gè rén**	seventeen or eighteen people
二、三十个老师	**èr | sān shí gè lǎoshī**	twenty to thirty teachers
一、二百个学生	**yī | èr bǎi gè xuésheng**	a hundred to two hundred students
两、三千(个)人	**liǎng | sān qiān (gè) rén**	two to three thousand people

Note: In relation to 'two', to say simply 'one or two' or 'two or three', 一、两 **yī \| liǎng** or 两、三 **liǎng \| sān** are generally used. For 'eleven or twelve' and 'twelve to thirteen' you must say 十一、二 **shí yī \| èr** or 十二、三 **shí èr \| sān**. 'Ten or twenty', 'twenty or thirty' must also be 一、二十 **yī \| èr shí** or 二、三十 **èr \| sān shí**. For higher numbers in these sequences 两 **liǎng** is usually preferred (e.g. 两、三百 **liǎng \| sān bǎi** 'two or three hundred', 一、两千 **yī \| liǎng qiān** 'one or two thousand') but 二 **èr** is also possible.

I To ask 'how many', 多少 **duōshao** 'how many; how much' (*lit.* many few) or 几 **jǐ** 'how many' with a measure are used. 几 **jǐ** implies that the number involved is below ten whereas 多少 **duōshao** is unlimited. 几 **jǐ** always requires a measure, whereas 多少 **duōshao** normally does not:

你有几个孩子？	**nǐ yǒu jǐ gè háizi**	How many children do you have?
你女儿今年几岁(了)？	**nǐ nǚ'ér jīnnián jǐ suì (le)**	How old is your daughter (this year)?
你喝了几杯啤酒？	**nǐ hē le jǐ bēi píjiǔ**	How many glasses of beer did you drink?

你身上带了多少钱？ **nǐ shēn shang dài le duōshao qián**
How much money do you have on you?

中国有多少人？ **zhōngguó yǒu duōshao rén**
How many people are there in China?

你去过多少国家？ **nǐ qù guo duōshao guójiā**
How many countries have you been to?

Note: 几 **jǐ** may be used with 十 **shí**, 百 **bǎi**, 千 **qiān**, etc.:

中国有几千年的历史？ **zhōngguó yǒu jǐ qiān nián de lìshǐ**
How many thousand years of history does China have?

那天晚会，你请了几十个同学？ **nà/nèi tiān wǎnhuì \| nǐ qǐng le jǐ shí gè tóngxué**
How many (*lit.* tens of) classmates did you invite to the party that evening?

Exercise 5.1

Express the following Chinese numbers in figures:

1 八十九 **bā shí jiǔ**   5 七百万 **qī bǎi wàn**
2 十六 **shí liù**   6 一万三千五百二十六
3 一万 **yī wàn**   **yī wàn sān qiān wǔ bǎi èr shí liù**
4 六亿 **liù yì**   7 十八万 **shí bā wàn**
8 六千九百三十四 **liù qiān jiǔ bǎi sān shí sì**
9 三千六百五十二 **sān qiān liù bǎi wǔ shí èr**
10 七亿八千万零四百六十九 **qī yì bā qiān wàn líng sì bǎi liù shí jiǔ**
11 六万四千五百零四 **liù wàn sì qiān wǔ bǎi líng sì**
12 四千零四点零零五 **sì qiān líng sì diǎn líng líng wǔ**

Exercise 5.2

Translate the figures below into Chinese:

1 80,205   7 3%
2 6,329,814   8 97%
3 600,000,000   9 4.1316
4 1,080   10 586.23
5 7/36   11 7,005
6 1/4   12 601.007

Exercise 5.3

Translate the following phrases into Chinese:

1 half a day   8 five and a half pears
2 two weeks   9 the fifth week
3 three and a half years   10 the fourth child
4 six months   11 the twelfth match
5 the first floor   12 the third year (at school)
6 half an orange   13 the second day
7 half a bottle of wine   14 seven and a half hours

Exercise 5.4

Fill in the blanks below with either 二 **èr** or 两 **liǎng** to complete the translation of the English:

1	_____ 次	_____ cì	twice
2	_____ 万人	_____ wàn rén	twenty thousand people
3	_____ 分之一	_____ fēn zhī yī	half
4	十 _____ 米	shí _____ mǐ	twelve metres
5	_____ 十五条金鱼	_____ shí wǔ tiáo jīnyú	twenty-five goldfish
6	_____ 条裙子	_____ tiáo qúnzi	two skirts
7	第 _____ 课	dì _____ kè	Lesson Two
8	_____ 、三打鸡蛋	_____	sān dá jīdàn	two or three dozen eggs
9	十 _____ 、三把牙刷	shí _____	sān bǎ yáshuā	twelve to thirteen toothbrushes
10	一、_____ 把雨伞	yī	_____ bǎ yǔsǎn	one or two umbrellas

Exercise 5.5

Translate the following phrases into Chinese:

1 one or two weeks
2 two hundred years
3 about sixty years old
4 thirty to forty bicycles
5 ten days and more
6 some two hundred shops
7 ten per cent
8 twenty or so
9 fifteen metres or so
10 a month or so
11 over ten thousand students
12 two or three children
13 about fifty friends and neighbours
14 about seventy miles
15 over eight kilograms
16 ten cities or more

Exercise 5.6

Translate the following sentences into Chinese:

1 There are three oranges, two pears, a loaf of bread and a bottle of wine in the cupboard.
2 There is a bowl, a mug and a pair of chopsticks on the table. (双 **shuāng** 'pair')
3 There are half a dozen eggs, a kilo of Chinese cabbage and some ice-cream in the fridge.

4 There are two sweaters and twelve skirts in the wardrobe.
5 Li Ming has invited (请了 **qǐng le**) thirty to forty friends and coursemates.
6 My boyfriend (男朋友 **nán péngyou**) has brought (带来了 **dài lái le**) a bunch of flowers and a few bottles of beer.
7 I have written (写了 **xiě le**) around five references. (封 **fēng** is the measure word for letters, etc.)
8 My girlfriend (女朋友 **nǚ péngyou**) has been to (去过 **qù guo**) ten countries or more.
9 I bumped into (碰见了 **pèng jiàn le**) over twenty coursemates.
10 My son saw (看了 **kàn le**) about a dozen films this year. (今年 **jīnnián** 'this year')
11 How much is that sweater?
12 How many younger sisters does he have?
13 How many people are there in Beijing?
14 How many Chinese people does your father know?
15 How many kilos of Chinese cabbage do you want to buy?

UNIT SIX
Measure words

A A measure word is always necessary when a noun is modified by a numeral or a demonstrative:

一本词典	**yī běn cídiǎn**	a/one dictionary
一支毛笔	**yī zhī máobǐ**	a/one writing brush
两只鸟	**liǎng zhī niǎo**	two birds
三条毛巾	**sān tiáo máojīn**	three towels
这杯牛奶	**zhè/zhèi bēi niúnǎi**	this glass of milk
那瓶啤酒	**nà/nèi píng píjiǔ**	that bottle of beer
哪个人	**nǎ/něi gè rén**	which person

One would not normally say:

*一笔	**yī bǐ**	(*lit.* a/one pen)
*两书	**liǎng shū**	(*lit.* two books)
*这鸟	**zhè niǎo**	(*lit.* this bird)
*哪车	**nǎ chē**	(*lit.* which car)

Some nouns may be associated with more than one measure word:

一座/所/幢/栋房子	**yī zuò/suǒ/zhuàng/dòng fángzi**	a/one house
这只/条/艘船	**zhè/zhèi zhī/tiáo/sōu chuán**	this boat/ship
三辆/部车	**sān liàng/bù chē**	three cars
哪幅/张画儿	**nǎ fú/zhāng huàr**	which picture or painting

B 个 **gè**, as we have seen (in Unit 1), is by far the most common of the measures and can be used with virtually any noun:

一个看法	**yī gè kànfǎ**	a view, opinion
两个客人	**liǎng gè kèren**	two visitors/guests

三个国家	**sān gè guójiā**	three countries
这个机会	**zhè/zhèi gè jīhuì**	this opportunity
哪个青年	**nǎ/něi gè qīngnián**	which young man

C   Most of the other measures can be placed in general categories, depending on their relationship to the nouns or sets of nouns they accompany:

(i)   Associated with particular nouns or sets of nouns

一顶帽子	**yī dǐng màozi**	a/one hat
两件衬衫	**liǎng jiàn chènshān**	two shirts
三、四家商店	**sān | sì jiā shāngdiàn**	three or four shops
一、两首歌	**yī | liǎng shǒu gē**	one or two songs
一架飞机	**yī jià fēijī**	a/one plane
几间学校	**jǐ jiān xuéxiào**	a few schools
一朵花儿	**yī duǒ huār**	a/one flower
那棵树	**nà/nèi kē shù**	that tree

Note: 几 **jǐ** means 'a few' when used in a statement but 'how many' in a question (see Unit 5):

我买了几件衬衫。 **wǒ mǎi le jǐ jiàn chènshān**
I bought a few shirts.

你买了几件衬衫? **nǐ mǎi le jǐ jiàn chènshān**
How many shirts have you bought (or did you buy)?

(ii) Portion of whole

三滴水	**sān dī shuǐ**	three drops of water
五片面包	**wǔ piàn miànbāo**	five slices of bread
这块肉	**zhè/zhèi kuài ròu**	this piece of meat
六块蛋糕	**liù kuài dàngāo**	six pieces of cake

Note: Observe the difference between 一个蛋糕 **yī gè dàngāo** 'a (whole) cake' and 一块蛋糕 **yī kuài dàngāo** 'a piece of cake' (i.e. a portion of a whole cake).

(iii) Container

两杯茶	**liǎng bēi chá**	two cups of tea
三碗饭	**sān wǎn fàn**	three bowls of (cooked) rice
四瓶酒	**sì píng jiǔ**	four bottles of wine

Note: Most containers occur as nouns themselves and then take on other measure words:

两个杯子	**liǎng gè bēizi**	two cups/glasses/mugs
三只碗	**sān zhī wǎn**	three bowls
四个瓶子	**sì gè píngzi**	four bottles

(iv) Shape

(a) 条 **tiáo** long and narrow; a strip

一条路	**yī tiáo lù**	a/one road (street)
一条毛巾	**yī tiáo máojīn**	a/one towel
这条裙子	**zhè/zhèi tiáo qúnzi**	this skirt
那条被子	**nà/nèi tiáo bèizi**	that quilt

(b) 根 **gēn** stick-like

一根火柴	**yī gēn huǒchái**	a/one match
一根绳子	**yī gēn shéngzi**	a rope/string
一根草	**yī gēn cǎo**	a/one blade of grass
一根线	**yī gēn xiàn**	a piece of thread

(c) 支 (枝) **zhī** like a branch or a twig

一支铅笔	**yī zhī qiānbǐ**	a/one pencil
两支烟	**liǎng zhī yān**	two cigarettes
一支部队	**yī zhī bùduì**	an/one army
一枝枪	**yī zhī qiāng**	a/one rifle/pistol

(d) 张 **zhāng** a flat surface

一张纸	**yī zhāng zhǐ**	a/one piece of paper
哪张桌子	**nǎ/něi zhāng zhuōzi**	which table
一张报纸	**yī zhāng bàozhǐ**	a/one newspaper
一张床	**yī zhāng chuáng**	a/one bed
一张地图	**yī zhāng dìtú**	a/one map

(e) 粒 **lì** granular

一粒沙	**yī lì shā**	a/one grain of sand
一粒米	**yī lì mǐ**	a/one grain of rice

(f) 颗 **kē** small and round

一颗珠子	**yī kē zhūzi**	a/one pearl
一颗黄豆	**yī kē huángdòu**	a/one soya bean

(v) Relating to noun groups

(a) 把 **bǎ** is used with nouns which indicate something held by the hand:

一把刀	**yī bǎ dāo**	a/one knife
这把椅子	**zhè/zhèi bǎ yǐzi**	this chair
一把(雨)伞	**yī bǎ (yǔ)sǎn**	an/one umbrella
一把牙刷	**yī bǎ yáshuā**	a/one toothbrush

(b) 座 **zuò** is used with nouns which indicate something large and imposing:

一座山	**yī zuò shān**	a/one hill/mountain
一座桥	**yī zuò qiáo**	a/one bridge
那座房子	**nà/nèi zuò fángzi**	that house/building

(c) 只 **zhī** is used with the following noun groups:

• animals, birds and insects

一只鸟	**yī zhī niǎo**	a/one bird
一只猫	**yī zhī māo**	a/one cat
一只老鼠	**yī zhī lǎoshǔ**	a/one mouse
一只羊	**yī zhī yáng**	a/one sheep
一只苍蝇	**yī zhī cāngying**	a/one fly

Note: The following animals take individual measure words:

一头牛	**yī tóu niú**	a/one cow
一匹马	**yī pǐ mǎ**	a/one horse
这条狗	**zhè/zhèi tiáo gǒu**	this dog

• utensils

一只碗	**yī zhī wǎn**	a/one bowl
一只锅	**yī zhī guō**	a/one wok

• one of a pair

一只手套	**yī zhī shǒutào**	a/one glove
那只鞋	**nà/nèi zhī xié**	that shoe
一只袜子	**yī zhī wàzi**	a/one sock
一只眼睛	**yī zhī yǎnjing**	a/one eye
一只耳朵	**yī zhī ěrduo**	a/one ear

(vi) Referring to weight, volume, length, etc.

两公斤马铃薯	**liǎng gōngjīn mǎlíngshǔ**	two kilos of potatoes
一磅牛肉	**yī bàng niúròu**	a/one pound of beef
八升汽油	**bā shēng qìyóu**	eight litres of petrol
五英里路	**wǔ yīnglǐ lù**	five miles (distance)

D Objects in pairs. In Chinese 'a pair of' is usually 一双 **yī shuāng** or 一对 **yī duì**:

一双鞋子	**yī shuāng xiézi**	a pair of shoes
一双筷子	**yī shuāng kuàizi**	a pair of chopsticks
一双手	**yī shuāng shǒu**	a pair of hands
一双手套	**yī shuāng shǒutào**	a pair of gloves
一对袜子	**yī duì wàzi**	a pair of socks
一对耳环	**yī duì ěrhuán**	which pair of earrings?

Note 1: 一双 **yī shuāng** and 一对 **yī duì** are generally interchangeable, although 一对 **yī duì** is more often used for people or animals forming partnerships:

一对夫妇	**yī duì fūfù**	husband and wife
一对鸽子	**yī duì gēzi**	a pair of pigeons
一对鸳鸯	**yī duì yuānyāng**	a pair of mandarin ducks/an affectionate couple

Note 2: In English one may use 'a pair of' with objects which are, in fact, a single entity. In Chinese these objects take specific measure words:

一把剪刀	**yī bǎ jiǎndāo**	a pair of scissors
一条裤子	**yī tiáo kuzl**	a pair of trousers
哪副眼镜	**nǎ/něi fù yǎnjìng**	which pair of glasses?

E Some nouns, particularly those referring to time, can be measure words in themselves and do not require a measure word:

一天 **yī tiān** a/one day   两年 **liǎng nián** two years

In some cases the measure word is optional:

一个星期	**yī gè xīngqī**	*or*	一星期	**yī xīngqī**	a/one week
三个小时	**sān gè xiǎoshí**	*or*	三小时	**sān xiǎoshí**	three hours

Note: 礼拜 **lǐbài**, an alternative for 'week' and 钟头 **zhōngtóu**, an alternative for 'hour', and 月 **yuè** 'month' always take the measure word 个 **ge**:

两个礼拜	**liǎng gè lǐbài**	*not*	*两礼拜	**liǎng lǐbài**	two weeks
三个钟头	**sān gè zhōngtóu**	*not*	*三钟头	**sān zhōngtóu**	three hours
六个月	**liù gè yuè**	*not*	*六月	**liù yuè**	six months

However, 月 **yuè** is used without 个 **gè** for the calendar months, e.g.

一月	**yī yuè**	January
二月	**èr yuè**	February
六月	**liù yuè**	June
十二月	**shí èr yuè**	December

F   A few Chinese measure words have a variety of translations in English according to context and to the noun they are linked with:

一杯茶	**yī bēi chá**	a cup of tea
一杯咖啡	**yī bēi kāfēi**	a mug of coffee
一杯水	**yī bēi shuǐ**	a glass of water
一群狼	**yī qún láng**	a pack of wolves
一群羊	**yī qún yáng**	a flock of sheep
一群人	**yī qún rén**	a crowd of people

Conversely some measure words in English have a range of translations in Chinese:

一条新闻	**yī tiáo xīnwén**	a piece of news
一块肥皂	**yī kuài féizào**	a piece of soap
一张纸	**yī zhāng zhǐ**	a piece of paper
一个信息	**yī gè xìnxī**	a piece of information
一支乐曲	**yī zhī yuèqǔ**	a piece of music
一支粉笔	**yī zhī fěnbǐ**	a piece of chalk

G   As we have seen from the examples in the unit, demonstratives 这 **zhè** and 那 **nà** and interrogative adjective 哪 **nǎ** are used with measure words in the same way as numerals:

这杯酒	**zhè/zhèi bēi jiǔ**	this glass of wine (or any alcoholic drink)
那瓶牛奶	**nà/nèi píng niúnǎi**	that bottle of milk
哪双鞋？	**nǎ/něi shuāng xié?**	which pair of shoes?

When 这 **zhè** or 那 **nà** or 哪 **nǎ** occurs together with a numeral, the former always precedes the latter:

这两杯酒	**zhè/zhèi liǎng bēi jiǔ**	these two glasses of wine, etc.
那三瓶牛奶	**nà/nèi sān píng niúnǎi**	those three bottles of milk
哪四双鞋？	**nǎ/něi sì shuāng xié?**	which four pairs of shoes?

这 **zhè**, 那 **nà** and 哪 **nǎ** are also used regularly with (一) 些 **(yī)xiē** 'some' to identify an indefinite plural number or amount:

这(一)些书	**zhè/zhèi (yī)xiē shū**	these books
那(一)些袜子	**nà/nèi (yī)xiē wàzi**	those socks/stockings
哪( )些钱？	**nǎ/něi (yī)xiē qián?**	which (amount of) money?

Note: 一些 (yī)xiē 'some' is a set expression. 些 xiē cannot be used with other numerals.

One cannot say:

*两些书   **liǎng xiē shū**

H There are a number of collective nouns which consist of a measure word suffixed to a noun:

车辆	**chēliàng**	vehicles	信件	**xìnjiàn**	correspondence
船只	**chuánzhī**	shipping	花朵	**huāduǒ**	flowers
书本	**shūběn**	books	马匹	**mǎpǐ**	horses
纸张	**zhǐzhāng**	paper			

These collective nouns *cannot* be modified by a 'numeral + measure word' phrase:

*两朵花朵	**liǎng duǒ huāduǒ**	(*lit.* two flowers)
*三只船只	**sān zhī chuánzhī**	(*lit.* three boats)

Exercise 6.1

Match each noun below with the correct measure word and translate the resulting phrase into English:

1	一匹	**yī pǐ**	商店	**shāngdiàn**
2	两架	**liǎng jià**	蛋糕	**dàngāo**
3	三个	**sān gè**	椅子	**yǐzi**
4	四、五把	**sì l wǔ bǎ**	山	**shān**
5	几张	**jǐ zhāng**	马	**mǎ**
6	六家	**liù jiā**	国家	**guójiā**
7	七所	**qī suǒ**	桌子	**zhuōzi**
8	八座	**bā zuò**	书	**shū**
9	九本	**jiǔ běn**	飞机	**fēijī**
10	十块	**shí kuài**	学校	**xuéxiào**

Exercise 6.2

See if you can find a measure word out of the eight below to replace the measure words in the following phrases:

部 **bù**   副 **fù**   对 **duì**   座 **zuò**   所 **suǒ**   个 **gè**   张 **zhāng**   床 **chuáng**

1 一份报纸	**yī fèn bàozhǐ**	a newspaper
2 一条被子	**yī tiáo bèizi**	a quilt
3 一间学校	**yī jiān xuéxiào**	a school
4 一对耳环	**yī duì ěrhuán**	a pair of earrings
5 一辆汽车	**yī liàng qìchē**	a car
6 一部电影	**yī bù diànyǐng**	a film
7 一幢房子	**yī zhuàng fángzi**	a house
8 一双筷子	**yī shuāng kuàizi**	a pair of chopsticks

Exercise 6.3

Translate the phrases below into Chinese:

 1 a day
 2 a bowl of (cooked) rice
 3 a year
 4 this pair of spectacles
 5 a pair of shoes
 6 a week
 7 an earring
 8 a sock
 9 a piece of bread
10 that pair of scissors
11 a piece of soap
12 a pair of trousers
13 a month
14 two pounds of apples
15 three miles
16 seven litres of petrol
17 which writing brush?
18 a boat
19 two songs
20 a map

Exercise 6.4

Translate the following phrases into Chinese (note that some nouns may share the same measure word):

1 a flock of sheep
2 a glass of beer
3 a crowd of people
4 an umbrella
5 a knife
6 that bird
7 those two bunches of flowers
8 a piece of music
 9 this newspaper
10 which three pencils?
11 an opportunity
12 a drop of water
13 a cup of tea
14 which flower?
15 a (piece of) string
16 a bed

17 a pair of trousers   19 this dog
18 a pair of scissors   20 these three cigarettes

Exercise 6.5

Complete the Chinese translations of the English sentences below, choosing
appropriate measures from the following list (note that some measure words
may be used more than once):

条 tiáo   本 běn   辆 liàng   碗 wǎn   些 xiē   张 zhāng
杯 bēi   把 bǎ   顶 dǐng   支 zhī   家 jiā   只 zhī
间 jiān   个 gè

1 There are only four tables and five chairs in this classroom.
———— ———— 教室里只有 ———— ———— 桌子和 ———— ———— 椅子。
———— ———— **jiàoshì li zhǐ yǒu** ———— **zhuōzi hé** ————
yǐzi

2 Our neighbour has two dogs and three cats.
我们邻居有 ———— ———— 狗和 ———— ———— 猫。
wǒmen línjū yǒu ———— ———— **gǒu hé** ———— ———— **māo**

3 We've got four cars in the family.
我家有 ———— ———— (汽)车。 **wǒ jiā yǒu** ———— ———— **(qì)chē**

4 My younger brother bought a new hat.
弟弟买了 ———— ———— 新帽子。 **dìdi mǎi le** ———— ———— **xīn màozi**

5 I had four cups of coffee today.
我今天喝了 ———— ———— 咖啡。 **wǒ jīntiān hē le** ———— ———— **kāfēi**

6 That person made a few suggestions.
———— ———— 人提了 ———— ———— 建议。
———— ———— **rén tí le** ———— ———— **jiànyì**

7 My uncle brought some fruit.
叔叔带来了 ———— ———— 水果。 **shūshu dài lái le** ———— ———— **shuǐguǒ**

8 Li Ming walked into a restaurant and ordered a bowl of fried noodles.
李明走进 ———— ———— 饭馆，叫了 ———— ———— 炒面。
lǐ míng zǒu jìn ———— **fànguǎn | jiào le** ———— ———— **chǎomiàn**

9 My uncle wants to go to France by car. He's borrowed a map of France.
我舅舅想开车去法国。他借了 ———— ———— 法国地图。
wǒ jiùjiu xiǎng kāi chē qù fǎguó | tā jiè le ———— ———— **fǎguó dìtú**

10 My younger sister likes birds. She keeps those two parrots.
妹妹喜欢鸟。她养了 ———— ———— ———— 鹦鹉。
mèimei xǐhuan niǎo | tā yǎng le ———— ———— **yīngwǔ**

Note: There is a difference in Chinese between 叔叔 **shūshu** 'uncle (on father's side)' and 舅舅
jiùjiu 'uncle (on mother's side)'.

UNIT SEVEN
Indefinite plurals

A A large (but unspecified) number or amount may be expressed in Chinese by using the adjectival phrases: 很多 **hěn duō** 'many; a lot of' and 不少 **bù shǎo** (*lit.* not few) 'many; quite a few'. They may modify all types of nouns:

很多钱	**hěn duō qián**	a lot of money	(material)
不少书	**bù shǎo shū**	many books	(common)
很多朋友	**hěn duō péngyou**	many friends	(common)
不少建议	**bù shǎo jiànyì**	quite a few suggestions	(abstract)
很多意见	**hěn duō yìjian**	a lot of opinions	(abstract)

B To express an unspecified number or quantity, 一些 **yīxiē** 'some; a few', is used, again with all types of nouns:

一些纸	**yīxiē zhǐ**	some paper	(material)
一些葡萄	**yīxiē pútáo**	a few grapes	(common)
一些水	**yīxiē shuǐ**	some water	(material)
有(一)些希望	**yǒu (yī)xiē xīwàng**	there is some hope	(abstract)

A smaller number or amount can be expressed respectively by '几 **jǐ** + measure word' 'some; a few' and 一点(儿) **yīdiǎn(r)** 'some; a little; a bit'. The former is generally used with common nouns and the latter, mostly with material nouns (e.g. 'iron, water, cloth', etc.) or abstract notions (e.g. ideas, feelings, etc.):

几个人	**jǐ gè rén**	a few people	(common)
几幅画儿	**jǐ fú huàr**	a few pictures	(common)
几辆自行车	**jǐ liàng zìxíngchē**	a few bicycles	(common)

Note: 几 **jǐ** functions like a number and is always followed by a measure (see Unit 2):

有几个客人在院子里等你。 **yǒu jǐ gè kèren zài yuànzi li děng nǐ**
A few guests are waiting for you in the courtyard.

我有几个问题想问你。 **wǒ yǒu jǐ gè wèntí xiǎng wèn nǐ**
I have a few questions which I would like to ask you.

| 一点(儿)盐 | **yīdiǎn(r) yán** | a bit of salt | (material) |
| 一点儿道埋 | **yīdiǎnr dàoli** | some sense | (abstract) |

有(一)点(儿)紧张 **yǒu (yī)diǎn(r) jǐnzhāng** (to be) a bit nervous
(*lit.* have/having a bit of nervousness)   (abstract)

没有一点(儿)希望 **méi yǒu yīdiǎn(r) xīwàng**
(to be) without any hope   (abstract)

Note: 有一些 **yǒu yīxiē**/有 ·点(儿) **yǒu yīdiǎn(r)** + nouns or noun phrases constitute adjectives or adjectival predicates (see *Intermediate Chinese*).

C   Though a '几 **jǐ** + measure word' phrase is usually used with common nouns, it may also be used with material nouns if the measure word is a container or a standard measurement (e.g. bottle, kilo, etc.):

| 几瓶酒 | **jǐ píng jiǔ** | a few bottles of wine | (container) |
| 几碗饭 | **jǐ wǎn fàn** | a few bowls of rice | (container) |

| 几升汽油 | **jǐ shēng qìyóu** | several litres of petrol | (standard measure) |
| 几公斤马铃薯 | **jǐ gōngjīn mǎlíngshǔ** | several kilos of potatoes | (standard measure) |

D   一点(儿) **yīdiǎn(r)** takes on a different emphasis in negative sentences:

| 这儿没有一点(儿)水。 | **zhèr méi yǒu yīdiǎn(r) shuǐ** | There isn't any water here. |
| 我没有一点(儿)钱。 | **wǒ méi yǒu yīdiǎn(r) qián** | I don't have any money. |

The emphasis is intensified if 一点(儿) **yīdiǎn(r)** and its noun is moved to a topic position before the verb and 也 **yě** is inserted before the verb:

这儿一点(儿)水也没有。 **zhèr yīdiǎn(r) shuǐ yě méi yǒu** (more emphatic)
There isn't any water here at all.

我一点(儿)钱也没有。 **wǒ yīdiǎn(r) qián yě méi yǒu** (more emphatic)
I don't have any money at all.

Note: 一点(儿) **yīdiǎn(r)** may, of course, occur without a noun:

她一点(儿)也不吃。 **tā yīdiǎn(r) yě bù chī**   She didn't eat anything at all.

This emphatic construction is also regularly used with '一 **yī** + measure (+ noun)' phrases:

这个人连一点(儿)道理也不讲。
zhè/zhèi gè rén lián yīdiǎn(r) dàoli yě bù jiǎng
This person was totally unreasonable.
(*lit.* This person was not concerned with reason in any way.)

这儿一个人也没有。 **zhèr yī gè rén yě méi yǒu**
There isn't anyone here at all.

我身上一分钱也没有。 **wǒ shēn shang yī fēn qián yě méi yǒu**
I don't have a cent/penny on me.

她一口饭也不想吃。 **tā yī kǒu fàn yě bù xiǎng chī**
She doesn't want to eat a single mouthful.

The emphasis can be increased still further by placing 连 **lián** 'even' before 一点(儿) **yīdiǎn(r)** or '一 **yī** + measure word (+ noun)' phrases:

这儿连一个人也没有。 **zhèr lián yī gè rén yě méi yǒu**
There isn't even one person here.

我身上连一分钱也没有。 **wǒ shēn shang lián yī fēn qián yě méi yǒu**
I've got absolutely no money at all on me.

E   Interrogative pronouns discussed in Unit 4 (e.g. 谁 **shéi/shuí**, 什么 **shénme**, 哪儿 **nǎr**, etc.) may also be used as indefinite plurals in topic positions in conjunction with 都 **dōu**/也 **yě**:

谁都来了。 **shéi/shuí dōu lái le**
Everybody has turned up.
谁也没(有)来。 **shéi/shuí yě méi(yǒu) lái**
Nobody has turned up.
他什么也没(有)买。 **tā shénme yě méi(yǒu) mǎi**
He did not buy anything.
她哪儿都去过。 **tā nǎr dōu qù guo**
She's been everywhere./There's no place she's not been to.

These interrogative pronouns may be used as objects in negative sentences in a similar way:

| 我没(有)碰见谁。 | **wǒ méi(yǒu) pèngjiàn shéi/shuí** | I did not bump into anybody. |
| 他不想吃什么。 | **tā bù xiǎng chī shénme** | He did not want to eat anything. |

F   Human nouns which take the suffix 们 **men** are of definite reference and cannot therefore be modified by indefinite plurals like 很多 **hěn duō**, 不少 **bù shǎo**, 一些 **yīxiē** or 一点(儿) **yīdiǎn(r)**.

One cannot say:

| *很多学生们 | **hěn duō xuéshengmen** | (*lit.* many students) |
| *一些朋友们 | **yīxiē péngyoumen** | (*lit.* some friends) |

Exercise 7.1

Pick out the Chinese phrases/sentences below that are incorrect and make necessary corrections:

1	不少学生	**bù shǎo xuésheng**	many students
2	不少个孩子	**bù shǎo gè háizi**	many children
3	不少朋友们	**bù shǎo péngyoumen**	many friends
4	一些葡萄	**yīxiē pútáo**	some grapes
5	很多个面包	**hěn duō gè miànbāo**	a lot of bread
6	很多意见	**hěn duō yìjian**	a lot of criticism (*lit.* opinions)
7	一点(儿)水	**yīdiǎn(r) shuǐ**	a little water
8	几个橙子	**jǐ gè chéngzi**	a few oranges
9	很多人们	**hěn duō rénmen**	quite a lot of people
10	一些工程师们	**yīxiē gōngchéngshīmen**	some engineers
11	一些盐	**yīxiē yán**	some salt
12	一些钱也没有	**yīxiē qián yě méi yǒu**	have no money at all
13	一点(儿)希望也没有	**yīdiǎn(r) xīwàng yě méi yǒu**	have no hope at all
14	没有一碗饭	**méi yǒu yī wǎn fàn**	there isn't a single bowl of (cooked) rice
15	连家里一粒米也没有。	**lián jiā li yī lì mǐ yě méi yǒu**	There isn't a single grain of rice at home.
16	花园里一朵花儿也没有。	**huāyuán li yī duǒ huār yě méi yǒu**	There isn't a single flower in the garden.

Exercise 7.2

Complete the Chinese sentences below by filling the gaps with one of the following expressions:

一些 **yīxiē** 很多 **hěn duō** 不少 **bù shǎo** 一点(儿) **yīdiǎn(r)** 一个 **yī gè**

1 弟弟买了 ＿＿＿ ＿＿＿ 玩具。 **dìdi mǎi le ＿＿＿ ＿＿＿ wánjù**
  My younger brother has bought a lot of toys.
2 奶奶没喝 ＿＿＿ ＿＿＿ (＿＿＿) 牛奶。 **nǎinai méi hē ＿＿＿ niúnǎi**
  Grandma didn't drink any milk at all.
3 爷爷吃了 ＿＿＿ ＿＿＿ 葡萄。 **yéye chī le ＿＿＿ ＿＿＿ pútáo**
  Grandpa ate quite a lot of grapes.
4 姐姐 ＿＿＿ ＿＿＿ 橙子也没吃。 **jiějie ＿＿＿ ＿＿＿ chéngzi yě méi chī**
  (My) elder sister didn't eat a single orange.
5 妈妈讲了 ＿＿＿ ＿＿＿ 故事。 **māma jiǎng le ＿＿＿ ＿＿＿ gùshi**
  Mother told many stories.
6 爸爸去过 ＿＿＿ ＿＿＿ 国家。 **bàba qù guo ＿＿＿ ＿＿＿ guójiā**
  My father has been to a lot of countries.
7 哥哥烤了 ＿＿＿ ＿＿＿ 面包。 **gēge kǎo le ＿＿＿ miànbāo**
  My elder brother baked some bread.
8 妹妹没带 ＿＿＿ ＿＿＿ (＿＿＿) 钱。 **mèimei méi dài ＿＿＿ qián**
  My younger sister hasn't got any money with her.
9 我在学校交了 ＿＿＿ ＿＿＿ 朋友。
  wǒ zài xuéxiào jiāo le ＿＿＿ ＿＿＿ péngyou
  I made a lot of friends at school.
10 爸爸写了 ＿＿＿ ＿＿＿ 信。 **bàba xiě le ＿＿＿ ＿＿＿ xìn**
  Father wrote quite a few letters.

Exercise 7.3

Rephrase the following Chinese sentences to make them more emphatic:

1 我身上没有一分钱。 **wǒ shēn shang méi yǒu yī fēn qián**
  I haven't got any money on me.
2 我家里没有一本词典。 **wǒ jiā li méi yǒu yī běn cídiǎn**
  I don't have a single dictionary in my house.
3 冰箱里没有一点儿水果。
  bīngxiāng li méi yǒu yīdiǎnr shuǐguǒ (水果 **shuǐguǒ** 'fruit')
  There aren't any fruit in the fridge.
4 她没说什么。 **tā méi shuō shénme**
  She didn't say anything.
5 他没吃什么东西。 **tā méi chī shénme dōngxi**
  He didn't eat anything.

6 妈妈没买什么肉。 **māma méi mǎi shénme ròu**
  Mother didn't buy any meat at all.
7 我们没去哪儿。 **wǒmen méi qù nǎr**
  We didn't go anywhere.
8 我昨天没碰见谁。 **wǒ zuótiān méi pèngjiàn shuí/shéi**
  I didn't bump into anybody yesterday.

Exercise 7.4

Fill in the gaps in the following exchanges with 一些 **yīxiē** or 一点(儿) **yīdiǎn(r)** as appropriate:

1 你想买两双新袜子吗？ **nǐ xiǎng mǎi liǎng shuāng xīn wàzi ma**
  Do you want to buy two new pairs of socks?
  不！我只要买一双。我只有 _____ _____ 钱了。
  bù | wǒ zhǐ yào mǎi yī shuāng | wǒ zhǐ yǒu _____ qián le
  No, I only want to buy one pair. I've only got a little money.
2 今天你喝过啤酒吗？ **jīntiān nǐ hē guo píjiǔ ma**
  Have you had any beer today?
  没有，今天我 _____ _____ 啤酒也没(有)喝。
  méi yǒu | jīntiān wǒ _____ píjiǔ yě méi(yǒu) hē
  No, I haven't had any beer today.
3 你妈妈好吗？ **nǐ māma hǎo ma**
  How is your mother?
  她病了！三天没吃 _____ _____ (_____) 东西了。
  tā bìng le | sān tiān méi chī __ __ dōngxi le
  She's ill. She hasn't touched anything for three days.
4 我饿了。 **wǒ è le** (饿 **è** 'to be hungry')
  I am hungry.
  我这儿还有 _____ _____ 面包。你想吃吗？
  wǒ zhèr hái yǒu _____ miànbāo | nǐ xiǎng chī ma
  I've got some bread here. Would you like it?
5 你带了钱吗？ **nǐ dài le qián ma**
  Have you any money with you?
  对不起。我身上 _____ _____ 钱也没带。
  duìbuqǐ | wǒ shēn shang _____ qián yě méi dài
  I'm sorry. I haven't brought any money with me.
6 这件事儿有希望吗？ **zhè/zhèi jiàn shìr yǒu xīwàng ma**
  (事儿 **shìr** 'affair; matter')
  Is there any hope with this?
  对不起。_____ _____ 希望也没有。
  duìbuqǐ | _____ xīwàng yě méi yǒu
  I'm sorry. There's no hope at all.

7 你要在茶里加糖吗？ **nǐ yào zài chá li jiā táng ma**
   (加 **jiā** 'to add'; 糖 **táng** 'sugar')
   Would you like some sugar in your tea?
   谢谢。_____ _____ 糖也不加。 **xièxie | _____ táng yě bù jiā**
   No, thank you. I won't have any sugar.

8 你喝了很多啤酒吗？ **nǐ hē le hěn duō píjiǔ ma**
   Have you had a lot of beer?
   不，我只喝了 _____ _____ 啤酒。 **bù | wǒ zhǐ hē le _____ píjiǔ**
   I have only had a little (beer).

UNIT EIGHT
Times and dates

A   The hours of the day are expressed by 点 **diǎn** or 点钟 **diǎn zhōng**. 点 **diǎn** 'hour' is essentially a measure and 钟 **zhōng** means 'clock':

| 两点 | **liǎng diǎn** | two o'clock |
| 十一点钟 | **shí yī diǎn zhōng** | eleven o'clock |

B   分 **fēn** 'minute' and 刻 **kè** 'quarter of an hour' are placed after 点 **diǎn**:

三点二十(分)	**sān diǎn èr shí (fēn)**	twenty minutes past three
六点一刻	**liù diǎn yī kè**	a quarter past six
八点三刻	**bā diǎn sān kè**	a quarter to nine
九点五十(分)	**jiǔ diǎn wǔ shí (fēn)**	nine fifty

Note: 零 **líng** 'zero' is used as a filler when the minutes after the hour are less than ten:

| 五点零五分 | **wǔ diǎn líng wǔ fēn** | five past five |
| 四点零二分 | **sì diǎn líng èr fēn** | two minutes past four |

C   For 'half past' 半 **bàn** 'half' comes immediately after 点 **diǎn**:

| 两点半 | **liǎng diǎn bàn** | half past two |
| 十点半 | **shí diǎn bàn** | half past ten |

D   Expressions for 'to' the hour use 差 **chà** (*lit.*) 'lack, be short of' which can form a phrase before or after 点 **diǎn**:

| 差十分四点 | **chà shí fēn sì diǎn** | *or* | 四点差十分 | **sì diǎn chà shí fēn** | ten to four |
| 差一刻七点 | **chà yī kè qī diǎn** | *or* | 七点差一刻 | **qī diǎn chà yī kè** | a quarter to seven |

Note: When other time units are mentioned with the hour, 点 **diǎn** is used for 'o'clock' and not 点钟 **diǎn zhōng**.

One does not say:

*三点钟二十(分)	sān diǎn zhōng èr shí (fēn)	
*六点钟一刻	liù diǎn zhōng yī kè	
*两点钟半	liǎng diǎn zhōng bàn	

E   To indicate a.m. and p.m., time expressions for particular periods of the day are used:

早上	**zǎoshang**	morning (early)
上午	**shàngwǔ**	morning (before noon)
下午	**xiàwǔ**	afternoon
晚上	**wǎnshang**	evening (night)
半夜	**bànyè**	midnight

晚上十一点半	**wǎnshang shí yī diǎn bàn**	half past eleven in the evening (11.30 p.m.)
下午三点	**xiàwǔ sān diǎn**	three o'clock in the afternoon (3 p.m.)
早上七点一刻	**zǎoshang qī diǎn yī kè**	a quarter past seven in the morning (7.15 a.m.)
上午十点二十分	**shàngwǔ shí diǎn èr shí fēn**	twenty past ten in the morning (10.20 a.m.)

F   With the exception of Sunday, days of the week, starting from Monday, are formed by placing the numbers one to six after 星期 **xīngqī** or 礼拜 **lǐbài** 'week' and for Sunday 天 **tiān** 'heaven' or 日 **rì** 'sun' come after 星期 **xīngqī**/礼拜 **lǐbài**:

星期/礼拜一	**xīngqī/lǐbài yī**	Monday
星期/礼拜二	**xīngqī/lǐbài èr**	Tuesday
星期/礼拜三	**xīngqī/lǐbài sān**	Wednesday
星期/礼拜四	**xīngqī/lǐbài sì**	Thursday
星期/礼拜五	**xīngqī/lǐbài wǔ**	Friday
星期/礼拜六	**xīngqī/lǐbài liù**	Saturday
星期/礼拜日/天	**xīngqī/lǐbài rì/tiān**	Sunday

G   Months are also formed numerically by putting the numbers one to twelve before 月 **yuè** 'month (or moon)':

一月	**yī yuè**	January
五月	**wǔ yuè**	May
八月	**bā yuè**	August
十二月	**shí èr yuè**	December

Note: January is also 正月 **zhēng yuè**.

H Dates of the month are expressed by 号 **hào** or, in written form, 日 **rì**:

| 二月三号/日 | **èr yuè sān hào/rì** | 3rd February |
| 十一月二十九号/日 | **shí yī yuè èr shí jiǔ hào/rì** | 29th November |

I Years, unlike English, are pronounced in numerical sequence:

一九九六年	**yī jiǔ jiǔ liù nián**	nineteen ninety-six	1996
一九四五年	**yī jiǔ sì wǔ nián**	nineteen forty-five	1945
一九一一年	**yī jiǔ yī yī nián**	nineteen eleven	1911

J Other common time expressions indicating the recent past, present or near future are:

今天	**jīntiān**	today
明天	**míngtiān**	tomorrow
后天	**hòutiān**	the day after tomorrow
大后天	**dà hòutiān**	in three days time
昨天	**zuótiān**	yesterday
前天	**qiántiān**	the day before yesterday
大前天	**dà qiántiān**	three days ago

这个月	**zhè/zhèi gè yuè**	this month
下个月	**xià gè yuè**	next month
下下个月	**xià xià gè yuè**	the month after next
上个月	**shàng gè yuè**	last month
上星期一	**shàng xīngqī yī**	last Monday
下礼拜五	**xià lǐbài wǔ**	next Friday

今年	**jīnnián**	this year
明年	**míngnián**	next year
后年	**hòunián**	the year after next
去年	**qùnián**	last year
前年	**qiánnián**	the year before last
大前年	**dà qiánnián**	three years ago

K Questions about time, apart from the general enquiry 什么时候 **shénme shíhou** or 几时 **jǐ shí** 'when?', are linked with the particular time expression and all involve the use of 几 **jǐ** 'how many':

几点(钟)？	**jǐ diǎn (zhōng)**	What time (of the day) is it?
今天星期/礼拜几？	**jīntiān xīngqī/lǐbài jǐ**	What day is it today?
今天几号？	**jīntiān jǐ hào**	What is the date today?
现在几月？	**xiànzài jǐ yuè**	What month is it (now)?

Note: 哪 **nǎ/něi** 'which?' can also be used with time words like 天 **tiān** 'day', 月 **yuè** 'month', 年 **nián** 'year'. With 月 **yuè** 'month', one can also use 哪个 **nǎ/něi gè**, which also occurs with 星期/礼拜 **xīngqī/lǐbài** 'week':

你哪天走？	**nǐ nǎ/něi tiān zǒu**	Which day are you leaving?
你们哪(个)月回来？	**nǐmen nǎ/něi (gè) yuè huí lái**	In which month are you (pl.) coming back?
你哪 (个)星期/礼拜回家？	**nǐ nǎ/něi (gè) xīngqī/lǐbài huí jiā**	Which week are you going home?

In questions (as above) or statements about time the link verb 是 **shì** 'to be' is not normally used:

现在九点半。	**xiànzài jiǔ diǎn bàn**	It's half past nine (now).
今天八月二十一号/日。	**jīntiān bā yuè èr shí yī hào/rì**	Today is 21st August.

However it is not wrong to say:

现在是六点半。	**xiànzài shì liù diǎn bàn**	It's half past six (now).
今天是星期三。	**jīntiān shì xīngqī sān**	Today is Wednesday.

Further question-and-answer examples:

你几点起床？ **nǐ jǐ diǎn qǐchuáng**
What time do you (usually) get up?
我早上七点半起床。 **wǒ zǎoshang qī diǎn bàn qǐchuáng**
I (usually) get up at half past seven.

客人们几点(钟)来？ **kèrenmen jǐ diǎn (zhōng) lái**
What time are the guests/visitors arriving?
他们下午三点(钟)来。 **tāmen xiàwǔ sān diǎn (zhōng) lái**
They are coming at three o'clock in the afternoon.

你几时回英国？ **nǐ jǐ shí huí yīngguó**
When are you going back to Britain?
我明年九月回去。 **wǒ míngnián jiǔ yuè huí qù**
I'm going back in September next year.

你几号动身到欧洲去？ **nǐ jǐ hào dòngshēn dào ōuzhōu qù**
Which day of the month are you setting out for Europe?
我四号走。 **wǒ sì hào zǒu**
I'm leaving on the fourth.

Note: 几 **jǐ** meaning 'a few' is discussed in Unit 7.

In dates and complex time expressions larger units always precede smaller ones:

一九九六年三月二十七号下午两点零五分
yī jiǔ jiǔ liù nián sān yuè èr shí qī hào xiàwǔ liǎng diǎn líng wǔ fēn
Five past two on the afternoon of the twenty-seventh of March nineteen ninety-six

L Time expressions in Chinese, like adverbs, go before the verbs and can be said to serve as their tense indicators:

你礼拜天做什么？ **nǐ lǐbài tiān zuò shénme**
What do you do on Sundays?/What are you going to do on Sunday?

你昨天下午做什么？ **nǐ zuótiān xiàwǔ zuò shénme**
What did you do yesterday afternoon?

我们今天晚上去酒吧间。 **wǒmen jīntiān wǎnshang qù jiǔbājiān**
We're going to a pub this evening.

我明年三月去北京。 **wǒ míngnián sān yuè qù běijīng**
I'm going to Beijing next March.

你明天来我家吗？ **nǐ míngtiān lái wǒ jiā ma**
Are you coming to my place tomorrow?

Exercise 8.1

Translate the following Chinese phrases into English:

1 三点钟	**sān diǎn zhōng**	
2 十二点钟	**shí èr diǎn zhōng**	
3 两点二十分	**liǎng diǎn èr shí fēn**	
4 七点五十五分	**qī diǎn wǔ shí wǔ fēn**	
5 差十分八点	**chà shí fēn bā diǎn**	
6 十一点一刻	**shí yī diǎn yī kè**	
7 九点半	**jiǔ diǎn bàn**	
8 十点零一分	**shí diǎn líng yī fēn**	
9 十二点零五分	**shí èr diǎn líng wǔ fēn**	
10 六点三刻	**liù diǎn sān kè**	

Exercise 8.2

Provide answers to the Chinese questions below using the information in brackets:

EXAMPLE
现在几点(钟)？ **xiànzài jǐ diǎn (zhōng)**
What time is it (now)? (7.15 a.m.)
现在上午七点一刻/十五分。 **xiànzài shàngwǔ qī diǎn yī kè/shí wǔ fēn**
It's 7.15 a.m.

1 你几点钟去学校？ **nǐ jǐ diǎn zhōng qù xuéxiào**
What time are you going to school? (8.30 a.m.)
2 你什么时候去游泳？ **nǐ shénme shíhou qù yóuyǒng**
What time are you going swimming? (8.55 a.m.)
3 你朋友下午几点下班？ **nǐ péngyou xiàwǔ jǐ diǎn xiàbān**
What time does your friend finish work in the afternoon? (5.45 p.m.)
4 你们几点吃晚饭？ **nǐmen jǐ diǎn chī wǎnfàn**
What time do you have your supper? (about 9.00 p.m.)
5 你哪天碰见我叔叔？ **nǐ nǎ/něi tiān pèngjiàn wǒ shūshu**
On which day of the month did you bump into my uncle? (the sixth)
6 你爸爸几号去中国？ **nǐ bàba jǐ hào qù zhōngguó**
Which day of the month is your father going to China? (the eleventh)
7 你妹妹几点钟睡觉？ **nǐ mèimei jǐ diǎn zhōng shuìjiào**
What time does your younger sister go to bed? (around 12 midnight)
8 你下个月几号给他写信？ **nǐ xià gè yuè jǐ hào gěi tā xiě xìn**
On which day of next month are you going to write to him? (the 21st)
9 你下星期几来这儿开座谈会？ **nǐ xià xīngqī jǐ lái zhèr kāi zuòtánhuì**
(开 **kāi** 'to attend (a meeting)') (座谈会 **zuòtánhuì** 'discussion; seminar')
On which day next week are you coming for a seminar? (Thursday)
10 你哪年毕业？ **nǐ nǎ/něi nián bìyè** (毕业 **bìyè** 'to graduate')
When will you graduate? (1999)
11 你几时到欧洲去？ **nǐ jǐ shí dào ōuzhōu qù**
When are you going to Europe? (next September)
12 你同学明年几月回国？ **nǐ tóngxué míngnián jǐ yuè huí guó**
Which month next year are your coursemates going back to their home country? (December)

Exercise 8.3

Form questions in Chinese that would elicit the answers specified in bold italics below, making appropriate adjustments, where necessary, to the personal pronouns involved:

EXAMPLE
我二月五号去我朋友家。 **wǒ *èr yuè wǔ hào* qù wǒ péngyou jiā**
I am going to my friend's house on the fifth of May.
你什么时候/几号去你朋友家？ **nǐ *shénme shíhou/jǐ hào* qù nǐ péngyou jiā**
When/what date are you going to your friend's house?

1 她六点半吃晚饭。 **tā** *liù diǎn bàn* **chī wǎnfàn**
  She has her dinner at half past six.
2 我礼拜五晚上七点来你家。 **wǒ lǐbài wǔ wǎnshang** *qī diǎn* **lái nǐ jiā**
  I'll come to your house at 7 o'clock on Friday evening.
3 我们八月十号去度假。 **wǒmen bā yuè** *shí hào* **qù dùjià**
  (度假 **dùjià** 'to go on holiday')
  We're going on holiday on the tenth of August.
4 我一九九五年第一次见到她。 **wǒ** *yī jiǔ jiǔ wǔ nián* **dì yī cì jiàn dào tā**
  I met her for the first time in 1995.
5 我妈妈五点半回家。 **wǒ māma** *wǔ diǎn bàn* **huí jiā**
  Mother comes home at half past five.
6 新经理下星期二来这儿上班。 **xīn jīnglǐ xià xīngqī** *èr* **lái zhèr shàngbān**
  The new manager will start work here next Tuesday.
7 我们下个月去找你。 **wǒmen** *xià gè yuè* **qù zhǎo nǐ**
  We'll go and see you next month.
8 他们明年毕业。 **tāmen** *míngnián* **bìyè**
  They will graduate next year.
9 我姐姐上星期三下午在学开车。
  wǒ jiějie shàng xīngqī *sān* **xiàwǔ zài xué kāichē**
  My elder sister was learning to drive last Wednesday afternoon.
10 我去年十一月买这幅画儿。 **wǒ qùnián** *shí yī yuè* **mǎi zhè/zhèi fú huàr**
   I bought this painting in November last year.
11 座谈会上午九点半开始。 **zuòtánhuì shàngwǔ** *jiǔ diǎn bàn* **kāishǐ**
   The discussion starts at half past nine in the morning.
12 我明天早上在家里休息。 **wǒ** *míngtiān zǎoshang* **zài jiā li xiūxi**
   I am resting at home tomorrow morning.

Exercise 8.4

Translate the following sentences into Chinese:

1 What time are you going to school tomorrow? (学校 **xuéxiào** 'school')
2 I am coming here to attend the seminar next month. (开座谈会 **kāi zuòtánhuì** 'to attend a seminar')
3 When are you going on a trip to Europe? (旅行 **lǚxíng** 'to travel')
4 What time are you going to work tomorrow? (上班 **shàngbān** 'to go to work')
5 What time in the afternoon are you going to the swimming-pool for a swim? (游泳池 **yóuyǒngchí** 'swimming-pool')
6 Which day are you going there to play football? (踢足球 **tī zúqiú** 'to play football')
7 Which month are you going to the seaside for a holiday? (海边 **hǎi biān** 'beach; seaside')

8 What time are you going to the railway station to buy the ticket? (火车站 **huǒchēzhàn** 'railway station')

9 What time in the morning are you going to the market? (买东西 **mǎi dōngxi** 'to do some shopping')

10 When are you going to the library to borrow books? (借书 **jiè shū** 'to borrow books')

UNIT NINE
More interrogative expressions

In the last unit we discussed interrogative time expressions which include 几点钟 **jǐ diǎn zhōng** 'what time (of the day)' and 几时 **jǐ shí** or 什么时候 **shénme shíhou** 'when', etc., and in Unit 4 we dealt with a number of interrogative pronouns including the interrogative location expression 哪儿 **nǎr** 'where'. In this unit we shall look at some more interrogative idioms and expressions.

A 多久 **duō jiǔ** and 多长时间 **duō cháng shíjiān** 'how long' are placed immediately after the verb, as are more precise questions such as 多少天(年)/几天(年) **duōshao tiān (nián)/jǐ tiān (nián)** 'how many days (years)', 多少个/几个月 (星期/礼拜) **duōshao gè/jǐ gè yuè (xīngqī/lǐbài)** 'how many months (weeks)', etc.:

你待(呆)了多长时间？ **nǐ dāi le duō cháng shíjiān**
How long did you stay?

他等了多久？ **tā děng le duō jiǔ**
How long did he wait?

你们在那个国家住了多少年？
nǐmen zài nà/nèi gè guójiā zhù le duōshao nián
How many years did you live in that country?

Note: These question phrases, like all time duration expressions, are placed after the verb and are essentially complements. For further discussion of duration expressions, see Unit 14.

When there is an object with the verb, if it is a pronoun it precedes the interrogative expression; if it is a noun it follows the interrogative expression with or without 的 **de**:

你等了他多久？ **nǐ děng le tā duō jiǔ**
How long did you wait for him?

你学了多长时间(的)中文？ **nǐ xué le duō cháng shíjiān (de) zhōngwén**
How long did you learn Chinese?

你姐姐当了多少年(的)护士？ **nǐ jiějie dāng le duōshao nián (de) hùshi**
How many years was your elder sister a nurse?

Another common way to formulate questions of this type where the verb has an object is to repeat the verb after the object and then place the question expression after this repeated verb (see Unit 14):

你学中文学了多久/多长时间？
nǐ *xué* zhōngwén *xué* le duō jiǔ/duō cháng shíjiān
How long did you learn Chinese?

你姐姐当护士当了多少年？ **nǐ jiějie *dāng* hùshi *dāng* le duōshao nián**
How many years was your elder sister a nurse?

A considerable number of common verbs in Chinese are intrinsically of a 'verb + object' construction, e.g. 游泳 **yóuyǒng** 'to swim', 跳舞 **tiàowǔ** 'to dance', 唱歌 **chàng gē** 'to sing', 睡觉 **shuìjiào** 'to sleep', 走路 **zǒulù** 'to walk', etc. With these verbs the same rule applies:

你和你朋友跳了几个钟头(的)舞？
nǐ hé nǐ péngyou tiào le jǐ gè zhōngtóu (de) wǔ

or

你和你朋友跳舞跳了几个钟头？
nǐ hé nǐ péngyou *tiàowǔ* tiào le jǐ gè zhōngtóu
How many hours did you dance with your friend?

One cannot say:

*你和你朋友跳舞了几个钟头？ **nǐ hé nǐ péngyou tiàowǔ le jǐ gè zhōngtóu**
(*lit.* How many hours did you dance with your friend?)

B   多 **duō** 'how' may in fact be used with many adjectives in questions of degree, for example, of size, weight, etc. The pattern of such enquiries is usually '有 **yǒu** + 多 **duō** + adjective':

中国有多大？ **zhōngguó yǒu duō dà**
How big is China?

你的行李有多重？ **nǐ de xínglǐ yǒu duō zhòng**
How heavy is your luggage?

你姐姐有多高？ **nǐ jiějie yǒu duō gāo**
How tall is your elder sister?

这个游泳池有多长？ **zhè/zhèi gè yóuyǒngchí yǒu duō cháng**
How long is this swimming-pool?

学校离这儿有多远？ **xuéxiào lí zhèr yǒu dōu yuǎn**
How far is the school from here?

Note: 离 **lí** in the last example is a coverb which occurs with other verbs or adjectives to mean 'distance (away) from (a place)' (see Unit 24).

C 多 **duō** may also be used in conjunction with an adjective as an adverbial or an attributive:

 (i) as an adverbial to modify a verb

> 你多快能完成这件工作？
> **nǐ duō kuài néng wánchéng zhè/zhèi jiàn gōngzuò**
> How fast can you finish this work?

(ii) as an attributive with 的 **de** to modify a noun

> 你穿多大的鞋？ **nǐ chuān duō dà de xié**
> What size (*lit.* how big) shoes do you take?

> Note: For more on attributives, see Unit 10. For 多 **duō** in 多少 **duōshao** 'how many' and comparisons with 几 **jǐ** + measure word 'how many', see Unit 5.

D 怎样 **zěn yàng**, 怎么 **zěnme** and 怎么样 **zěnme yàng** are used adverbially before verbs to mean 'how; in what way':

我怎么样去伦敦？	**wǒ zěnme yàng qù lúndūn**	How do I get to London?
去游泳池怎么走？	**qù yóuyǒngchí zěnme zǒu**	How do you get to the swimming-pool?

Note: Observe the different meanings of 走 **zǒu**:

 (i) to walk; to come/go on foot

> 我走路去。 **wǒ zǒulù qù**   I'll go on foot.

 (ii) to leave

> 他走了。 **tā zǒu le**   He's left.

(iii) to get to (a place) (often with 怎么 **zěnme** or 怎样 **zěn yàng**)

> 去车站怎样走？ **qù chēzhàn zěn yàng zǒu**   How do you get to the station?

E   怎么样 **zěnme yàng** can be used predicatively and is placed after the topic of the sentence to mean 'what is (something or somebody) like'/'how is (somebody or something)':

那儿的天气怎么样？	**nàr de tiānqì zěnme yàng**	What's the weather like there?
你弟弟怎么样？	**nǐ dìdi zěnme yàng**	How is your younger brother?
工作怎么样？	**gōngzuò zěnme yàng**	How's work?

F   怎么样 **zěnme yàng** in addition, can occur after a statement and convert that statement into a question 'what/how about . . .' (It is often used when making suggestions about future actions or activities):

晚上我们去看电影，怎么样？
wǎnshang wǒmen qù kàn diànyǐng | zěnme yàng
How about going to the cinema this evening?

咱们明天去跳舞，怎么样？ **zánmen míngtiān qù tiàowǔ | zěnme yàng**
What about going dancing tomorrow?

G   为什么 **wèi shénme** 'why' is usually placed before the verb:

你为什么学中文？ **nǐ wèi shénme xué zhōngwén**
Why do you study Chinese?

小李昨天为什么不来？ **xiǎo lǐ zuótiān wèi shénme bù lái**
Why didn't Xiao Li come yesterday?

Note: 小 **xiǎo** is often used before the family name or given name (which must be a monosyllable) of a person who is younger than the speaker. It implies a degree of familiarity with the person addressed.

H   怎么 **zěnme** is also used colloquially to mean 'how is it? how come?':

你怎么不去看他？	**nǐ zěnme bù qù kàn tā**	Why aren't you going to see him?
她怎么会讲日语？	**tā zěnme huì jiǎng rìyǔ**	How come she can speak Japanese?

Exercise 9.1

Convert the Chinese statements below into questions, focusing on the highlighted elements. Please also make adjustments to the pronouns as necessary:

EXAMPLE

我在这儿住了六年。 **wǒ zài zhèr zhù le** *liù nián*
I lived here for six years.

你在这儿住了多久/多长时间？ **nǐ zài zhèr zhù le** *duō jiǔ/duō cháng shíjiān*
How long did you live here?

1 我在路上花了两小时。 **wǒ zài lù shang huā le** *liǎng xiǎoshí*
   It took me two hours to get here.
2 我在教室里看了一个多小时的书。
   wǒ zài jiàoshì li kàn le *yī gè duō xiǎoshí* **de shū**
   I read for over an hour in the classroom.
3 足球比赛开始半个钟头了。 **zúqiú bǐsài kāishǐ** *bàn gè zhōngtóu* **le**
   The soccer match has been started for half an hour.
4 我和姐姐在花园里坐了十来分钟。
   wǒ hé jiějie zài huāyuán li zuò le *shí lái fēn zhōng*
   My elder sister and I sat in the garden for over ten minutes.
5 妈妈在厨房里忙了几个钟头。
   māma zài chúfáng li máng le *jǐ gè zhōngtóu*
   Mother was busy cooking in the kitchen for several hours.
6 妹妹帮了我两天的忙。 **mèimei bāng le wǒ** *liǎng* **tiān de máng**
   My younger sister helped me for two days.
7 我开了一年车，骑了两年自行车。
   wǒ kāi le *yī nián* **chē | qí le** *liǎng nián* **zìxíngchē**
   I drove for a year and travelled by bike for two years.
8 足球场有八十米长。 **zúqiúchǎng yǒu** *bā shí mǐ cháng*
   The football pitch is 80 metres long.
9 我哥哥有一米七高。 **wǒ gēge yǒu** *yī mǐ qī gāo*
   My elder brother is 1 metre 70 tall.
10 巴黎离伦敦有二百英里远。 **bālí lí lúndūn yǒu** *èr bǎi yīnglǐ yuǎn*
   Paris is two hundred miles from London.

Exercise 9.2

Translate into English the following sentences with 怎么 **zěnme**, 怎样 **zěn yàng** or 怎么样 **zěnme yàng**:

1 咱们下星期一去他家看他，怎么样？
   zánmen xià xīngqī yī qù tā jiā kàn tā | zěnme yàng
2 去汽车站怎样/怎么走？ **qù qìchēzhàn zěn yàng/zěnme zǒu**
3 伦敦的交通怎么样？
   lúndūn de jiāotōng zěnme yàng (交通 **jiāotōng** 'transport; traffic')
4 去电影院怎么/怎样走？ **qù diànyǐngyuàn zěnme/zěn yàng zǒu**
5 明晚咱们去酒吧间喝啤酒，怎么样？
   míng wǎn zánmen qù jiǔbājiān hē píjiǔ | zěnme yàng

6 北京的天气怎么样？ **běijīng de tiānqì zěnme yàng**
7 那家商店的东西怎么样？ **nà/nèi jiā shāngdiàn de dōngxi zěnme yàng**
8 咱们下个月去度假，怎么样？
  zánmen xià gè yuè qù dùjià | zěnme yàng

Exercise 9.3

Translate the following questions into Chinese:

1 How much did you eat?
2 How did you get to London?
3 Why did he leave?
4 How long are you going to stay?
5 How did you make this cake?
6 What's your new house like?
7 How much money have you got?
8 What was the film like?
9 How about a drink?
10 Why are you learning Chinese?
11 How do I get to know Xiao Li?
12 What do you think of the Chinese teacher?
13 How do you go to work?
14 How long have you been waiting for her?
15 How many hours did she sleep?
16 How many days did you (pl.) drive?
17 How long did you wait for the bus?
18 How far did you walk?

Exercise 9.4

Complete the Chinese translations of the English sentences below with '多 **duō** + adjective' (as appropriate):

1 How far is it to London?
   去伦敦有 ＿＿＿＿ ＿＿＿＿？ **qù lúndūn yǒu** ＿＿＿＿ ＿＿＿＿
2 How tall is your younger brother?
   你弟弟有 ＿＿＿＿ ＿＿＿＿？ **nǐ dìdi yǒu** ＿＿＿＿ ＿＿＿＿
3 How many people are there in Beijing?
   北京有 ＿＿＿＿ ＿＿＿＿ 人？ **běijīng yǒu** ＿＿＿＿ **rén**
4 How far is the post-office from here?
   邮局离这儿有 ＿＿＿＿ ＿＿＿＿？ **yóujú lí zhèr yǒu** ＿＿＿＿ ＿＿＿＿
5 How heavy is this piece of luggage?
   这件行李有 ＿＿＿＿ ＿＿＿＿？
   zhè/zhèi jiàn xínglǐ yǒu ＿＿＿＿ ＿＿＿＿

6 How heavy is the rain outside?

外面的雨有 ___ ___? **wàimian de yǔ yǒu** _____ _____

7 How much is that pair of trousers?

(买)那条裤子要 _____ _____ 钱？

(mǎi) nà/nèi tiáo kùzi yào ___ **qián**

8 What size is that pair of shoes?

那双鞋有 _____ _____? **nà/nèi shuāng xié yǒu** _____ _____

9 How many miles did he run?

他跑了 _____ _____ 英里路？ **tā páo le** _____ **yīnglǐ lù**

10 How long has Li Ming been gone?

李明走了 _____ _____/_____ _____ _____ _____ 了？

lǐ míng zǒu le _____ _____/_____ _____ _____ **le**

11 Have you been dancing the whole evening?

你们跳了 _____ _____/_____ _____ _____ _____ (的)舞？

nǐmen tiào le _____ _____/_____ _____ _____ **(de) wǔ**

12 How much time have we still got?

我们还有 _____ _____ 时间？ **wǒmen hái yǒu** _____ **shíjiān**

13 How long have you been here?

你们在这儿待了 _____ _____/_____ _____ _____ _____?

nǐmen zài zhèr dāi le _____ _____/_____ _____ _____

14 How much work have you done?

你们做了 _____ _____ 工作？ **nǐmen zuò le** _____ **gōngzuò**

UNIT TEN
Adjectives: attributive and predicative

Attributives are words placed before nouns to qualify or describe them. Adjectives are obvious examples of attributives.

A When a monosyllabic adjective is used as an attributive, it is placed directly before the noun it qualifies:

红花	**hóng huā**	red flowers
白云	**bái yún**	white clouds
长裙子	**cháng qúnzi**	a long skirt
脏衣服	**zāng yīfu**	dirty clothes

Disyllabic adjectives, on the other hand, are normally followed by 的 **de**:

干净的街道	**gānjìng de jiēdào**	a clean street
漂亮的车	**piàoliang de chē**	a beautiful car
古老的楼房	**gǔlǎo de lóufáng**	ancient buildings

Where there is a 'numeral + measure' phrase or a 'demonstrative + measure' phrase, it always precedes the adjectival attributive:

一所新房子	**yī suǒ xīn fángzi**	a new house
两本旧书	**liǎng běn jiù shū**	two old books
这家大商店	**zhè/zhèi jiā dà shāngdiàn**	this big store
那匹黑马	**nà/nèi pǐ hēi mǎ**	that black horse
一场精彩的比赛	**yī chǎng jīngcǎi de bǐsài**	an exciting match
两个有趣的故事	**liǎng gè yǒuqù de gùshi**	two interesting stories

Note: When a disyllabic adjective qualifies a disyllabic noun, 的 **de** may sometimes be omitted, especially when the combination becomes a set expression:

新鲜蔬菜	**xīnxiān shūcài**	fresh vegetables
精彩表演	**jīngcǎi biǎoyǎn**	excellent performance

B   Adjectives themselves are commonly modified by degree adverbs such as
很 **hěn** 'very', 太 **tài** 'too', 十分 **shífēn** 'extremely', 非常 **fēicháng** 'extremely'
(*lit.* 'unusually'):

很大	**hěn dà**	(very) big
太小	**tài xiǎo**	too small
十分干净	**shífēn gānjìng**	extremely clean
非常古老	**fēicháng gǔlǎo**	incredibly ancient

Note: Adjectives modified by degree adverbs also require the particle 的 **de** when used as attributives:

很大的屋子	**hěn dà de wūzi**	a (very) big room
非常古老的城市	**fēicháng gǔlǎo de chéngshì**	a really ancient city

An exception to this rule are the indefinite plurals like 很多 **hěn duō** and 不少 **bù
shǎo** 'many' (see Unit 7):

他们有很多钱。 **tāmen yǒu hěn duō qián**
They have a lot of money.

不少人来这儿看风景。 **bù shǎo rén lái zhèr kàn fēngjǐng**
Quite a number of people come here for the scenery.

C   A distinctive feature of Chinese is that when an adjective is used as a
predicative, it follows the subject/topic immediately and does not require the
link verb 'to be'. In addition, it should *always* be modified by a degree adverb:

那条街道很干净。	**nà/nèi tiáo jiēdào hěn gānjìng**	The street is (very) clean.
这双鞋子太小。	**zhè/zhèi shuāng xiézi tài xiǎo**	This pair of shoes is too small.
这个故事非常有趣。	**zhè/zhèi gè gùshi fēicháng yǒuqù**	This story is extremely interesting.
那场比赛十分精彩。	**nà/nèi chǎng bǐsài shífēn jīngcǎi**	That match was extremely exciting.

One does not normally say (unless speaking emphatically to reiterate or contradict a statement):

街道是干净。 **jiēdào shì gānjìng**
(*lit.* The street IS clean.)
[implying, e.g. who says it isn't *or* I did say that it was clean]

Note: The degree adverb 很 **hěn**, though when stressed it means 'very', otherwise carries little
meaning.

An unmodified adjective, when used as a predicative, always implies some form of contrast.

街道干净。 **jiēdào gānjìng**
The street is clean. [perhaps the shops aren't]

这双鞋子小。 **zhè/zhèi shuāng xiézi xiǎo**
This pair of shoes is small. [perhaps another pair is the right size]

D   An adjectival predicative is negated by 不 **bù** 'not':

这双鞋子不贵。	**zhè/zhèi shuāng xiézi bù guì**	This pair of shoes isn't expensive.
那瓶牛奶不新鲜。	**nà/nèi píng niúnǎi bù xīnxiān**	That bottle of milk isn't fresh.
今天的天气不好。	**jīntiān de tiānqì bù hǎo**	Today's weather is bad.

The negator 不 **bù** and a degree adverb may both come before the adjectival predicative. When this happens, the positioning of 不 **bù** in relation to the degree adverb affects the meaning of the adjective:

这所房子不很好。 **zhè/zhèi suǒ fángzi bù hěn hǎo**
This house isn't very good/nice.

这所房子很不好。 **zhè/zhèi suǒ fángzi hěn bù hǎo**
This house is really bad. (*lit.* This house is very not good.)

这瓶牛奶不太新鲜。 **zhè/zhèi píng niúnǎi bù tài xīnxiān**
This bottle of milk isn't very/too fresh.

这瓶牛奶太不新鲜了。 **zhè píng niúnǎi tài bù xīnxiān le**
This bottle of milk isn't fresh at all.

The negator 不 **bù** is regularly linked with 够 **gòu** 'enough' to modify an adjectival predicative:

这条裙子不够长。 **zhè/zhèi tiáo qúnzi bù gòu cháng**
This skirt isn't long enough.

我这杯咖啡不够甜。 **wǒ zhè/zhèi bēi kāfēi bù gòu tián**
This cup of coffee (of mine) isn't sweet enough.

E   Most monosyllabic adjectives may be reduplicated to intensify their meaning. Reduplicated adjectives take the particle 的 **de** when qualifying nouns:

蓝蓝的天	**lánlán de tiān**	a really blue sky (*lit.* blue blue sky)
高高的楼房	**gāogāo de lóufáng**	really tall buildings (*lit.* tall tall buildings)
一些红红的桔子	**yīxiē hónghóng de júzi**	some bright red tangerines (*lit.* some red red tangerines)

A limited number of disyllabic adjectives may also be reduplicated. The pattern for reduplication is: AB > AABB

干净	**gānjìng**	clean and tidy	>
干干净净	**gāngānjìngjìng**	spotlessly clean	
整齐	**zhěngqí**	orderly/tidy	>
整整齐齐	**zhěngzhěngqíqí**	very orderly/tidy	
老实	**lǎoshí**	honest; naïve	>
老老实实	**lǎolǎoshíshí**	very honest/very naïve	

一张干干净净的桌子	**yī zhāng gāngānjìngjìng de zhuōzi**	a spotlessly clean table
一个整整齐齐的房间	**yī gè zhěngzhěngqíqí de fángjiān**	an extremely tidy room
一个老老实实的人	**yī gè lǎolǎoshíshí de rén**	a very honest person

Reduplicated adjectives, being already emphatic in form, cannot be further modified by a degree adverb or a negator.

One cannot say:

| *很红红 | **hěn hónghóng** | (*lit.* very red) |
| *不干干净净 | **bù gāngānjìngjìng** | (*lit.* not spotlessly clean) |

Exercise 10.1

Translate the following phrases into Chinese, paying attention to the inclusion or omission of 的 **de**:

1 a very big swimming-pool
2 new buildings
3 white cats
4 a large bowl
5 a beautiful garden
6 a little child
7 an interesting film
8 an exciting match

9 fresh vegetables
10 a lot of money
11 an old car
12 extremely heavy luggage
13 clean clothes
14 a tidy room
15 very narrow streets (狭窄 **xiázhǎi** 'narrow')
16 ancient cities
17 an extremely good concert
18 dirty shoes

Exercise 10.2

Indicate which of the Chinese translations given for the English sentences below is correct:

1 The weather is nice today.
今天天气很好。   **jīntiān tiānqì hěn hǎo**
今天天气是好。   **jīntiān tiānqì shì hǎo**

2 She is rich.
她很有钱。   **tā hěn yǒu qián**
她是有钱。   **tā shì yǒu qián**

3 This armchair isn't very comfortable.
这个沙发不很舒服。   **zhè/zhèi gè shāfā bù hěn shūfu**
这个沙发很不舒服。   **zhè/zhèi gè shāfā hěn bù shūfu**

4 The classroom is really clean.
那个教室非常干干净净。   **nà/nèi gè jiàoshì fēicháng gāngānjìngjìng**
那个教室是非常干净。   **nà/nèi gè jiàoshì shì fēicháng gānjìng**
那个教室非常干净。   **nà/nèi gè jiàoshì fēicháng gānjìng**

5 My younger brother isn't very tall.
我弟弟不太高。   **wǒ dìdi bù tài gāo**
我弟弟太不高。   **wǒ dìdi tài bù gāo**
我弟弟不高高。   **wǒ dìdi bù gāogāo**

6 This match isn't particularly exciting.
这场比赛不十分精彩。   **zhè/zhèi chǎng bǐsài bù shífēn jīngcǎi**
这场比赛不精彩彩。   **zhè/zhèi chǎng bǐsài bù jīngjingcǎicai**
这场比赛十分不精彩。   **zhè/zhèi chǎng bǐsài shífēn bù jīngcǎi**

7 There were toys of all colours on the floor.
地上都是红红绿绿玩具。   **dì shang dōu shì hónghónglǜlǜ wánjù**
地上都是红红绿绿的玩具。   **dì shang dōu shì hónghónglǜlǜ de wánjù**
地上都有红红绿绿的玩具。   **dì shang dōu yǒu hónghónglǜlǜ de wánjù**

8 Mr Wang is a very interesting person.
王先生是一个非常有趣人。   **wáng xiānsheng shì yī gè fēicháng yǒuqù rén**
王先生一个非常有趣的人。   **wáng xiānsheng yī gè fēicháng yǒuqù de rén**
王先生是个非常有趣的人。   **wáng xiānsheng shì gè fēicháng yǒuqù de rén**

Exercise 10.3

Translate the following into Chinese:

1 Beijing is an extremely ancient city.
2 That old book is not too expensive.
3 The library is extremely big.
4 I don't have any new clothes.
5 Those fresh flowers are very beautiful.
6 That pair of shoes is too large.
7 The weather here is really nice.
8 That street is not clean enough.
9 I don't like milk which isn't fresh.
10 That cup of coffee is too sweet.

Exercise 10.4

Add emphasis to the highlighted adjectives by means of reduplication:

1 路旁坐着一个高大的小伙子。
   lù páng zuò zhe yī gè *gāodà* de xiǎohuǒzi
   A tall young man sat by the roadside.
2 小王长着弯眉毛，高鼻子，小嘴巴和一双大眼睛，留着一头整齐的短发。
   xiǎo wáng zhǎng zhe *wān* méimao | *gāo* bǐzi | *xiǎo* zuǐba hé yī shuāng *dà* yǎnjing | liú zhe yī tóu *zhěngqí* de duǎn fà
   Xiao Wang had curved eyebrows, a straight nose, a small mouth, big eyes and hair cut in a neat bob.
3 这是一间干净的房间。白床单，蓝窗帘，红炉火，给你一种舒适的感觉。
   zhè shì yī jiān *gānjìng* de fángjiān | *bái* chuángdān | *lán* chuānglián | *hóng* lúhuǒ | gěi nǐ yī zhǒng *shūshì* de gǎnjué
   This is a neat and tidy room. The white sheets, blue curtains and warm fire make it feel very cosy.

4 她那朴素的衣着，大方的举止，甜美的声音给人留下了深刻的印象。

tā nà *pǔsù* **de yīzhuó |** *dàfāng* **de jǔzhǐ |** *tiánměi* **de shēngyīn gěi rén liú xià le shēnkè de yìnxiàng**

Her plain clothes, dignified bearing and clear, sweet voice made a deep impression on people.

UNIT ELEVEN
是 **shì** and 有 **yǒu**

A The verb 是 **shì** 'to be' in Chinese is not exactly equivalent to the English verb 'to be'. It is similar to its English counterpart in that it may generally be followed by a noun which defines the subject/topic:

我们是学生。	**wǒmen shì xuésheng**	We are students.
他是老师。	**tā shì lǎoshī**	He is a teacher.
今天是星期日。	**jīntiān shì xīngqī rì**	Today is Sunday.

The noun which follows 是 **shì** may, of course, be modified in many ways. It may, for instance, be preceded by a possessive adjective or pronoun, another noun usually with or without 的 **de**, a 'numeral/demonstrative + measure word' phrase or an adjective qualifier:

他是我丈夫。 **tā shì wǒ zhàngfu**
He is my husband.

那是他的大衣。 **nà shì tā de dàyī**
That is his coat.

这位是张先生的朋友。 **zhè/zhèi wèi shì zhāng xiānsheng de péngyou**
This is Mr Zhang's friend.

这些是中国画儿。 **zhè/zhèi xiē shì zhōngguó huàr**
These are Chinese paintings.

那是一个馒头。 **nà shì yī gè mántou**
That is a steamed bun.

这是一本很有意思的书。 **zhè shì yī běn hěn yǒu yìsi de shū**
This is a very interesting book.

If the noun is qualified by an attributive and repeats the topic or is understood from the context, it may be omitted:

这支笔是我的。 **zhè/zhèi zhī bǐ shì wǒ de** (pronoun attributive)
This pen is mine.

那匹马是张先生的。 **nà/nèi pǐ mǎ shì zhāng xiānsheng de** (noun attributive)
That horse is Mr Zhang's.

这一个是好的。 **zhè/zhèi yī gè shì hǎo de** (adjective attributive)
This is a good one.

B   However, 是 **shì** is not normally followed by an adjective on its own unless one is speaking emphatically to reiterate a case, contradict a previous speaker, etc. (see Unit 10):

这本书是贵。 **zhè/zhèi běn shū shì guì**
This book *is* expensive. (I admit, but another may be more expensive, etc.)

她是非常聪明。 **tā shì fēicháng cōngming**
She *is* extremely intelligent. (The problem is that she isn't really conscientious.)

Normal unemphasized sentences have an adjectival predicative without 是 **shì** (see previous unit):

| 这本书很贵。 | **zhè/zhèi běn shū hěn guì** | This book is (very) expensive. |
| 她非常聪明。 | **tā fēicháng cōngming** | She's extremely intelligent. |

Note: There is however a group of adjectives which can be called 'non-gradable' in that they are not purely descriptive but define an 'either–or' quality or situation (e.g. 活 **huó** 'alive', i.e. 'not dead'; 黑 **hēi** 'black', i.e. not of any other colour, etc.). These adjectives, when used predicatively, require 是 **shì** to link them to the topic and they are followed by the particle 的 **de**:

| 这条鱼是活的。 | **zhè/zhèi tiáo yú shì huó de** | This fish is alive. |
| 这辆车是黑的。 | **zhè/zhèi liàng chē shì hēi de** | This car is black. |

C   是 **shì** is negated by 不 **bù**:

今天不是星期天。 **jīntiān bù shì xīngqī tiān**
Today is not Sunday.

明年不是猪年。 **míngnián bù shì zhū nián**
Next year is not the year of the pig.

这是绿茶，不是红茶。 **zhè shì lǜchá | bù shì hóngchá**
This is green tea, not black tea. (*lit.* this is green tea, not red tea)

那张桌子是方的，不是圆的。
nà/nèi zhāng zhuōzi shì fāng de | bù shì yuán de
That table is square, not round.

这些都不是我的，是李太太的。
zhè/zhèi xiē dōu bù shì wǒ de | shì lǐ tàitai de
None of these are mine, they're Mrs Li's.

Note 1: Notice that if the adverb 都 **dōu** 'both; all' is also present, the positioning of the negator 不 **bù** with reference to 都 **dōu** may affect the meaning of the sentence:

| 这些不都是我的。 | **zhè/zhèi xiē bù dōu shì wǒ de** | Not all of these are mine. |
| 这些都不是我的。 | **zhè/zhèi xiē dōu bù shì wǒ de** | None of these are mine. |

Note 2: The twelve animals of the Chinese zodiac, which are often used to identify the year of one's birth, come in the following order: (老)鼠 **(lǎo)shǔ** 'rat', 牛 **niú** 'ox', (老)虎 **(lǎo)hǔ** 'tiger', 兔(子) **tù(zi)** 'rabbit', 龙 **lóng** 'dragon', 蛇 **shé** 'snake', 马 **mǎ** 'horse', 羊 **yáng** 'goat', 猴(子) **hóu(zi)** 'monkey', 鸡 **jī** 'rooster', 狗 **gǒu** 'dog', 猪 **zhū** 'pig'.

D   是 **shì** is also used as an intensifier to highlight the initiator, recipient, time, place, means, purpose, etc. of the action expressed in the verb. It is placed immediately before the word or phrase to be highlighted, which may mean that it is placed at the beginning of the sentence:

你是早上洗澡吗？	**nǐ shì zǎoshang xǐzǎo ma**	Do you take a bath *in the morning*?
她明天是坐船去。	**tā míngtiān shì zuò chuán qù**	She is going *by boat* tomorrow.
是谁在敲门？	**shì shéi zài qiāo mén**	*Who* is it knocking at the door?
我们是来找经理。	**wǒmen shì lái zhǎo jīnglǐ**	We are coming to see *the manager*.

If the action to be emphasized took place in the past, 是 **shì** is used with 的 **de**:

| 他是昨天走的吗？ | **tā shì zuótiān zǒu de ma** | Did he leave *yesterday*? |
| 我们不是走路来的。 | **wǒmen bù shì zǒulù lái de** | We did not come *on foot*. |

To highlight the object, 是 **shì** is placed before the verb while 的 **de** is inserted between the verb and the object:

我小时候是学的中文。 **wǒ xiǎo shíhou shì xué de zhōngwén**
I studied *Chinese* when I was little.

我们刚才是叫的炒面。 **wǒmen gāngcái shì jiào de chǎomiàn**
What we ordered just now was *fried noodles*.

E 有 **yǒu** indicates *either* possession 'to have':

她有一个电脑。	**tā yǒu yī gè diànnǎo**	She's got a computer.
他只有两个儿子。	**tā zhǐ yǒu liǎng gè érzi**	He only has two sons.

or existence 'there is/are'. A regular pattern is 'location phrase + 有 **yǒu** + noun', which normally translates into English as 'There is/are (something/some things) (somewhere)':

抽屉里有信纸。 **chōuti li yǒu xìnzhǐ**
There is some writing paper in the drawer.

操场上有很多运动员。 **cāochǎng shang yǒu hěn duō yùndòngyuán**
There are a lot of athletes on the sportsfield.

树下有一只兔子。 **shù xià yǒu yī zhī tùzi**
There is a hare under the tree.

湖上有一群鸭子。 **hú shang yǒu yī qún yāzi**
There is a flock of ducks on the lake.

Note: The noun following 有 **yǒu** is always of indefinite reference (see Unit 2).

F 有 **yǒu** is negated by 没 **méi**:

我没有电脑。 **wǒ méi yǒu diànnǎo**
I haven't got a computer.

屋子里没有人。 **wūzi li méi yǒu rén**
There isn't anybody in the room.

抽屉里只有信纸，没有信封。 **chōuti li zhǐ yǒu xìnzhǐ | méi yǒu xìnfēng**
There is only writing paper in the drawer, and no envelopes.

Note: When 有 **yǒu** is negated, the noun object is not usually modified by a 'numeral + measure word' phrase unless the number is the central issue:

柜子里只有一件毛衣，没有两件毛衣。 **guìzi li zhǐ yǒu yī jiàn máoyī | méi yǒu liǎng jiàn máoyī**
There is only one sweater in the wardrobe, not two.

G 是 **shì** may also be used to indicate existence like 有 **yǒu**, but it differs from 有 **yǒu** in two ways.

(i) 是 **shì** (but not 有 **yǒu**) may be preceded by 全 **quán** or 都 **dōu** 'all; entirely' to suggest that the location is occupied solely by one kind of being or thing:

地上全是水。 **dì shang quán shì shuǐ**
The ground was covered with water.

街上都是人。 **jiē shang dōu shì rén**
The street was full of people.

(ii) while 有 **yǒu** only focuses on what exists, 是 **shì** tends to emphasize the location as well:

电影院对面有几家商店。 **diànyǐngyuàn duìmiàn yǒu jǐ jiā shāngdiàn**
There are a few shops opposite the cinema.

房子后面是个菜园。 **fángzi hòumian shì gè càiyuán**
Behind the house is a vegetable garden.

Exercise 11.1

Translate the following sentences into Chinese, bearing in mind that 是 **shì** may, or may not, have to be present:

1 She is my neighbour.
2 My younger sister is beautiful.
3 Yesterday was Tuesday.
4 My car is red.
5 This fish is alive.
6 Our room is clean.
7 That story is very interesting.
8 These vegetables are fresh.
9 This skirt isn't too dirty.
10 The concert was wonderful.
11 All these clothes are old.
12 Whose is that pair of glasses?

Exercise 11.2

Rewrite the Chinese sentences below in the negative to match the English:

1 小王有一条狗。 **xiǎo wáng yǒu yī tiáo gǒu**
   Xiao Wang hasn't got a dog.
2 花园里有很多花儿。 **huāyuán li yǒu hěn duō huār**
   There aren't many flowers in the garden.

3 他们都是英国人。 **tāmen dōu shì yīngguó rén**
None of them is English.

4 这幢房子是他的。 **zhè/zhèi zhuàng fángzi shì tā de**
This house isn't his.

5 那杯咖啡是我朋友的。 **nà/nèi bēi kāfēi shì wǒ péngyou de**
That cup of coffee isn't my friend's.

6 楼下有人。 **lóuxià yǒu rén**
There's no one downstairs.

7 她是经理。 **tā shì jīnglǐ**
She isn't the manager.

8 他有两件行李。 **tā yǒu liǎng jiàn xíngli**
He doesn't have two pieces of luggage.

9 我的同学都是中国人。 **wǒ de tóngxué dōu shì zhōngguó rén**
Not all my classmates are Chinese.

10 图书馆后面是电影院。 **túshūguǎn hòumian shì diànyǐngyuàn**
It isn't the cinema behind the library.

Exercise 11.3

Indicate which of the two Chinese translations for the English sentences below is correct in each case:

1 There is some writing paper in the drawer.
抽屉里是信纸。 **chōuti li shì xìnzhǐ**
抽屉里有信纸。 **chōuti li yǒu xìnzhǐ**

2 The picture is beautiful.
那幅画儿很美。 **nà/nèi fú huàr hěn měi**
那幅画儿是美的。 **nà/nèi fú huàr shì měi de**

3 This snake is alive. (蛇 **shé** 'snake')
这条蛇是活。 **zhè/zhèi tiáo shé shì huó**
这条蛇是活的。 **zhè/zhèi tiáo shé shì huó de**

4 I haven't got a pair of gloves.
我没有手套。 **wǒ méi yǒu shǒutào**
我没有一双手套。 **wǒ méi yǒu yī shuāng shǒutào**

5 He isn't a manager.
他没是经理。 **tā méi shì jīnglǐ**
他不是经理。 **tā bù shì jīnglǐ**

6 There aren't any rabbits under the tree.
树下不有兔子。 **shù xià bù yǒu tùzi**
树下没有兔子。 **shù xià méi yǒu tùzi**

7 Those trousers aren't mine.
那条裤子不是我的。 **nà/nèi tiáo kùzi bù shì wǒ de**
那条裤子没是我的。 **nà/nèi tiáo kùzi méi shì wǒ de**

8 The bookshelf was filled with books.
书架上都是书。 **shūjià shang dōu shì shū**
书架上都有书。 **shūjià shang dōu yǒu shū**

Exercise 11.4

Translate the following sentences into Chinese:

1 There are two red jumpers in the wardrobe.
2 There is a large cooker in the kitchen. (炉子 **lúzi** 'cooker')
3 There are many books on the bookshelf.
4 There are many students in the classroom.
5 The swimming-pool is full of people.
6 There isn't a single chair in the room.
7 There is nothing in the drawer.
8 There are no flowers in the garden.
9 There isn't a telephone in the office.
10 There is a flock of sheep at the foot of the hill.
11 Opposite the restaurant is the cinema.
12 There is quite a lot of cooked rice in the pot.
13 There is only a little milk in the bottle.
14 There are toys all over the floor. (地板 **dìbǎn** 'floor')
15 There is nobody in the house.

Exercise 11.5

Translate the sentences below into Chinese:

1 This is a bus ticket, not a cinema ticket.
2 That is a pair of mandarin ducks, not ordinary ducks.
  (普通 **pǔtōng** 'ordinary')
3 Those are potatoes, not sweet potatoes. (番薯 **fānshǔ** 'sweet potato')
4 These are bees, not flies. (蜜蜂 **mìfēng** 'bee')
5 This is petrol, not vegetable oil. (菜油 **càiyóu** 'vegetable oil')
6 That is Mr Zhang, the manager, not Mr Li, the engineer.
7 There is only a bicycle outside, not a car.
8 There are pearls but no earrings in the box. (盒子 **hézi** 'box')
9 There is only a map on the wall, not a picture.
10 I have a packet of cigarettes, but not a box of matches. (包 **bāo** 'packet')
11 There is a cooker but no fridge in the kitchen.
12 I have only got a knife, but not a pair of scissors.
13 None of these is hers.
14 Not all of those are good.
15 Those are all bad/no good.

UNIT TWELVE
Comparisons

A   The standard way to express a comparison in Chinese is to use the coverb 比 **bǐ** 'to compare with' in conjunction with an adjectival predicate (for a full discussion of coverbs see Unit 24). 'X is better/larger, etc. than Y' therefore follows the pattern 'X + 比 **bǐ** + Y + adjective (e.g. good/large, etc.)':

这个比那个好。 **zhè/zhèi gè bǐ nà/nèi gè hǎo**
This one is better than that one.

这个学校比那个学校大。 **zhè/zhèi gè xuéxiào bǐ nà/nèi gè xuéxiaò dà**
This school is larger than that school.

这个箱子比那个箱子重。 **zhè/zhèi gè xiāngzi bǐ nà/nèi gè xiāngzi zhòng**
This box is heavier than that box.

Note: To negate such a construction, 不 **bù** 'not' is placed directly before 比 **bǐ**:

这个不比那个好。 **zhè/zhèi gè bù bǐ nà/nèi gè haǒ**
This one isn't better than that one.

这个学校不比那个学校大。 **zhè/zhèi gè xuéxiào bù bǐ nà/nèi gè xuéxiào dà**
This school isn't larger than that school.

这个箱子不比那个箱子重。 **zhè/zhèi gè xiāngzi bù bǐ nà/nèi gè xiāngzi zhòng**
This box isn't heavier than that box.

An adjective in the predicative position implies a comparison if it stands alone (see Unit 10), and in 比 **bǐ** comparisons it therefore naturally does not have an adverbial modifier. However, the adjective may be modified by degree adverbs like 更 **gèng** and 还(要) **hái (yào)** 'even (more)' or followed by degree complements like 一点儿 **yīdiǎnr** 'slightly', 一些 **yīxiē** 'a little' and 得多 **de duō** or 多了 **duō le** 'much':

 (i) with degree adverbs:

这个比那个更好。 **zhè/zhèi gè bǐ nà/nèi gè gèng hǎo**
This one is even better than that one.

这个学校比那个(学校)更大。
zhè/zhèi gè xuéxiào bǐ nà/nèi gè (xuéxiào) gèng dà
This school is even larger than that school.

这个箱子比那个(箱子)还(要)重。
zhè/zhèi gè xiāngzi bǐ nà/nèi ge (xiāngzi) hái (yào) zhòng
This box is even heavier than that box.

(ii) with degree complements:

这个比那个好多了。 **zhè/zhèi gè bǐ nà/nèi gè hǎo duō le**
This one's much better than that one.

这幢房子比那幢(房子)大一点儿。
zhè/zhèi zhuàng fángzi bǐ nà/nèi zhuàng (fángzi) dà yīdiǎnr
This house is slightly larger than that house.

这件行李比那件(行李)重得多。
zhè/zhèi jiàn xíngli bǐ nà/nèi jiàn (xíngli) zhòng de duō
This case is much heavier than that one. (*lit.* This piece of luggage is
much heavier than that piece.)

上海比北京暖一些。 **shànghǎi bǐ běijīng nuǎn yīxiē**
Shanghai is a bit warmer than Beijing.

两件大衣都很长，红大衣比蓝大衣更长。
liǎng jiàn dàyī dōu hěn cháng | hóng dàyī bǐ lán dàyī gèng cháng
Both coats are very long, but the red one is even longer than the blue one.

这种帽子很贵，那种帽子还(要)贵。
zhè/zhèi zhǒng màozi hěn guì | nà/nèi zhǒng màozi hái (yào) guì
A hat like this is very expensive, but one like that hat is even more
expensive.

Sometimes a degree complement registers an actual amount or extent:

我比爸爸矮一寸。 **wǒ bǐ bàba ǎi yī cùn**
I'm an inch shorter than my father.

哥哥比弟弟重两公斤。 **gēge bǐ dìdi zhòng liǎng gōngjīn**
(The) elder brother is two kilos heavier than the younger brother.

B Similarity is conveyed by 一样 **yīyàng** 'the same' (*lit.* 'one type'), in conjunction with the coverb 跟 **gēn** (or 和 **hé**, 同 **tóng**, 与 **yǔ**) 'with; and'. 一样
yīyàng functions itself as an adjectival predicative:

那两个一样。	**nà/nèi liǎng gè yīyàng**	Those two are the same.
我跟你一样。	**wǒ gēn nǐ yīyàng**	I'm the same as you.
这个跟那个一样。	**zhè/zhèi gè gēn nà/nèi gè yīyàng**	This (one) is the same as that (one).

一样 **yīyàng** is also followed by an adjective to express more specific similarity, in the pattern: 'X + 跟 **gēn** (和 **hé**, 同 **tóng**, 与 **yǔ**) + Y + 一样 **yīyàng** + adjective':

我跟你一样大。 **wǒ gēn nǐ yīyàng dà**
I'm as old as you.

这个跟那个一样好。 **zhè/zhèi gè gēn nà/nèi gè yīyàng hǎo**
This (one) is as good as that (one).

小吴跟小红一样重。 **xiǎo wú gēn xiǎo hóng yīyàng zhòng**
Xiao Wu and Xiao Hong are the same weight./Xiao Wu weighs as much as Xiao Hong.

妈妈和爸爸一样高。 **māma hé bàba yīyàng gāo**
Mother and Father are the same height./Mother is as tall as Father.

Note: In the negative form of this pattern, 不 **bù** comes before 一样 **yīyàng**. It expresses a precise negation of the similarity and no more. 小吴跟小红不一样大。 **xiǎo wú gēn xiǎo hóng bù yīyàng dà** therefore means 'Xiao Wu and Xiao Hong are not the same age.' It *does not* mean 'Xiao Wu is not as young (or old) as Xiao Hong' (see section C).

C Negative comparison is also expressed by the pattern: 'X + 没(有) **méi(yǒu)** + Y + 那么 **nàme**/这么 **zhème** 'so' + adjective':

我没(有)你那么/这么聪明。 **wǒ méi(yǒu) nǐ nàme/zhème cōngming**
I'm not as intelligent as you.

这个没(有)那个那么/这么好。
zhè/zhèi gè méi(yǒu) nà/nèi gè nàme/zhème hǎo
This (one) is not as good as that (one).

我姐姐没(有)我这么高。 **wǒ jiějie méi(yǒu) wǒ zhème gāo**
My elder sister isn't as tall as I am.

老鼠没(有)松鼠那么大。 **lǎoshǔ méi(yǒu) sōngshǔ nàme dà**
Mice aren't as big as squirrels.

The pattern can occur in the positive (i.e. with 有 **yǒu**), usually when a question is being asked:

你姐姐有你这么高吗？ **nǐ jiějie yǒu nǐ zhème gāo ma**
Is your elder sister as tall as you are?

老鼠有松鼠那么大吗？ **lǎoshǔ yǒu sōngshǔ nàme dà ma**
Are mice as big as squirrels?

D   So far, the comparison/similarity expressions discussed above have all been
used as adjectival predicates. If the expression is associated with an action, it
then becomes a complement to that action verb. The complement construction
involves placing 得 **de** after the verb and the required adjectival expression after
得 **de** to indicate comparison or similarity as a result of the action of the verb
(for a full discussion of complements see Unit 22):

我做得比你好。 **wǒ zuò de bǐ nǐ hǎo**
I did it better than you.
我做得跟你一样好。 **wǒ zuò de gēn nǐ yīyàng hǎo**
I did it as well as you.

一号运动员跑得比二号(运动员)快。
yī hào yùndòngyuán pǎo de bǐ èr hào (yùndòngyuán) kuài
Athlete No. 1 ran faster than athlete No. 2.
一号运动员跑得跟二号(运动员)一样快。
yī hào yùndòngyuán pǎo de gēn èr hào (yùndòngyuán) yīyàng kuài
Athlete No. 1 ran as fast as athlete No. 2.

他吃得比我多。 **tā chī de bǐ wǒ duō**
He ate more than I did./He eats more than I do.
他吃得跟我一样多。 **tā chī de gēn wǒ yīyàng duō**
He ate as much as I did./He eats as much as I do.

The '比 **bǐ** + noun'/'跟 **gēn** + noun' phrase may also precede the verb:

我比你做得好。	**wǒ bǐ nǐ zuò de hǎo**	I did it better than you.
他跟我吃得一样多。	**tā gēn wǒ chī de yīyàng duō**	He ate as much as I did.

Note: If the action verb has an object, the verb is repeated after the verb-object expression in either
of the above patterns:

她跳舞跳得比我好。 **tā tiàowǔ tiào de bǐ wǒ hǎo**
她跳舞比我跳得好。 **tā tiàowǔ bǐ wǒ tiào de hǎo**
She dances better than I do./She is a better dancer than I am.

他爬山爬得跟我一样快。 **tā páshān pá de gēn wǒ yīyàng kuài**
他爬山跟我爬得一样快。 **tā páshān gēn wǒ pà de yīyàng kuài**
He climbs a hill as fast as I do.

E   The superlative degree is expressed simply by placing the adverb 最 **zuì** before the adjective:

这三种花儿，白花最香。 **zhè/zhèi sān zhǒng huār | bái huā zuì xiāng**
Of these three flowers, the white one smells the nicest.
(*lit.* is the most fragrant)

班上二十几个学生，小张最勤奋。
bān shang èr shí jǐ gè xuésheng | xiǎo zhāng zuì qínfèn
Out of the twenty or so pupils in the class, Xiao Zhang is the most diligent.

我有四个孩子。第二个孩子考得最好。
wǒ yǒu sì gè háizi | dì èr gè háizi kǎo de zuì hǎo
I have four children. The second child did best in the examination.

F   Increasing or intensifying comparison in the pattern 'more . . . and more . . .' follows the pattern: '越来越 **yuè lái yuè** + adjective':

白天/黑夜越来越长。 **báitiān/hēiyè yuè lái yùe cháng**
The days/nights are growing longer and longer.

天气越来越热/冷。 **tiānqì yuè lái yuè rè/lěng**
The weather is getting hotter and hotter/colder and colder.

我们的生活越来越好。 **wǒmen de shēnghuó yuè lái yuè hǎo**
Our life is getting better and better.

The '越 **yuè** . . . 越 **yuè** . . .' pattern is in fact used in a number of ways:

(i) '越 **yuè** + adjective + 越 **yuè** + adjective':

越多越好。 **yuè duō yuè hǎo**
The more the better (merrier).

姜越老越辣。 **jiāng yuè lǎo yuè là**
The older ginger gets the hotter it is (i.e. old ginger gets hotter).

(ii) '越 **yuè** + verb + 越 **yuè** + adjective':

她越跳越高。 **tā yuè tiào yuè gāo**
She jumped higher and higher.

他越跑越快。 **tā yuè pǎo yuè kuài**
He ran faster and faster.

(iii) '越 **yuè** + verb + 越 **yuè** + verb':

他越赌越输，越输越赌。 **tā yuè dǔ yuè shū | yuè shū yuè dǔ**
The more he gambled the more money he lost, and the more money he lost the more he gambled.

她越说越气。 **tā yuè shuō yuè qì**
The more she spoke, the angrier she became.

(iv) where meaning allows, each '越 **yuè** + verb' construction may have its own subject:

她越说我越气。 **tā yuè shuō wǒ yuè qì**
The more she spoke, the angrier I became.

咖啡越甜我越喜欢。 **kāfēi yuè tián wǒ yuè xǐhuan**
The sweeter the coffee, the better I like it.

Exercise 12.1

Using the words supplied, construct Chinese sentences expressing comparison or similarity and then translate them into English.

EXAMPLE
我 **wǒ**   你 **nǐ**   大 **dà**   跟 **gēn**   一样 **yīyàng**

我跟你一样大。 **wǒ gēn nǐ yīyàng dà**
You and I are the same age.

1	飞机	火车	比	快	
	fēijī	**huǒchē**	**bǐ**	**kuài**	
	plane	train		fast	
2	法国	美国	不一样	大	跟
	fǎguó	**měiguó**	**bù yīyàng**	**dà**	**gēn**
	France	America			
3	冬天	春天	比	暖和	
	dōngtiān	**chūntiān**	**bǐ**	**nuǎnhuo**	
	winter	spring		warm	
4	猫	老虎	得多	小	比
	māo	**lǎohǔ**	**de duō**	**xiǎo**	**bǐ**
	cat	tiger	a lot		

5	阿尔卑斯山	喜马拉雅山	高	那么	没有
	ā'ěrbēisī shān	**xǐmǎlāyǎ shān**	**gāo**	**nàme**	**méiyǒu**
	The Alps	The Himalayas	high		
6	中国的人口	俄国的人口	多	比	
	zhōngguó de	**éguó de rénkǒu**	**duō**	**bǐ**	
	rénkǒu	Russia's	many		
	China's	population			
	population				
7	长城	金字塔	有名	和	一样
	chángchéng	**jīnzìtǎ**	**yǒumíng**	**hé**	**yīyàng**
	The Great Wall	The Pyramids	well-known		
8	小李	老张	那么	勤奋	没有
	xiǎo lǐ	**lǎo zhāng**	**nàme**	**qínfèn**	**méiyǒu**
	Xiao Li	Lao Zhang		industrious	
9	炒饭	炒面	好吃	得多	比
	chǎofàn	**chǎomiàn**	**hǎochī**	**de duō**	**bǐ**
	fried rice	fried noodles	delicious	a lot	
10	我的行李	你的行李	两公斤	重	比
	wǒ de xíngli	**nǐ de xíngli**	**liǎng gōngjīn**	**zhòng**	**bǐ**
	my luggage	your luggage	two kilos	heavy	

Exercise 12.2

Rewrite the following negative comparison sentences using 比 **bǐ** without changing the meaning, and then translate them into English.

EXAMPLE

弟弟没有我这么高。 **dìdi méiyǒu wǒ zhème gāo**
My younger brother isn't as tall as I am.

我比弟弟高。 **wǒ bǐ dìdi gāo**
I am taller than my younger brother.

1 鲨鱼没有鲸鱼那么大。 **shāyú méiyǒu jīngyú nàme dà**
   Sharks are not as big as whales.
2 照相机没有摄象机那么贵。 **zhàoxiàng jī méiyǒu shèxiàngjī nàme guì**
   Cameras aren't as expensive as video cameras.
3 桃子没有苹果那么硬。 **táozi méiyǒu píngguǒ nàme yìng**
   Peaches are not as hard as apples.
4 这个城市没有那个城市那么美丽。
   zhè/zhèi gè chéngshì méiyǒu nà/nèi gè chéngshì nàme měilì
   This city isn't as beautiful as that one.

5 英国的春天没有夏天这么热。
yīngguó de chūntiān méiyǒu xiàtiān zhème rè
The spring isn't as hot as the summer in Britain.
6 法语没有德语这么难。 **fǎyǔ méiyǒu déyǔ zhème nán**
French is not as difficult as German.
7 你没有我那么重。 **nǐ méiyǒu wǒ nàme zhòng**
You are not as heavy as me.
8 黄河没有长江那么长。 **huánghé méiyǒu chángjiāng nàme cháng**
The Yellow River is not as long as the Yangtze River.
9 他的肩膀没有你的那么宽。
tā de jiānbǎng méiyǒu nǐ de nàme kuān (宽 **kuān** 'broad')
His shoulders are not as broad as yours.
10 这首歌没有那首歌么好听。
zhè/zhèi shǒu gē méiyǒu nà/nèi shǒu gē nàme hǎotīng
This song is not as nice as that one.

Exercise 12.3

Complete the Chinese sentences below with either: '(adjective) + 一些 **yīxiē**/
一点儿 **yīdiǎnr**/得多 **de duō**' or '(adjective) + numeral + measure word',
to match the English translations (Note: 一点儿 **yīdiǎnr** is represented as two
spaces ＿＿＿ ＿＿＿):

1 那个厨师比我 ＿＿＿ ＿＿＿ ＿＿＿。
nà/nèi gè chúshī bǐ wǒ ＿＿＿ ＿＿＿ ＿＿＿ (胖 **pàng** 'fat')
That cook is much fatter than I am.
2 猫的尾巴比兔子的尾巴 ＿ ＿＿ ＿＿＿ ＿＿＿。
māo de wěiba bǐ tùzi de wěiba ＿＿＿ ＿＿＿ ＿ ＿＿
A cat's tail is much longer than a rabbit's tail.
3 球鞋比皮鞋 ＿＿＿ ＿＿＿ ＿＿＿ ＿＿＿ (＿＿＿)。
qiúxié bǐ píxié ＿＿＿ ＿＿＿
Sports shoes are slightly cheaper than leather shoes.
4 妹妹比姐姐 ＿＿＿ ＿＿＿ ＿＿＿。
mèimei bǐ jiějie ＿＿＿ ＿＿＿ (瘦 **shòu** 'thin')
The younger sister is slightly thinner than the older sister.
5 爷爷比奶奶 ＿＿＿ ＿＿＿ ＿＿＿。
yéye bǐ nǎinai ＿＿＿ ＿＿＿ ＿＿＿
Grandma is two years younger than Grandpa.
6 这件衣服比那件衣服 ＿＿＿ ＿＿＿ ＿＿＿。
zhè/zhèi jiàn yīfu bǐ nà/nèi jiàn yīfu ＿＿＿ ＿＿＿ ＿＿＿
This dress is two pounds more expensive than that one.
7 这个故事比那个故事 ＿＿＿ ＿＿＿ ＿＿＿ ＿＿＿。
zhè/zhèi gè gùshi bǐ nà/nèi gè gùshi ＿＿＿ ＿＿＿ ＿＿＿
This story is much more interesting than that one.

8 这幢房子比那幢 _____ _____ _____ _____ 。
   zhè/zhèi zhuàng fángzi bǐ nà/nèi zhuàng _____ _____
   This house is slightly prettier than that one.

9 那些香蕉比这些 _____ _____ _____ _____ 。
   nà/nèi xiē xiāngjiāo bǐ zhè/zhèi xiē _____ _____ _____
   Those bananas are much fresher than these.

10 我的牛仔裤比你的 _____ _____ _____ 。
   wǒ de niúzǎikù bǐ nǐ de _____ _____
   My jeans are a little cleaner than yours.

Exercise 12.4

Complete these sentences with either 更 **gèng**/还要 **hái yào** or 最 **zuì**:

1 这么多的鞋子，黑的那双 _____ 漂亮。
   zhème duō de xiézi | hēi de nà/nèi shuāng _____ **piàoliang**
   Of all these shoes that black pair is the most beautiful.

2 这些书都很有意思，那本 _____ 有意思。
   zhè/zhèi xiē shū dōu hěn yǒu yìsi | nà/nèi běn _____ **yǒu yìsi**
   All these books are interesting, but that book is even more interesting.

3 那三个西瓜都很甜，这个 _____ _____ 甜一点儿。
   nà/nèi sān gè xīguā dōu hěn tián | zhè/zhèi gè _____ _____ **tián yīdiǎnr**
   Those three water melons are sweet, but this one is even sweeter.

4 到市中心去，这条路 _____ 近。
   dào shìzhōngxīn qù | zhè/zhèi tiáo lù _____ **jìn**
   This is the quickest way to the city centre.

5 我去过的城市中，布拉格 _____ 美丽。
   wǒ qù guo de chěngshì zhōng | bùlāgé _____ **měilì**
   Of all the cities I have been to, Prague is the most beautiful.

6 三年级五十个学生，她 _____ 勤奋。
   sān niánjí wǔ shí gè xuésheng | tā _____ **qínfèn**
   Amongst the fifty students of the Third Year, she is the most industrious.

7 这些菜都很好吃，可是那个菜 _____ 好吃。
   zhè/zhèi xiē cài dōu hěn hǎochī | kěshì nà/nèi gè cài _____ **hǎochī**
   (菜 **cài** 'dish (of food)')
   These dishes are tasty, but that dish is even more tasty.

8 那首歌很好听，可是这首歌 _____ 好听。
   nà/nèi shǒu gē hěn hǎotīng | kěshì zhè/zhèi shǒu gē _____ **hǎotīng**
   That song is nice, but this song is even nicer.

9 这种花很香，那种花 _____ _____ 香。
   zhè/zhèi zhǒng huā hěn xiāng | nà/nèi zhǒng huā _____ _____ **xiāng**
   This kind of flower is fragrant; but that kind is even more fragrant.

10 二号运动员跑得比一号运动员 _____ _____ 快。
èr hào yùndòngyuán pǎo de bǐ yī hào yùndòngyuán _____ _____ **kuài**
Athlete No. 2 runs even faster than athlete No. 1.

Exercise 12.5

Translate the sentences below into Chinese (more than one version of the translation may be possible):

1 He came earlier than others. (早 **zǎo** 'early') (其他人 **qítā rén** 'others/other people')
2 She walks more slowly than he does. (走路 **zǒulù** 'to walk')
3 Yesterday he went to bed later than I did. (晚 **wǎn** 'late')
4 My wife is a better driver than I am. (妻子 **qīzi** 'wife')
5 One of my coursemates sings better than I do. (唱歌 **chàng gē** 'sing')
6 My husband is a better tennis player than I am.
   (丈夫 **zhàngfu** 'husband'; 打网球 **dǎ wǎngqiú** 'to play tennis')
7 My elder brother is an inch taller than I am. (高 **gāo** 'tall')
8 (The) younger sister is a half kilo lighter than the elder sister.
   (轻 **qīng** 'light')
9 Is a squirrel as big as a mouse?
10 This house isn't as pretty as that one. (房子 **fángzi** 'house')

Exercise 12.6

Translate the following sentences into Chinese, using the patterns for intensifying comparison:

1 I am growing more and more hungry.
2 The chef was getting fatter and fatter. (厨师 **chúshī** 'chef')
3 That horse runs more and more slowly in races.
   (在比赛中 **zài bǐsài zhōng** 'in races')
4 The soccer match became more and more exciting.
5 The road gets wider and wider.
6 Grandfather's illness was growing more and more serious.
   (严重 **yánzhòng** 'serious')
7 The more he drinks the more drunk he becomes.
8 The quicker the better.
9 The more he sings, the unhappier I become.
10 The more peppery the food, the more I like it.

UNIT THIRTEEN
Verbs and location expressions

A A number of the most commonplace words link the root words 里 **lǐ**, 外 **wài**, 上 **shàng**, 下 **xià**, 前 **qián** and 后 **hòu** with 边 **bian**, 面 **mian** or 头 **tou**:

里边	**lǐbian**	(里面 **lǐmian**,	里头 **lǐtou**)	inside
外边	**wàibian**	(外面 **wàimian**,	外头 **wàitou**)	outside
上边	**shàngbian**	(上面 **shàngmian**,	上头 **shàngtou**)	above
下边	**xiàbian**	(下面 **xiàmian**,	下头 **xiàtou**)	below
前边	**qiánbian**	(前面 **qiánmian**,	前头 **qiántou**)	in front
后边	**hòubian**	(后面 **hòumian**,	后头 **hòutou**)	behind

Others are linked with 边 **bian** or 面 **mian**:

左边	**zuǒbian**	(左面 **zuǒmiàn**)	left
右边	**yòubian**	(右面 **yòumiàn**)	right
东边	**dōngbian**	(东面 **dōngmiàn**)	east
南边	**nánbian**	(南面 **nánmiàn**)	south
西边	**xībian**	(西面 **xīmiàn**)	west
北边	**běibian**	(北面 **běimiàn**)	north

Others have only one form:

旁边	**pángbiān**	at/by the side of
对面	**duìmiàn**	opposite
中间	**zhōngjiān**	in the middle/between

Note: A colloquial variant of 下边 **xiàbian**/下头 **xiàtou**/下面 **xiàmian** is 底下 **dǐxia**.

B These location words may all be used as postpositions placed after nouns to form more complex location expressions:

桌子上边	**zhuōzi shàngbian**	on the table
学校前面	**xuéxiào qiánmian**	in front of the school

柜子里头	**guìzi lǐtou**	in(side) the cupboard
房子外面	**fángzi wàimian**	outside the house
游泳池旁边	**yóuyǒngchí pángbiān**	next to/by the side of the swimming-pool
礼堂对面	**lǐtáng duìmiàn**	opposite the auditorium
大厅中间	**dàtīng zhōngjiān**	in the centre of the hall
客厅和卧室中间	**kètīng hé wòshì zhōngjiān**	between the sitting-room and the bedroom
我家南面	**wǒ jiā nánmiàn**	(to the) south of my home
上海北边	**shànghǎi běibian**	(to the) north of Shanghai

There are a few other place words which can function as postpositions but which convey less specific locations:

四周/周围	**sìzhōu/zhōuwéi**	around
附近	**fùjìn**	near
那儿	**nàr**	at the home of/where someone is

For example,

大学附近	**dàxué fùjìn**	near the university
李先生那儿	**lǐ xiānsheng nàr**	at Mr Li's place or over there where Mr Li is
花园四周	**huāyuán sìzhōu**	on all sides of/around the garden

C   For some of these disyllabic postpositions discussed in A and B, there are a number of monosyllabic variants, which are in fact the root or stem of these disyllabic forms:

里	**li**	in/inside
外	**wài**	outside
上	**shang**	on/above/over
下	**xià**	under/below/beneath
前	**qián**	in front of
后	**hòu**	behind
中	**zhōng**	in/among/between
旁	**páng**/边 **biān**	by/beside

里 **li** and 上 **shang** are the most widely used of these monosyllabic postpositions, but they all regularly occur:

| 椅子上 | **yǐzi shang** | on the chair |
| 房子里 | **fángzi li** | in the house |

城外	**chéng wài**	outside the city
门前	**mén qián**	in front of the door
树下	**shù xià**	under the tree
朋友中	**péngyou zhōng**	amongst friends
路边	**lù biān**	by the side of the road
背后	**bèi hòu**	behind someone's back

Note: As we can see from the last example, these monosyllabic postpositions may also be used in contexts where something more than the locational relationship is implied:

| 心中 | **xīn zhōng** | in one's heart |
| 会上 | **huì shang** | at the meeting |

D　Location expressions are used in the following positions in a Chinese sentence:

(i)　before the verb, in conjunction with a preposition (or coverb – see Units 23 and 24), such as 在 **zài** 'in; at', 到 **dào** 'to', 从 **cóng** 'from', etc., to indicate location, destination or direction:

他们在墙上写标语。 **tāmen zài qiáng shang xiě biāoyǔ**
They are writing slogans on the wall.

孩子们在草地上玩儿。 **háizimen zài cǎodì shang wánr**
The children are playing on the grass.

我们到城里去买书。 **wǒmen dào chéng li qù mǎi shū**
We went to town to buy some books.

请在里面等他。 **qǐng zài lǐmian děng tā**
Please wait for him inside.

她从盒子里拿出一支铅笔来。 **tā cóng hézi li ná chū yī zhī qiānbǐ lái**
She took a pencil out of the box.

他们在学校旁边盖一座新房子。
tāmen zài xuéxiào pángbiān gài yī zuò xīn fángzi
They are putting up a new building next to the school.

Note: The postposition 里 **li** (or 里边 **lǐbian**/里头 **lǐtou**/里面 **lǐmiàn**) is not used after geographical names. For example,

| 他们在中国旅游。 | **tāmen zài zhōngguó lǚyóu** | They are on a tour in China. |
| 北京有很多剧场。 | **běijīng yǒu hěn duō jùchǎng** | There are a lot of theatres in Beijing. |

One cannot say:

| *他们在中国里旅游。 | **tāmen zài zhōngguó li lǚyóu** |
| *北京里有很多剧场。 | **běijīng li yǒu hěn duō jùchǎng** |

里 **li** and its variants are also optional after a noun (phrase) indicating a particular place:

她在花园(里)种花。 **tā zài huāyuán (li) zhòng huā**
She is planting flowers in the garden.

弟弟从学校(里)出来。 **dìdi cóng xuéxiào (li) chū lái**
(My) younger brother came out of the school.

姐姐和朋友在饭馆(里)吃饭。 **jiějie hé péngyou zài fànguǎn (li) chīfàn**
(My) elder sister and her friends are having a meal in a restaurant.

(ii) after a verb which leads to location in a particular place (see Unit 21):

爷爷坐在沙发上。 **yéye zuò zài shāfā shang**
Grandpa is sitting on the sofa.

她待(呆)家里。 **tā dāi zài jiā li**
She stayed at home.

他们都住在城外。 **tāmen dōu zhù zài chéng wài**
All of them live in the outskirts. (*lit.* out of the town)

很多人躺在草地上晒太阳。
hěn duō rén tǎng zài cǎodì shang shài tàiyáng
There are many people lying on the grass, sunbathing.

请坐在前面。 **qǐng zuò zài qiánmian**
Please sit in front.

别扔到窗外去。 **bié rēng dào chuāng wài qù**
Don't throw it out of the window.

Note: Location verbs in this category may also be used in the pattern specified in (i), e.g. 爷爷坐在沙发上。 **yéye zuò zài shāfā shang** 'Grandad sat on the sofa' may be rephrased as 爷爷在沙发上坐着。 **yéye zài shāfā shang zuò zhe** 'Grandad was sitting on the sofa'. However, verbs which do not lead to location in a particular place cannot, of course, follow the pattern discussed in (ii), therefore

One cannot say:

*他们学习在图书馆。   **tāmen xuéxí zài túshūguǎn**   (*lit.* They are studying at the library.)

(iii) at the beginning of a sentence to indicate the location of something or someone (see Unit 11):

动物园右边是植物园。 **dòngwùyuán yòubian shì zhíwùyuán**
To the right of the zoo is the botanical garden.

站台上有很多人。 **zhàntái shang yǒu hěn duō rén**
There are a lot of people on the (station) platform.

外边没有椅子。 **wàibian méi yǒu yǐzi**
There are no chairs outside.

E   Where location expressions with 在 **zài** come before the verb (see examples under D (i) above), the verb that follows usually consists of more than one syllable:

他在教室里学习。 **tā zài jiàoshì li xuéxí** (a disyllabic verb)
He is studying in the classroom.

病人在床上躺着。 **bìngrén zài chuáng shang tǎng zhe**
(a monosyllabic verb with an aspect marker)
The patient is lying in bed.

有很多人在站台上等车。 **yǒu hěn duō rén zài zhàntái shang děng chē**
(a verb with an object)
There are a lot of people on the platform waiting for the train.

One cannot say:

*他在教室里学。	**tā zài jiàoshì li xué**	(*lit.* He is studying in the classroom.)
*病人在床上躺。	**bìngrén zài chuáng shang tǎng**	(*lit.* The patient is lying in bed.)

Note: The exception to this rule is that monosyllabic verbs may be used in questions (and their associated answers) and in imperatives:

你在哪儿等？	**nǐ zài nǎr děng**	Where are you going to wait?
我在火车站等。	**wǒ zài huǒchēzhàn děng**	I'll wait at the railway station.
你在这儿坐。	**nǐ zài zhèr zuò**	You sit here!

Exercise 13.1

Complete the sentences below by adding correct postpositions:

1 风很大，路 _____ 行人很少。 **fēng hěn dà | lù _____ xíngrén hěn shǎo**
(行人 **xíngrén** 'pedestrian')
The wind was strong and there were very few people on the street.
2 鸡在烤箱 _____ 烤着。 **jī zài kǎoxiāng _____ kǎo zhe**
The chicken was cooking in the oven.

3 她站在门 _____ (_____)，看着爸爸离去。
   tā zhàn zài mén _____(_____) kàn zhe bàba lí qù
   She stood by the door and watched her father leave.

4 窗 _____ 传来汽车的喇叭声。
   chuāng _____ chuán lái qìche de lǎba shēng (喇叭 **lǎba** 'horn (of a car)')
   The sound of a car horn came from outside./A car horn sounded outside the window.

5 老鼠躲在床 _____ _____。
   lǎoshǔ duǒ zài chuáng _____ (躲 **duǒ** 'to hide')
   The mouse hid under the bed.

6 车站在学校 _____ _____。 **chēzhàn zài xuéxiào _____**
   The station is near the school.

7 我们的作业本子在老师 _____ _____。 **wǒmen de zuòyè běnzi zài lǎoshī**
   _____
   Our course-work books are with the teacher.

8 英国 _____ _____ 都是海。 **yīngguó _____ dōu shì hǎi**
   Britain is surrounded by sea.

9 日本在中国 _____ _____。 **rìběn zài zhōngguó _____**
   Japan is east of China.

10 银行 _____ _____ 是鞋店，_____ _____ 是服装店。
   yínháng _____ shì xié diàn | _____ shì fúzhuāng diàn
   On the left of the bank is a shoe shop and on the right, a clothes shop.

11 厕所在电梯 _____ _____。 **cèsuǒ zài diàntī _____**
   The toilet is next to the lift.

12 英吉利海峡在英国和法国 _____ _____。
   yīng jílì hǎixiá zài yīngguó hé fǎguó _____
   The English Channel lies between England and France.

13 袜子和手套都放在柜子 _____ (_____)。
   wàzi hé shǒutào dōu fàng zài guìzi _____(_____)
   (放 **fàng** 'put; keep') Socks and gloves are all kept in the wardrobe.

14 冰箱在洗衣机 _____ _____。 **bīngxiāng zài xǐyījī _____**
   The fridge is on the left of the washing-machine.

15 病人坐在医生和护士 _____ _____。
   bìngrén zuò zài yīshēng hé hùshi _____ (医生 **yīshēng** 'doctor: either physician or surgeon')
   The patient was sitting between the doctor and the nurse.

16 地图挂在黑板 _____ _____。 **dìtú guà zài hēibǎn _____**
   The map is hanging on the right-hand side of the blackboard.

17 博物馆在银行 _____ _____。
   bówùguǎn zài yínháng _____ (博物馆 **bówùguǎn** 'museum')
   The museum is behind the bank.

18 一群人站在大楼 _____ _____。
   yī qún rén zhàn zài dàlóu _____
   A crowd of people were standing all around the building.

Exercise 13.2

Translate the following phrases into Chinese. In some cases there may be two possible versions:

 1 at the university
 2 at the bus-stop
 3 in the wardrobe
 4 in the north of the city
 5 in a box
 6 in bed
 7 in the middle of the room
 8 at the foot of the mountain
 9 on the bus
10 under a tree
11 next to Mother
12 above the swimming-pool
13 in front of the library
14 behind the house
15 by the river
16 on the table
17 near the park
18 around the child
19 at my grandpa's house
20 in the west

Exercise 13.3

Decide which of the following sentences is incorrect and make corrections where necessary, paying special attention to the use of appropriate postpositions:

 1 报纸在桌子。 **bàozhǐ zài zhuōzi**
    The newspaper is on the table.
 2 屋子里他们在开会。 **wūzi li tāmen zài kāihuì**
    They are having a meeting in the room.
 3 泰晤士河是英国里有名的河。 **tàiwùshì hé shì yīngguó li yǒumíng de hé**
    The Thames is a famous river in Britain.
 4 医生在病人的床站了一会儿，没有说话。
    yīshēng zài bìngrén de chuáng zhàn le yīhuìr | méiyǒu shuō huà
    The doctor stood by the patient's bed for a while without saying a word.
 5 妹妹在图书馆看书。 **mèimei zài túshūguǎn kàn shū**
    My younger sister was reading in the library.
 6 爷爷在床上躺着。 **yéye zài chuáng shang tǎng zhe**
    Grandpa was lying in bed.

7 你的钥匙在门里。 **nǐ de yàoshi zài mén li**
  Your key is in the door.
8 叔叔工作在伦敦。 **shūshu gōngzuò zài lúndūn**
  My uncle works in London.
9 她在门前站。 **tā zài mén qián zhàn**
  She was standing in front of the house. (*lit.* in front of the door)
10 奶奶坐在沙发上。 **nǎinai zuò zài shāfā shang**
  Grandmother is sitting on the sofa.
11 金鱼游在水池里。 **jīnyú yóu zài shuǐchí li**
  The goldfish are swimming in the pool.
12 电影院在鞋店左。 **diànyǐngyuàn zài xiédiàn zuǒ**
  The cinema is to the left of the shoe shop.
13 报纸里有不少广告。 **bàozhǐ li yǒu bù shǎo guǎnggào**
  There are quite a few advertisements in the newspaper.
14 天里没有云。 **tiān li méi yǒu yún**
  There are no clouds in the sky.

Exercise 13.4

Six people have rooms in a block of flats. The diagram shows where they live in relation to one another. Complete these sentences with the words in the list. (Each word may only be used once):

左边 **zuǒbian**   楼下 **lóuxià**   下面 **xiàmian**
中间 **zhōngjiān**   东面 **dōngmiàn**   楼上 **lóushang**

	A	B	C (upstairs)	
WEST	D	E	F (downstairs)	EAST

1 **B** 住在 _____ _____，住在 **A** 和 **C** _____ _____。
  B zhù zài _____ **l zhù zài A hé C** _____
2 **E** 住在 **D** _____ _____，住在 **F** _____ _____。 **E zhù zài D** _____ **l zhù zài F** _____
3 **F** 住在 _____ _____，住在 **C** _____ _____。 **F zhù zài** _____ **l zhù zài C** _____

Exercise 13.5

Tick the correct Chinese translation(s) for each of the English sentences below, paying particular attention to the positioning of the location phrase:

1 The beef is cooking in the pot. (牛肉 **niúròu** 'beef')
  牛肉在锅里煮着。 **niúròu zài guō li zhǔ zhe**
  牛肉在锅煮着。 **niúròu zài guō zhǔ zhe**
  牛肉煮在锅里。 **niúròu zhǔ zài guō li**

2 A friend of mine works in a hospital.
我的一个朋友在一家医院工作。
wǒ de yī gè péngyou zài yī jiā yīyuàn gōngzuò
我的一个朋友工作在一家医院。
wǒ de yī gè péngyou gōngzuò zài yī jiā yīyuàn
我的一个朋友在一家医院里工作。
wǒ de yī gè péngyou zài yī jiā yīyuàn li gōngzuò

3 We live in Paris.
我们住在巴黎。   **wǒmen zhù zài bālí**
我们住在巴黎里。   **wǒmen zhù zài bālí li**
我们在巴黎住。   **wǒmen zài bālí zhù**

4 She is waiting for you at the museum.
她在博物馆等你。   **tā zài bówùguǎn děng nǐ**
她等你在博物馆里。   **tā děng nǐ zài bówùguǎn li**
她在博物馆里等你。   **tā zài bówùguǎn li děng nǐ**

5 A flock of sheep is feeding at the foot of the hill.
有一群羊在山脚下吃草。   **yǒu yī qún yáng zài shānjiǎo xià chī cǎo**
有一群羊吃草在山脚下。   **yǒu yī qún yáng chī cǎo zài shānjiǎo xià**

6 My uncle is sunbathing by the sea.
我叔叔在海边晒太阳。   **wǒ shūshu zài hǎi biān shài tàiyáng**
我叔叔晒太阳在海边。   **wǒ shūshu shài tàiyáng zài hǎi biān**

UNIT FOURTEEN
Verbs and time expressions

A Expressions which indicate the time at which something happens are generally placed before the verb. They have an important relationship with the verb,
which in Chinese does not inflect or change its form to indicate tense (see also
Unit 15). They therefore set the time context for the action of the verb. The
following examples illustrate this:

我们明天去散步。 **wǒmen míngtiān qù sànbù**
We'll go for a walk tomorrow.

我们昨天去散步。 **wǒmen zuótiān qù sànbù**
We went for a walk yesterday.

我们每天(都)去散步。 **wǒmen měi tiān (dōu) qù sànbù**
We go for a walk every day.

We can see from the above that the verbal phrase 去散步 **qù sànbù** 'go for a
walk' remains unchanged in each case though the English translations differ to
convey tense.

Note: A time expression may also be placed before the subject at the beginning of the sentence,
where it tends to have a slightly more emphatic meaning:

明天我们去散步。 **míngtiān wǒmen qù sànbù** We are going for a walk *tomorrow*.
夏天我们每天(都)去散步。 **xiàtiān wǒmen měi tiān (dōu) qù sànbù**
We go for a walk every day *in the summer*.

An unmarked verb in Chinese without a preceding time expression usually indicates either habit or intention:

我走路上班。	**wǒ zǒulù shàngbān**	I go to work on foot.	(habit)
我们去散步。	**wǒmen qù sànbù**	We are going for a walk.	(intention)

B Time expressions may take a number of different forms from the simple, as in the examples in A above, to the more complex (see also Unit 8). Other examples of simple time expressions are:

现在	**xiànzài**	now/nowadays
以前	**yǐqián**	previously
以后	**yǐhòu**	afterwards
过去	**guòqù**	in the past
将来	**jiānglái**	in the future
月初	**yuèchū**	at the beginning of the month
月底	**yuèdǐ**	at the end of the month
周末	**zhōumò**	at the weekend
前几年	**qián jǐ nián**	over/in the past few years
过几天	**guò jǐ tiān**	in a few days' time
上个世纪	**shàng gè shìjì**	in the last century

他们周末去海边度假。 **tāmen zhōumò qù hǎibiān dùjià**
They are going on holiday by the sea at the weekend.

我的大儿子现在在邮局工作。 **wǒ de dà érzi xiànzài zài yóujú gōngzuò**
My eldest son is working at the post-office now.

过几天我的父母来这儿探望我们。
guò jǐ tiān wǒ de fùmǔ lái zhèr tànwàng wǒmen
In a few days my parents will come here to visit us.

Other more complex phrases indicating before, after and during an action or (period of) time are formed by putting one of the following at the end of the time or verb phrase: . . . (以/之)前 . . . **(yǐ/zhī) qián** 'ago/before'; . . . (以/之)后 . . . **(yǐ/zhī) hòu** 'later/after'; and . . . (的) 时(候) . . . **(de) shí(hou)** 'when . . . / while . . .':

三个星期以前	**sān gè xīngqī yǐ qián**	three weeks ago/three weeks before
回家之前	**huí jiā zhī qián**	before going home
两个月前	**liǎng gè yuè qián**	two months ago/two months before
五分钟之后	**wǔ fēn zhōng zhī hòu**	five minutes later/in five minutes' time/after five minutes
吃晚饭以后	**chī wǎnfàn yǐ hòu**	after (eating) supper
一年后	**yī nián hòu**	a year later/in a year's time/ after a year
采草莓的时候	**cǎi cǎoméi de shíhou**	while picking strawberries

| 我们去中国的时候 | **wǒmen qù zhōngguó de shíhou** | when we went to China |
| 看书时 | **kàn shū shí** | when reading |

两个月以后我去看他们。 **liǎng gò yuè yǐ hòu wǒ qù kàn tāmen**
I went to see them two months later.

她吃晚饭以后去看电影。 **tā chī wǎnfàn yǐ hòu qù kàn diànyǐng**
After (she's had) supper she is going to see a film./After supper she went to see a film.

我下班的时候碰见他。 **wǒ xiàbān de shíhou pèngjiàn tā**
I met him when I came off work.

回家之前她去图书馆借书。 **huí jiā zhī qián tā qù túshūguǎn jiè shū**
She is going to borrow some books from the library before she goes home./
She went to borrow some books from the library before she went home.

C   Time words like 常常 **chángcháng** 'frequently/often', 已经 **yǐjing** 'already'
and 马上 **mǎshàng** 'immediately/at once' etc., which indicate less specific time,
must follow (and not precede) the subject, if there is one:

他常常去游泳。 **tā chángcháng qù yóuyǒng** He often goes swimming.
我马上(就)来。 **wǒ mǎshàng (jiù) lái** I'll be with you in a minute.
(*lit.* I immediately come)

One cannot say:

*常常他去游泳。 **chǎngcháng tā qù yóuyǒng**
*马上我(就)来。 **mǎshàng wǒ (jiù) lái**

D   Time words or expressions are sometimes used in conjunction with aspect
markers which indicate the completion, the continuation, the experience, etc. of
an action (see Unit 15):

我已经看完了那本小说。 **wǒ yǐjing kàn wán le nà/nèi běn xiǎoshuō**
I've already finished reading that novel.

他三岁的时候生过痢疾。 **tā sān suì de shíhou shēng guo lìjí**
(痢疾 **lìjí** dysentery)
He suffered from dysentery when he was three.

E   Duration expressions, which indicate the length of time an action lasts or the
time since an action has taken place, are generally placed immediately *after* the
verb (compare the discussion of the time duration question in Unit 9):

他在这儿住了半年。 **tā zài zhèr zhù le bàn nián**
He stayed here for six months. (*lit.* He stayed here for half a year.)

我今天工作了八小时。 **wǒ jīntiān gōngzuò le bā xiǎoshí**
I worked for eight hours today.

你的朋友已经等了二十分钟了。
nǐ de péngyou yǐjing děng le èr shí fēn zhōng le
Your friend has already been waiting twenty minutes.

我们到了/来了一个半月了。 **wǒmen dào le/lái le yī gè bàn yuè le**
It's one month and a half since we arrived./We've been here for a month and
a half.

李先生离开了三个多星期了。 **lǐ xiānsheng líkāi le sān gè duō xīngqī le**
It's over three weeks now since Mr Li left./Mr Li has been gone for over
three weeks.

Note 1: In the last two examples, the verbs 到 **dào** 'to arrive', 来 **lái** 'to come', 离开 **líkāi** 'to leave'
do not themselves express any duration of action, but the time phrase that follows indicates the time
since the action took place.

Note 2: The implication of the presence of 了 **le** at the end of the sentence, as seen in a number of
the sentences above, is analysed in *Intermediate Chinese*, Unit 1.

If the verb has a noun object, the duration expression is placed between the verb
and the noun object with or without 的 **de**:

我看了两个小时(的)书。 **wǒ kàn le liǎng gè xiǎoshí (de) shū**
I read for two hours.

我们跳了一个晚上(的)舞。 **wǒmen tiào le yī gè wǎnshang (de) wǔ**
We danced all evening.

他学过三年(的)中文。 **tā xué guo sān nián (de) zhōngwén**
He's studied Chinese for three years.

However, if the object is a personal (pro)noun or a noun indicating location, the
duration expression is normally placed after the object:

王老师教了我们/我们孩子两年。
wáng lǎoshī jiāo le wǒmen/wǒmen háizi liǎng nián
Mr/Miss Wang, our teacher, taught us/our children for two years.

我父母来北京五个月了。 **wǒ fùmǔ lái běijīng wǔ gè yuè le**
My parents have been in Beijing for five months now.

An alternative for that is to repeat the verb after the verb object phrase and then follow this verb with the duration expression (compare duration questions in Unit 9):

我们谈天谈了一个钟头。 **wǒmen tántiān tán le yī gè zhōngtóu**
We chatted for an hour.

他们学中文足足学了三年。 **tāmen xué zhōngwén zúzu xué le sān nián**
They studied Chinese for fully three years.

In this format the emphasis is more on the actual period of time and involves some degree of comment on the part of the speaker.

F   Brief duration is generally expressed by the idiomatic expression 一下 **yīxià** 'a moment' or 一会儿 **yīhuìr** 'a while':

请你先坐一下。 **qǐng nǐ xiān zuò yīxià**
Please first take a seat for a moment.

请等一下。 **qǐng děng yīxià**
Please wait a minute.

咱们休息一会儿吧！ **zánmen xiūxī yīhuìr ba**
Let's rest for a while.

你能在这儿等我一下吗？ **nǐ néng zài zhèr děng wǒ yīxià ma**
(following a pronoun object)
Can you wait here a minute for me?

If the verb has a noun object, the brief duration expression is likewise placed between the verb and the noun object but without 的 **de**:

我们在公园里散了一会儿/一下步。
wǒmen zài gōngyuán li sàn le yīhuìr/yīxià bù
We went for a walk in the park.

One does not usually say:

*我们在公园里散了一会儿的/一下的步。
  wǒmen zài gōngyuán li sàn le yīhuìr de/yīxià de bù

An alternative way of expressing brief duration is to repeat the verb. If the verb is a monosyllable, 一 **yī** may be placed between the two verbs, or 了 **le** if a past action is referred to:

咱们研究研究。 **zánmen yánjiū yánjiū**
We'll look into/consider it.

请你在外面等一等。 **qǐng nǐ zài wàimian děng yī děng**
Please wait outside for a moment.

请大家看一看今天的报纸。 **qǐng dàjiā kàn yī kàn jīntiān de bàozhǐ**
Will everyone please have a look at today's newspaper.

姑娘笑了笑。 **gūniang xiào le xiào**
The girl gave a smile.

他点了点头。 **tā diǎn le diǎn tóu**
He nodded.

咱们去散散步。 **zánmen qù sàn sàn bù**
Let's go for a walk.

G If the duration expression emphasizes a specific period of time within which an action took place or has taken place, it is placed immediately before the verb and is normally followed by 都 **dōu**. It also goes before the verb if it refers to a period of time when something has not or did not take place, and, in this case, it is followed by a negator.

她整天都在家里看管孩子。 **tā zhěngtiān dōu zài jiā li kānguǎn háizi**
All day she was looking after the children at home.

他一个礼拜(都)没抽烟了。 **tā yī gè lǐbài (dōu) méi chōuyān le**
He hasn't smoked for a whole week.

H Frequency expressions, like those indicating duration, are placed immediately after the verb:

我们谈过两次。 **wǒmen tán guo liǎng cì**
We have talked to each other twice./We've had a couple of talks.

他们来了三趟。 **tāmen lái le sān tàng**
They came three times.

If the verb has a noun object, the frequency expression is placed between the verb and the noun object:

我复习了两遍课文。 **wǒ fùxí le liǎng biàn kèwén**
I revised my lessons twice.

她已经开过三次刀了。 **tā yǐjing kāi guo sān cì dāo le**
She's been operated on three times already.

我们见过很多次面。 **wǒmen jiàn guo hěn duō cì miàn**
We have met many times.

Note: Unlike duration expressions, 的 **de** is not used with frequency expressions.

One cannot say:

*我复习了两遍的课文。 **wǒ fùxí le liǎng biàn de kèwén**

If the object is a noun indicating place, the frequency expression may also follow the object:

我去了银行两趟。 **wǒ qù le yínháng liǎng tàng**
I went to the bank twice. (*lit.* I made two trips to the bank)

If the object is a personal (pro)noun the frequency expression must normally follow the pronoun:

队长找了你/你哥哥几次。 **duìzhǎng zhǎo le nǐ/nǐ gēge jǐ cì**
The team captain looked for you/your elder brother several times.

Note: 次 **cì** indicates the number of times (in general), 趟 **tàng**, the number of trips made and 遍 **biàn** the number of times from beginning to the end.

It is also possible, but not particularly common, for the frequency expression to follow a repeated verb (as with duration expressions discussed above):

我找他找了三次。 **wǒ zhǎo tā zhǎo le sān cì**
I looked for him three times.

他们去北京去过好几趟。 **tāmen qù běijīng qù guo hǎo jǐ tàng**
They have been to Beijing quite a number of times.

I   As with duration expressions, if a frequency expression is specific (that is of definite reference), it is placed immediately before the verb and is usually followed by 都 **dōu** and/or a negator:

他们每次都带孩子来。 **tāmen měi cì dōu dài háizi lái**
They brought (their) children each time.

队长三场比赛都没进球了。 **duìzhǎng sān chǎng bǐsài dōu méi jìn qiú le**
The team captain hasn't scored in the last three matches.

他十次都没中。 **tā shí cì dōu méi zhòng**
He hasn't won (a prize) in ten attempts. (*lit.* for ten times)

Exercise 14.1

Place the time/duration/frequency expression or expressions given in brackets, in the Chinese sentences below, to provide a correct translation of the English:

1 I am going to Beijing tomorrow.
   我去北京。 **wǒ qù běijīng** (明天 **míngtiān** 'tomorrow')
2 I am going to Beijing for two days.
   我去北京。 **wǒ qù běijīng** (两天 **liǎng tiān** 'for two days')
3 I went to Beijing last year.
   我去了北京。 **wǒ qù le běijīng** (去年 **qùnián** 'last year')
4 I am going to Beijing in two days' time.
   我去北京。 **wǒ qù běijīng** (两天后 **liǎng tiān hòu** 'two days later')
5 I am going to Beijing before I get married.
   我去北京。 **wǒ qù běijīng** (结婚前 **jiéhūn qián** 'before getting married')
6 I am going to Beijing twice next year.
   我要去北京。 **wǒ yào qù běijīng**
   (明年 **míngnián** 'next year'; 两次 **liǎng cì** 'twice')
7 I have not been to Beijing for six months.
   我没去北京了。 **wǒ méi qù běijīng le**
   (半年 **bàn nián** 'half a year; six months')
8 I go to Beijing for a fortnight every summer.
   我去北京。 **wǒ qù běijīng**
   (半个月 **bàn gè yuè** 'half a month; a fortnight'; 每年夏天 **měi nián xiàtiān** 'every summer' (*lit.* every year summer))

Exercise 14.2

Re-write the following sentences to include the time expressions given in brackets:

1 他去了上海。 **tā qù le shànghǎi**
   He went to Shanghai. (the year before last)
2 妈妈离开英国。 **māma líkāi yīngguó**
   My mother left Britain. (last month)
3 哥哥去游泳。 **gēge qù yóuyǒng**
   (My) elder brother went swimming. (on Tuesday)
4 爷爷每天都看小说。 **yéye měi tiān dōu kàn xiǎoshuō**
   Grandpa reads novels every day. (for 2 or 3 hours)
5 我在学习汉语。 **wǒ zài xuéxí hànyǔ**
   I'm learning Chinese. (now)

6 我们全家去海滨。 **wǒmen quán jiā qù hǎibīn**
Our whole family are going to the seaside. (next weekend)
7 我们去跳舞。 **wǒmen qù tiàowǔ**
We go to a dance. (every Thursday evening)
8 小张去银行。 **xiǎo zhāng qù yínháng**
Xiao Zhang is going to the bank. (next Monday)
9 请在这儿等我。 **qǐng zài zhèr děng wǒ**
Please wait for me here. (for five minutes)
10 我去年去探望我父母。 **wǒ qùnián qù tànwàng wǒ fùmǔ**
I went to see my parents last year. (twice)

Exercise 14.3

Decide which of these sentences are incorrect and make corrections as required:

1 他们常常去看电影。 **tāmen chángcháng qù kàn diànyǐng**
They often go to see a film.
2 他在海里游了泳一会儿。 **tā zài hǎi li yóu le yǒng yīhuìr**
He swam in the sea for a while.
3 马上我上班。 **mǎshàng wǒ shàngbān**
I am going to work immediately.
4 音乐会刚刚开始。 **yīnyuèhuì gānggāng kāishǐ**
The concert has just started.
5 我们记得他永远。 **wǒmen jìde tā yǒngyuǎn** (永远 **yǒngyuǎn** 'for ever')
We will remember him for ever.
6 我爸爸总是很晚睡觉。 **wǒ bàba zǒngshì hěn wǎn shuìjiào**
(总是) **zǒngshì** 'always')
My father always goes to bed late.
7 我写了信已经了。 **wǒ xiě le xìn yǐjing le**
I have already written the letter.
8 队长看见刚刚小李。 **duìzhǎng kànjiàn gānggāng xiǎo lǐ**
The team captain saw Xiao Li just now.
9 这对夫妇整年都在外地旅游。
zhè/zhèi duì fūfù zhěng nián dōu zài wàidì lǚyóu
This couple were away travelling all the year round.
10 她两次都来了。 **tā liǎng cì dōu lái le**
She turned up both times.
11 她两次来了这儿。 **tā liǎng cì lái le zhèr**
She's been here twice.
12 爷爷和奶奶今天半个钟头散步。
yéye hé nǎinai jīntiān bàn gè zhōngtóu sànbù
My grandparents went for a walk for half an hour today.

Exercise 14.4

Translate these sentences into English, paying attention to the way in which Chinese time expressions affect the tenses of the English verb.

1　今天早上我游了两个小时(的)泳。
   jīntiān zǎoshang wǒ yóu le liǎng gè xiǎoshí (de) yǒng
2　我的英国朋友在中国住了两个月。
   wǒ de yīngguó péngyou zài zhōngguó zhù le liǎng gè yuè
3　他们已经学了两年中文了。
   tāmen yǐjing xué le liǎng nián zhōngwén le
4　会议开始了四十分钟了。
   huìyì kāishǐ le sì shí fēn zhōng le (会议 **huìyì** 'meeting')
5　明天下午我和同学去踢足球。
   míngtiān xiàwǔ wǒ hé tóngxué qù tī zúqiú
   (踢足球 **tī zúqiú** 'to play football' (*lit.* to kick football))
6　妹妹整晚都在那儿写信。
   mèimei zhěng wǎn dōu zài nàr xiě xìn
   (整晚 **zhěng wǎn** 'the whole evening')
7　王先生和他的妻子明年去中国度假。
   wáng xiānsheng hé tā de qīzi míngnián qù zhōngguó dùjià
8　他去年六月毕业。
   tā qùnián liù yuè bìyè (毕业 **bìyè** 'to graduate')
9　弟弟买了一双很漂亮的球鞋。
   dìdi mǎi le yī shuāng hěn piàoliang de qiúxié (球鞋 **qiúxié** 'sports shoes')
10　我爸爸常常骑自行车去上班。
   wǒ bàba chángcháng qí zìxíngchē qù shàngbān
11　我三次都在他家待了半个钟头。
   wǒ sān cì dōu zài tā jiā dāi le bàn gè zhōngtóu
12　那天晚上她跳了三个钟头的舞。
   nà/nèi tiān wǎnshang tā tiào le sān gè zhōngtóu de wǔ

Exercise 14.5

Translate the following sentences into Chinese:

1 Did you try steamed bread when you were in China?
2 Can you wait outside for a minute?
3 Let's sit in the park for a while.
4 Can you look after my child for a while?
5 We went strawberry-picking for an hour.

6 She glanced briefly at that photograph. (照片 **zhàopiàn** 'photograph')
7 Please have a look at today's paper first.
8 He hasn't touched alcohol for the whole year.
9 I have known him for three years.
10 I've already had a bath. (洗澡 **xǐzǎo** 'to have a bath')

UNIT FIFTEEN
Verbs and aspect markers

A Although as indicated in Unit 14 Chinese verbs do not express tense they are often linked with an aspect marker which may indicate the completion, experience, continuation, etc. of an action. With the exception of 在 **zài** (see below) aspect markers are placed directly after the verb.

The most common aspect markers are:

了	**le**	completed action
过	**guo**	past experience
在	**zài**	an action in progress
着	**zhe**	a continuous state resulting from an action/an accompanying action
起来	**qǐlái**	an action/a state which has just started
下去	**xiàqù**	an action which is to be continued
下来	**xiàlái**	an action/a state which is gradually changing into non-action or a quieter state

B 了 **le** indicates that the action of the verb has been completed:

我写了两封信。 **wǒ xiě le liǎng fēng xìn**
I wrote two letters.

他买了很多苹果。 **tā mǎi le hěn duō píngguǒ**
He bought a lot of apples.

The object of the completed action verb is generally specified in one way or another. In the above sentences, 信 **xìn** is modified by 两封 **liǎng fēng** and 苹果 **píngguǒ** by 很多 **hěn duō**. If 了 **le** is followed by an unmodified noun, for example: *我写了信。 **wǒ xiě le xìn** or *他买了苹果。 **tā mǎi le píngguǒ**, the sentence sounds incomplete and one needs to add another clause to round it off:

我写了信就去寄信了。 **wǒ xiě le xìn jiù qù jì xìn le**
As soon as I had written the letter, I went to post it.

我买了苹果就回家了。 **wǒ mǎi le píngguǒ jiù huí jiā le**
I went home as soon as I had bought the apples.

Note: The unmodified object of a completed action verb is always of definite reference. In the above examples, 信 **xìn** means 'the letter' and 苹果 **píngguǒ** 'the apples'.

Completed action of course in most cases refers to something completed in the past and an English translation would naturally use the past tense. A completed action, however, may take place in the future, as the following examples show:

我下了班就去找你。 **wǒ xià le bān jiù qù zhǎo nǐ**
When I finish work I will come (*lit.* go) and see you.

请你看了医生就去打针。 **qǐng nǐ kàn le yīshēng jiù qù dǎzhēn**
When you have seen the doctor, please go and have the injection.

Note 1: 就 **jiù** is usually placed before the verb in the second part of the sentence and implies that the action of this verb follows from the action of the verb in the first part of the sentence.

Note 2: 了 **le** is also used after adjectives, intransitive verbs or verbs indicating or incorporating complements of results to indicate a situation or state, which has emerged or is emerging. This use of 了 **le**, particularly when it occurs at the end of a statement, links with the sentence particle 了 **le**, which is generally used at the end of sentences to indicate a change of state as the speaker sees it. (For a full discussion of sentence 了 **le** see *Intermediate Chinese*, Unit 1.)

爷爷的病好了。 **yéye de bìng hǎo le** (adjective)
Grandpa is well again.

我的表停了。 **wǒ de biǎo tíng le** (intransitive verb)
My watch has stopped.

他的裤子破了。 **tā de kùzi pò le** (verb indicating result)
His trousers are torn.

弟弟的衣服全淋湿了。 **dìdi de yīfu quán lín shī le** (verb incorporating result complement)
(My) younger brother got soaked.

C   过 **guo** implies past experience:

我吃过饺子。 **wǒ chī guo jiǎozi**
I have had (tried) Chinese dumplings (before).

我妹妹去过长城。 **wǒ mèimei qù guo chángchéng**
My younger sister has been to the Great Wall.

这三个月我只见过经理一次。 **zhè/zhèi sān gè yuè wǒ zhǐ jiàn guo jīnglǐ yī cì**
I have seen the manager only once in the last three months.

Note: From the last example you can see that the experience indicated by *guo* can refer to a specified period – 'the last three months'. Hence the common enquiry or greeting: 你吃过饭没有？

nǐ chī guo fàn méiyǒu 'Have you eaten?', which is referring in the speaker's mind to the immediate past. The distinction between completed action 了 **le** and experience 过 **guo** can be seen from the following:

他们去了中国了。 **tāmen qù le zhōngguó le**
They have gone to China (and they are in China now).

他们去过中国。 **tāmen qù guo zhōngguó**
They have been to China before (and they are now back here or somewhere else).

D (正)在 (**zhèng**)**zài**, which precedes the verb, indicates that an action is in progress:

爸爸(正)在修(理)汽车。	**bàba (zhèng)zài xiū(lǐ) qìchē**	Father is repairing his car.
他们(正)在开会。	**tāmen (zhèng)zài kāihuì**	They are having a meeting.

Note 1: If a location phrase with 在 **zài** precedes the verb the aspect marker 在 **zài** is not needed:

他(正)在花园里割草。 **tā (zhèng)zài huāyuán li gē cǎo**
He is/was in the garden mowing the grass.

One does not say:

*他(正)在在花园里割草。 **tā (zhèng)zài zài huāyuán li gē cǎo**
(*lit.* He is/was mowing the grass in the garden.)

Note 2: Like 了 **le**, (正)在 (**zhèng**)**zài** itself carries no indication of tense, since the action may be in progress at any time, in the past, present or future (other particles indicating progress will be discussed in *Intermediate Chinese*):

她现在(正)在学习中文。 **tā xiànzài (zhèng)zài xuéxí zhōngwén**
She is studying Chinese now.

她那年(正)在学习中文。 **tā nà/nèi nián (zhèng)zài xuéxí zhōngwén**
She was studying Chinese that year.

明天早上她一定在学习中文。 **míngtiān zǎoshang tā yídìng zài xuéxí zhōngwén**
She'll certainly be studying Chinese tomorrow morning.

E   着 **zhe** conveys either

(i) a continuous state resulting from an action:

她穿着一条红裙子。 **tā chuān zhe yī tiáo hóng qúnzi**
She is/was wearing a red skirt.

他戴着一顶白帽子。 **tā dài zhe yī dǐng bái màozi**
He is/was wearing a white hat.
(The action of 'putting on' the skirt or the hat results in the 'wearing' of them.)

墙上挂着一幅山水画。 **qiáng shang guà zhe yí fú shānshuǐ huà**
A Chinese landscape painting is hanging on the wall. (*lit.* On the wall is hanging a Chinese landscape painting.)
(The action of 'hanging a picture' results in the picture 'being hung'.)

or

(ii) an accompanying action (an action which takes place at the same time as another action):

他坐着谈天。 **tā zuò zhe tántiān**
He sits/sat chatting./He is/was sitting there chatting.

她笑着点了点头。 **tā xiào zhe diǎn le diǎn tóu**
She nodded smiling.

他们哼着歌儿走了进来。 **tāmen hēng zhe gēr zǒu le jìnlái**
They came in humming a tune.

F 起来 **qǐlái** implies that an action or state has just started:

他们吵起来了。 **tāmen chǎo qǐlái le**
They (have) started to quarrel.

她哭起来了。 **tā kū qǐlái le**
She (has) started crying.

天冷起来了。 **tiān lěng qǐlái le**
It began/has begun to get colder.

When an object follows the verb, it is placed between 起 **qǐ** and 来 **lái**:

他们打起架来了。 **tāmen dǎ qǐ jià lái le**
They (have) started fighting.

他们唱起歌来了。 **tāmen chàng qǐ gē lái le**
They (have) started to sing.

外面下起雨来了。 **wàimian xià qǐ yǔ lái le**
It began/has begun to rain (outside).

One cannot say:

*打架起来 **dǎjià qǐlái**/*打起来架 **dǎ qǐlái jià** (*lit.* start/have started fighting)
*唱歌起来 **chàng gē qǐlái** (*lit.* start/have started singing)

G   下去 **xiàqù** indicates the continuation of an action:

你说下去！   **nǐ shuō xiàqù**   Go on!/Carry on (talking)!
他们会待下去吗？   **tāmen huì dāi xiàqù ma**   Will they stay on?

下去 **xiàqù** is not used where the verb has an object.

One cannot say:

*你说下话去。 **nǐ shuō xià huà qù**/*你说话下去。 **nǐ shuōhuà xiàqù**
(*lit.* Go on!/Carry on (talking)!)

H   下来 **xiàlái** implies that an action has gradually ceased or subsided or a
situation has become more settled or quiet:

车停下来了。 **chē tíng xiàlái le**
The car came to a stop.
(originally, the car was moving.)

我想在这儿住下来。 **wǒ xiǎng zài zhèr zhù xiàlái**
I would like to settle down here.
(originally, I was always on the move.)

大家都静下来了。 **dàjiā dōu jìng xiàlái le**
Everybody has become quiet.
(originally there was a lot of noise.)

As with 起来 **qǐlái**, if the verb has an object, the object comes between 下 **xià**
and 来 **lái**:

他停下车来。 **tā tíng xià chē lái**
He brought the car to a stop.

她安下心来。 **tā ān xià xīn lái**
She feels at ease (now)./She is no longer worried.

Note: In most of the examples for 起来 **qǐlái** and 下来 **xiàlái**, 了 **le** occurs at the end of the sentence.
Here 了 **le** is functioning as a sentence particle, not an aspect marker, and implies a change of
circumstance (see *Intermediate Chinese*, Unit 1). For further uses of 起来 **qǐlái**, 下去 **xiàqù** and 下来
xiàlái as directional complements, see Unit 21.

Exercise 15.1

Add 着 **zhe**, 了 **le**, 过 **guo** or 在 **zài** to the sentences below to complete the
translation of the English in each case. In some cases there may be more than
one possibility:

1 他 ——— 唱歌。 **tā ——— chàng gē**
 He is singing.
2 爷爷戴 ——— 一副眼镜。 **yéye dài ——— yī fù yǎnjìng**
 Grandpa is wearing a pair of glasses
3 我见 ——— 大熊猫。 **wǒ jiàn ——— dà xióngmāo**
 I have seen a giant panda.
4 她笑 ——— 说话。 **tā xiào ——— shuōhuà**
 She spoke smiling.
5 他背 ——— 背包去爬山。 **tā bēi ——— bèibāo qù pá shān**
 He went climbing with a rucksack on his back.
6 我丢 ——— 一把钥匙。 **wǒ diū ——— yī bǎ yàoshi**
 I (have) lost a key.
7 我朋友喝 ——— 中国啤酒。 **wǒ péngyou hē ——— zhōngguó píjiǔ**
 My friend has tried Chinese beer.
8 老师 ——— 讲解课文。 **lǎoshī ——— jiǎngjiě kèwén**
 The teacher is explaining the text.
9 姐姐买 ——— 一双皮鞋。 **jiějie mǎi ——— yī shuāng píxié**
 (My) elder sister bought a pair of leather shoes.
10 他们去 ——— 北京。 **tāmen qù ——— běijīng**
 They have been to Beijing.
11 世界 ——— 变化。 **shìjiè ——— biànhuà**
 The world is changing.
12 谁 ——— 帮你的忙？ **shéi/shuí ——— bāng nǐ de máng**
 Who is helping you?
13 她 ——— 减肥。 **tā ——— jiǎnféi**
 She is slimming/trying to lose weight.
14 我已经吃 ——— 晚饭了。 **wǒ yijīng chī ——— wǎnfàn le**
 I've already had dinner.
15 小王刚生 ——— 一个小孩。
 xiǎo wáng gāng shēng ——— yī gè xiǎohái
 Xiao Wang has just had a baby.

Exercise 15.2

Translate the following sentences into Chinese, paying particular attention to the
use of appropriate aspect markers:

1 He was wiping the window. (擦窗(户) **cā chuāng(hu)** 'to wipe the window')
2 They have been here.
3 I was watering the flowers. (浇 **jiāo** 'to water')
4 My friend is drinking beer.
5 The teacher was standing teaching the lesson.
 (站 **zhàn** 'to stand', 讲课 **jiǎngkè** 'to teach the lesson')

6 He started dancing.
7 He is driving.
8 She bought a pair of shoes. (一双 **yī shuāng** 'a pair of')
9 Grandfather is watching television.
  (看电视 **kàn diànshì** 'to watch television')
10 Mother is wearing a beautiful hat.

Exercise 15.3

Complete these sentences with either 起来 **qǐlái**, 下去 **xiàqù** or 下来 **xiàlái**, according to the English translation:

1 他们唱 —— —— 了。 **tāmen chàng** _____ **le**
  They began to sing.
2 火车停 —— —— 了。 **huǒchē tíng** _____ **le**
  The train came to a halt.
3 你们做 —— —— 吧。 **nǐmen zuò** _____ **ba**
  Carry on (with what you are doing).
4 天气热 —— —— 了。 **tiānqì rè** _____ **le**
  The weather got warmer.
5 大家静 —— —— 了。 **dàjiā jìng** _____ **le**
  Everyone quietened down.
6 请你说 —— ——！ **qǐng nǐ shuō** _____
  Please go on!
7 小孩哭 —— —— 了。 **xiǎohái kū** _____ **le**
  The child began to cry.
8 两条运河连 —— —— 了。 **liǎng tiáo yùnhé lián** _____ **le**
  The two canals were connected together.
9 这件事我想 —— —— 了。 **zhè/zhèi jiàn shì wǒ xiǎng** _____ **le**
  I recalled this matter.
10 计划定 —— —— 了。 **jìhuà dìng** _____ **le**
  The plan was decided upon.

Exercise 15.4

Decide which of the following Chinese phrases are wrong and make corrections as necessary:

1 讲下来 **jiǎng xiàlái** Carry on (with your story)!
2 学起习来 **xué qǐ xí lái** begin to study
3 写起来信 **xiě qǐlái xìn** start to write letters
4 学下来 **xué xiàlái** carry on lcarning
5 雨停下来了 **yǔ tíng xiàlái le** the rain stopped

6 吵起来架 **chǎo qǐlái jià** start quarrelling
7 游泳起来 **yóuyǒng qǐlái** start swimming
8 暖和起来 **nuǎnhuo qǐlái** get warmer
9 聪明下来 **cōngming xiàlái** become more intelligent
10 慢下来 **màn xiàlái** gradually become slower

UNIT SIXTEEN
Modal verbs

Modal verbs in Chinese are very much like those in English (e.g. can, must, should, etc.). They are placed directly before other verbs to indicate particular moods or attitudes. They are generally negated by 不 **bù**.

A   要 **yào** and 想 **xiǎng** are used to express wishes or desires:

我要/想喝杯茶。 **wǒ yào/xiǎng hē bēi chá**
I would like a cup of tea. (*lit.* I would like to drink a cup of tea.)

我要/想喝咖啡，不要/想喝茶。
wǒ yào/xiǎng hē kāfēi | bù yào/xiǎng hē chá
I'd like coffee not tea. (*lit.* I would like to drink coffee not tea.)

你要/想学中文/英文吗？ **nǐ yào/xiǎng xué zhōngwén/yīngwén ma**
Do you want/Are you going to learn Chinese/English?

Note: In a statement 要 **yào** used with a second-person pronoun can only express obligation:

你要早点回来。 **nǐ yào zǎo diǎn huí lái**
You must come back early.

你要小心。 **nǐ yào xiǎoxīn**
You must take care.

B   愿意 **yuànyì** and 肯 **kěn** both indicate 'willingness':

他肯/愿意帮助你吗？ **tā kěn/yuànyì bāngzhù nǐ ma**
Is he willing to help you?

她不肯/愿意认错。 **tā bù kěn/yuànyì rèncuò**
She is unwilling to admit her mistakes.

C 敢 **gǎn** 'dare':

他敢提出自己的看法。 **tā gǎn tí chū zìjǐ de kànfǎ**
He dares/dared to put forward his own ideas.

我不敢去见她。 **wǒ bù gǎn qù jiàn tā**
I daren't go and see her.

D (应)该 **(yīng)gāi** 'ought to' and 得 **děi** 'have to':

你(应)该睡了/起床了。 **nǐ (yīng)gāi shuì le/qǐchuáng le**
You ought to go to bed/get up.

我得走了。 **wǒ děi zǒu le**
I must be off now.

Negative sentences with (应)该 **(yīng)gāi**, on the other hand, imply reproach or blame for something that has already happened, and those with 得 **děi** indicate (official) prohibition:

你不该告诉他。 **nǐ bù gāi gàosu tā**
You shouldn't have told him.

你不该骂她。 **nǐ bù gāi mà tā**
You shouldn't have scolded her.

闲人不得入内。 **xiánrén bù dé rù nèi**
No admittance./Admittance to staff only. (*lit.* casual people shouldn't enter)

Note: Note the change in pronunciation from 得 **děi** to 得 **dé** in the negative.

E 必须 **bìxū** 'must'; 'have to' is, strictly speaking, an adverb but is used like a modal verb:

明天我必须到达那儿。 **míngtiān wǒ bìxū dàodá nàr**
I must get there by tomorrow.

我们今天必须完成这个工作。
wǒmen jīntiān bìxū wánchéng zhè/zhèi gè gōngzuò
We must finish this work today.

Note: As 必须 **bìxū** is an adverb, it does not have a negative form, and 不必 **bù bì** /不用 **bù yòng** 'need not' are used instead:

你不必/不用去了。 **nǐ bù bì/bù yòng qù le**
You needn't go. (*lit.* There is no need for you to go.)

F 能 **néng** 'can; may; be able to; be capable of' and 可以 **kěyǐ** 'can; may' to some extent overlap in function:

你现在可以走了。 **nǐ xiànzài kěyǐ zǒu le**
You may leave/can go now.

他十分钟能跑一英里。 **tā shí fēn zhōng néng pǎo yī yīnglǐ**
He can run a mile in ten minutes.

我能进来吗？ **wǒ néng jìn lái ma**
May I come in?

Note: 可以 **kěyǐ** implies permission from an outside authority, whereas 能 **néng** refers to the ability to do something in particular circumstances:

你不可以在这儿吸烟/抽烟。 **nǐ bù kěyǐ zài zhèr xīyān/chōuyān**
You can't smoke here.

我昨晚不能来。 **wǒ zuó wǎn bù néng lái**
I wasn't able to come last night [because something cropped up, I missed the train, etc.].

G 会 **huì** indicates either probability: 'be likely to; be sure to' or inherent or acquired ability/skill: 'can; be able to; be good at; be skilful in':

明天会下雨/下雪吗？ **míngtiān huì xià yǔ/xià xuě ma**
Will it rain/snow tomorrow? (probability)

你会说中文吗？ **nǐ huì shuō zhōngwén ma**
Can you speak Chinese? (ability)

Note: The difference between 会 **huì** and 能 **néng** which both mean 'can'; 'be able to' can be illustrated by the following:

我会开车，但是现在喝了酒，我不能开。
wǒ huì kāichē | dànshì xiànzài hē le jiǔ | wǒ bù néng kāi
I can drive, but, as I have been drinking, I can't.

我会喝酒，但是现在要开车，我不能喝。
wǒ huì hē jiǔ | dànshì xiànzài yào kāichē, wǒ bù néng hē
I can drink, but, as I am going to drive, I can't have one.

Exercise 16.1

Replace 要 **yào** with 想 **xiǎng** in the following where it is appropriate to do so:

1 我要休息一会儿。 **wǒ yào xiūxi yīhuìr**
I would like to have a rest.

2 你要早点儿起床。 **nǐ yào zǎo diǎnr qǐchuáng**
You must get up early.

3 他要去中国旅游。 **tā yào qù zhōngguó lǚyóu**
He wants to go travelling in China.

4 你要喝点儿什么？ **nǐ yào hē diǎnr shénme**
What would you like to drink?

5 你要好好儿学习。 **nǐ yào hǎohāor xuéxí**
You must study hard.

6 妈妈要买一件外套。 **māma yào mǎi yī jiàn wàitào**
Mother would like to buy a coat.

Exercise 16.2

Choose the appropriate modal verb for the Chinese sentences so that they match
the English translations:

1 你 _____ 帮我的忙吗？ **nǐ _____ bāng wǒ de máng ma**
Can you help me?
　　a 会 **huì**　　b 能 **néng**　　c 要 **yào**

2 今晚 _____ 刮风吗？ **jīn wǎn _____ guā fēng ma**
Is it going to be windy tonight?
　　a 会 **huì**　　b 能 **néng**　　c 要 **yào**

3 很晚了。我 _____ 回家了。 **hěn wǎn le | wǒ _____ huí jiā le**
It's getting very late. I must go home now.
　　a 要 **yào**　　b 该 **gāi**　　c 可以 **kěyi**

4 对不起。你不 _____ 在这儿抽烟。
duìbuqǐ | nǐ bù _____ zài zhèr chōuyān
I'm sorry. You can't smoke here.
　　a 要 **yào**　　b 能 **néng**　　c 会 **huì**

5 我 _____ _____ 在这儿停车吗？
wǒ _____ zài zhèr tíng chē ma
May I park my car here?
　　a 可以 **kěyi**　　b 必须 **bìxū**　　c 应该 **yīnggāi**

6 他 _____ 说中文，可是他现在不 _____ 说。
tā _____ shuō zhōngwén | kěshì tā xiànzài bù _____ shuō
He can speak Chinese, but he's not willing to speak it at this moment.
　　a 能 **néng**; 要 **yào**　　b 会 **huì**; 肯 **kěn**　　c 会 **huì**; 能 **néng**

7 我感冒了。我今天 _____ _____ 呆/待在家里。
wǒ gǎnmào le | wǒ jīntiān _____ dāi/dāi zài jiā li
I have a cold. I should stay at home today.
   a 必须 **bìxū**   b 应该 **yīnggāi**   c 愿意 **yuànyì**

8 她搭公共汽车来。你不 _____ 去接她了。
tā dā gōnggòng qìchē lái | nǐ bù _____ qù jiē tā le
She'll come by bus. You don't have to go and meet her.
   a 得 **děi**   b 必 **bì**   c 该 **gāi**

Exercise 16.3

Add modal verbs with negatives, where necessary, to the Chinese sentences below so that they are a correct translation of the English:

1 He is not willing to do this.
   他 _____ _____ _____ 做这件事。
   tā _____ _____ zuò zhè/zhèi jiàn shì
2 She doesn't dare to go climbing at night.
   她 _____ _____ 在夜里爬山。 **tā _____ _____ zài yè li pá shān**
3 You may go home now.
   你现在 _____ _____ 回家了。 **nǐ xiànzài _____ huí jiā le**
4 He is not willing to admit his mistakes.
   他 _____ _____ 认错。 **tā _____ _____ rèncuò**
5 I wouldn't want to write a novel.
   我 _____ _____ 写小说。 **wǒ _____ _____ xiě xiǎoshuō**
6 She wants to go and see her friend in hospital.
   她 _____ 去医院看朋友。 **tā _____ qù yīyuàn kàn péngyou**
7 Don't you dare ask her?
   你 _____ 问她吗？ **nǐ _____ wèn tā ma**
8 I have to tell her the truth about the matter.
   我 _____ 告诉她事情的真相。 **wǒ _____ gàosu tā shìqing de zhēnxiàng**
9 You don't have to go to school.
   你今天 _____ _____ 去上学。 **nǐ jīntiān _____ _____ qù shàngxué**
10 I ought to phone her this evening.
   今晚我 _____ 给她打电话。 **jīn wǎn wǒ _____ gěi tā dǎ diànhuà**
11 We must call the doctor.
   我们 _____ _____ 叫医生。 **wǒmen _____ jiào yīshēng**
12 The prize shouldn't have gone to him/been his.
   这个奖 _____ _____ 是他的。 **zhè/zhèi gè jiǎng _____ _____ shì tā de**
13 Can I bring my cat?
   我 _____ _____ 带猫来吗？ **wǒ _____ dài māo lái ma**
14 Do you know how to use chopsticks?
   你 _____ 用筷子吗？ **nǐ _____ yòng kuàizi ma**

15 Can the patient go jogging?

病人 _____ 去跑步吗？ **bìngrén _____ qù pǎobù ma**

16 Please may I have a piece of cake.

请问，我 _____ _____吃一块蛋糕吗？

qǐng wèn | wǒ _____ chī yī kuài dàngāo ma

17 Mr Wang was ill and wasn't able to come to class.

王老师病了， _____ _____ 来上课。

wáng lǎoshī bìng le | _____ _____ lái shàngkè

18 Will it snow tomorrow?

明天 _____下雪吗？ **míngtiān _____ xià xuě ma**

19 He can swim.

他 _____ 游泳。 **tā _____ yóuyǒng**

20 I can dance, but the floor was too slippery so I couldn't dance on it.

我 _____ 跳舞，但是地板太滑，我 _____ _____ 在上面跳舞。

wǒ _____ tiàowǔ | dànshì dìbǎn tài huá | wǒ _____ _____ zài shàngmian tiàowǔ

21 You can speak both English and Chinese so you can be our interpreter.

你 _____ 说英语和汉语，你 _____ 做我们的翻译。

nǐ _____ shuō yīngyǔ hé hànyǔ | nǐ _____ zuò wǒmen de fānyì

22 You can't cheat me.

你 _____ _____ 欺骗我。 **nǐ _____ _____ qīpiàn wǒ**

23 I shall be able to come tomorrow.

明天我 _____ 来。 **míngtiān wǒ _____ lái**

24 This girl is small but she can eat a lot.

这个女孩子很小，但是她 _____ 吃很多。

zhè/zhèi gè nǚ háizi hěn xiǎo | dànshì tā _____ chī hěn duǒ

25 Do you know how to repair cars?

你 _____ 修理汽车吗？ **nǐ _____ xiūlǐ qìchē ma**

26 Is Manager Li likely to turn up tomorrow?

李经理明天 _____ 来吗？ **lǐ jīnglǐ míngtiān _____ lái ma**

27 Can you wait for me here?

你 _____ 在这儿等我吗？ **nǐ _____ zài zhèr děng wǒ ma**

28 You shouldn't quarrel (with each other).

你们 _____ _____ _____ 吵架。 **nǐmen _____ _____ chǎojià**

Exercise 16.4

Translate the following sentences into Chinese:

1 Do you know how to drive?
2 Is it likely to rain at the weekend?
3 Do you want to go and visit your parents?
4 You must go and revise your lessons.

 5 Can we go to the beach this week?
 6 I must remember the time of the concert.
 7 You shouldn't have come to blows (with each other).
 8 May I take a holiday next March?
 9 Are you willing to help him?
10 She daren't fly in a plane.

UNIT SEVENTEEN
Negators: 不 **bù** and 没(有) **méi(yǒu)**

We have already discussed some uses of 不 **bù** and 没(有) **méi(yǒu)** in previous units (see Units 11 and 12). Here we shall review the functions of these two negators and draw attention to differences in the ways they are employed.

A 不 **bù** generally refers to the present or the future. It precedes the verb to indicate that something does not happen *habitually* or *intentionally* or that something will not happen in the future:

我不去看电影。 **wǒ bù qù kàn diànyǐng**
I don't go and see films./I'm not going to see the film.

那个运动员不穿运动鞋。 **nà/nèi gè yùndòngyuán bù chuān yùndòngxié**
That athlete doesn't wear sports shoes.

图书馆明天不开门。 **túshūguǎn míngtiān bù kāimén**
The library isn't/won't be open tomorrow.

陈小姐不抽烟，不喝酒，不打牌。
chén xiǎojie bù chōuyān | bù hē jiǔ | bù dǎ pái
Miss Chen doesn't smoke or drink or play mahjong.

Note: 不 **bù** is also used to negate habitual or intentional action if the context is set in the past:

那个运动员以前不穿运动鞋。 **nà/nèi gè yùndòngyuán yǐqián bù chuān yùndòngxié**
That athlete didn't wear sports shoes in the past.

小时候我常常不去上课。 **xiǎo shíhou wǒ chángcháng bù qù shàngkè**
When I was a child, I often missed classes.

B In contrast with 不 **bù**, 没(有) **méi(yǒu)**, which likewise goes before the verb, refers to the past and indicates that something has not taken place or did not take place *on one particular occasion* or, if 过 **guo** is suffixed to the verb, *as a past experience*:

她上个月没(有)碰见李先生。
tā shàng gè yuè méi(yǒu) pèngjiàn lǐ xiānsheng
She didn't bump into Mr Li last month.

弟弟那天没(有)去游泳。 **dìdi nà/nèi tiān méi(yǒu) qù yóuyǒng**
(My) younger brother didn't go swimming that day.

我没(有)吃过北京烤鸭。 **wǒ méi(yǒu) chī guo běijīng kǎoyā**
I've never had/eaten Peking duck.

Note: 没有 **méiyǒu** may be abbreviated to 没 **méi**:

那个孩子昨天没吃饭。 **nà/nèi gè háizi zuótiān méi chīfàn**
That child didn't eat (any food) yesterday.

C   The two negators are different in the way they are used with aspect markers:

(i) 不 **bù**, and not 没(有) **méi(yǒu)**, is normally used with the continuous action marker 在 **zài**:

妈妈不在吸尘。 **māma bù zài xīchén**
Mother is not vacuuming (at the moment).
那时候妈妈不在吸尘。 **nà /nèi shíhou māma bù zài xīchén**
Mother was not vacuuming at that moment.

It is unusual to say:

*那时候妈妈没在吸尘。 **nà/nèi shíhou māma méi zài xīchén**

However, 不 **bù** does not usually occur with the aspect markers 着 **zhe**, 下去 **xiàqù** and 下来 **xiàlái** except in the form of 不要 **bù yào** or 别 **bié** 'don't' in prohibitions:

不要唱下去了！	**bù yào chàng xiàqù le**	Don't sing any more!
别停下来！	**bié tíng xiàlái**	Don't stop!
别站着！	**bié zhàn zhe**	Don't just stand there. (Do something!)

不 **bù** may not be used with 了 **le**, 过 **guo** or 起来 **qǐlái** though it does occur with 了 **le** as sentence particle (see *Intermediate Chinese*, Unit 1):

他不咳嗽了。	**tā bù késòu le**	He's not coughing any more.
她不抽烟了。	**tā bù chōuyān le**	She's quit smoking. (*lit.* She's no longer smoking.)

(ii) 没(有) **méi(yǒu)** may only be used with the aspect markers 过 **guo**, 起来 **qǐlái**, 下去 **xiàqù** and 下来 **xiàlái**:

我没(有)见过他。	**wǒ méi(yǒu) jiàn guo tā**	I have never met him.
他们没(有)打起来。	**tāmen méi(you) dǎ qǐlái**	They did not fight with each other.
老大爷没(有)待下去。	**lǎodàyé méi(yǒu) dāi xiàqù**	The old man didn't stay on.
钱太太没(有)安下心来。	**qián tàitai méi(yǒu) ān xià xīn lái**	Mrs Qian did not stop worrying.

没(有) **méi(yǒu)** is not used with 了 **le** and 着 **zhe**. It must be emphasized that as a negator of past actions, 没(有) **méi(yǒu)** replaces 了 **le** and does not occur with it:

Compare:

摄影师拍了很多照片。 **shèyǐngshī pāi le hěn duō zhàopiàn**
The photographer took a lot of photographs.

摄影师没(有)拍很多照片。
shèyǐngshī méi(yǒu) pāi hěn duō zhàopiàn
The photographer didn't take many photographs.

One does not say:

*她没碰见了李先生。 **tā méi pèngjiàn le lǐ xiānsheng**
(*lit.* She didn't bump into Mr Li.)

Compare also:

他穿着大衣。	**tā chuān zhe dàyī**	He's wearing an overcoat.
他没(有)穿大衣。	**tā méi(yǒu) chuān dàyī**	He did not wear/was not wearing an overcoat.

One does not usually say:

*他没(有)穿着大衣。 **tā méi(yǒu) chuān zhe dàyī**
(*lit.* He wasn't wearing his overcoat.)

D   Time expressions like 昨天 **zuótiān**, 已经 **yǐjing**, 刚才 **gāngcái**, etc. usually come before 不 **bù** or 没(有) **méi(yǒu)**:

约翰已经不学中文了。 **yuēhàn yǐjing bù xué zhōngwén le**
John doesn't study Chinese any more.

我们刚才没有看见她。 **wǒmen gāngcái méiyǒu kànjiàn tā**
We didn't see her just now.

玛丽昨晚没睡觉。 **mǎlì zuó wǎn méi shuìjiào**
Mary didn't sleep last night.

Note: The time expression 从来 **cónglái** 'all along' is always linked with a negator:

这个人我从来没见过。	**zhè/zhèi gè rén wǒ cónglái méi jiàn guo**	I have never met this person (before).
他从来不赌博。	**tā cónglái bù dǔbó**	He has never gambled.

E   If there are location expressions in the sentence, they usually come after 不 **bù** or 没(有) **méi(yǒu)**:

我爸爸不在大使馆工作。 **wǒ bàba bù zài dàshǐguǎn gōngzuò**
My father doesn't work at the Embassy.

我家没在美国住过。 **wǒ jiā méi zài měiguó zhù guo**
Our family has never lived in America.

F   Monosyllabic adverbs like 都 **dōu** 'both'; 'all', 也 **yě** 'also', 又 **yòu** 'once again', 还 **hái** 'still; yet', etc. usually come before 不 **bù** or 没(有) **méi(yǒu)**:

他们都没来。	**tāmen dōu méi lái**	None of them came.
我也不喜欢乌鸦。	**wǒ yě bù xǐhuan wūyā**	I don't like crows either.
他又不来上课了。	**tā yòu bù lái shàngkè le**	He did not turn up for his class again.
我弟弟还没上学。	**wǒ dìdi hái méi shàngxué**	My younger brother hasn't started school yet.

Note: The only exception is 都 **dōu** which may also come after the negator when it has a different meaning. Compare the following sentences:

他们都没去。	**tāmen dōu méi qù**	None of them went.
他们没都去。	**tāmen méi dōu qù**	Not all of them went./They didn't all go.

G   不 **bù**, and not 没(有) **méi(yǒu)**, is used with modal verbs or verbs that express attitude.

(i) It is generally placed before the modal/attitudinal verb:

他们不愿意帮助我。 **tāmen bù yuànyi bāngzhù wǒ**
They are/were not willing to help me.

那个小偷不敢说实话。 **nà/nèi gè xiǎotōu bù gǎn shuō shíhuà**
That thief doesn't/didn't dare to tell the truth.

我不喜欢吃肉。 **wǒ bù xǐhuan chī ròu**
I don't like meat. (*lit.* I don't like eating meat.)

(ii) However, it may also occur between the modal verb and the main verb
when the meaning requires it:

我想不喝酒，喝汽水。 **wǒ xiǎng bù hē jiǔ | hē qìshuǐ**
I would rather have a fizzy drink than alcohol.
(*lit.* I would like not to drink alcohol (but) to drink a fizzy drink.)

Compare:

你不可以走。 **nǐ bù kěyǐ zǒu**   You can't leave (now).
你可以不走。 **nǐ kěyǐ bù zǒu**   You can stay. (*lit.* You can not leave.)

H Adjectival predicatives may only be negated by 不 **bù**:

那条裙子不漂亮。 | **nà/nèi tiáo qúnzi bù** | That skirt isn't pretty.
 | **piàoliang** |
这间屋子不干净。 | **zhè/zhèi jiān wūzi bù** | This room isn't clean.
 | **gānjìng** |
我的办公室不大。 | **wǒ de bàngōngshì bù dà** | My office isn't big.
这儿的空气不新鲜。 | **zhèr de kōngqì bù xīnxiān** | The air here isn't fresh.
那儿的人不多。 | **nàr de rén bù duō** | There aren't many people
 | | there.

Note: Only adjectival idioms beginning with 有 **yǒu** will have to be negated by 没 **méi**:

这本小说没(有)意思。 **zhè/zhèi běn xiǎoshuō méi(yǒu) yìsi** This novel isn't interesting.
我今晚没(有)空。 **wǒ jīn wǎn méi(yǒu) kòng** I am busy tonight. (*lit.* I tonight
am not free.)

I 没(有) **méi(yǒu)**, however, is generally used to negate adjectives which
are used as state verbs with sentence particle 了 **le** (see *Intermediate Chinese*,
Unit 1). Compare the following pairs of sentences:

他的病好了。 | **tā de bìng hǎo le** | He's well again.
他的病还没(有)好。 | **tā de bìng hái méi(yǒu) hǎo** | He isn't well yet.

天晴了。 | **tiān qíng le** | The sky has cleared up.
天还没(有)晴。 | **tiān hái méi(yǒu) qíng** | It is still raining. (*lit.* The sky
 | | hasn't cleared up yet.)

Exercise 17.1

Complete the sentences below with either 不 **bù** or 没 **méi** to provide a correct translation of the English:

1 爸爸 ———— 喝酒。 **bàba** ———— **hē jiǔ**
   Father doesn't drink.
2 他 ———— 去看京剧。 **tā** ———— **qù kàn jīngjù**
   He didn't go to watch the Beijing Opera.
3 昨天 ————下雪。 **zuótiān** ———— **xià xuě**
   It didn't snow yesterday.
4 以前我 ———— 学过汉语。 **yǐqián wǒ** ———— **xué guo hànyǔ**
   I have never studied Chinese before.
5 她从来 ———— 抽过烟。 **tā cónglái** ———— **chōu guo yān**
   She has never smoked.
6 过去王先生常常 ———— 戴帽子。
   guòqù wáng xiānsheng chángcháng ———— **dài màozi**
   Mr Wang didn't often wear a hat before.
7 我 ———— 去游泳。 **wǒ** ———— **qù yóuyǒng**
   I am not going swimming.
8 他已经 ———— 骑自行车了。 **tā yǐjing** ———— **qí zìxíngchē le**
   He has stopped riding a bike.
9 姐姐那天 ———— 跳舞。 **jiějie nà/nèi tiān** ———— **tiàowǔ**
   My elder sister didn't dance that day.
10 妹妹 ———— 买裙子。 **mèimei** ———— **mǎi qúnzi**
   My younger sister didn't buy a skirt.
11 我 ———— 读昨天的报纸。 **wǒ** ———— **dú zuótiān de bàozhǐ**
   I didn't read yesterday's newspaper.
12 哥哥 ———— 喜欢唱歌。 **gēge** ———— **xǐhuan chàng gē**
   My older brother doesn't like singing.
13 我从来 ———— 吃牛肉。 **wǒ cónglái** ———— **chī niúròu**
   I have never eaten beef.
14 我从来 ———— 喝过绿茶。 **wǒ cónglái** ———— **hē guo lǜchá**
   I have never drunk green tea before.
15 弟弟 ———— 会开车。 **dìdi** ———— **huì kāichē**
   My younger brother can't drive.

Exercise 17.2

Add the adverb in brackets to the Chinese sentences below and then adjust the English translation to take account of this:

1 孩子们不喜欢吃蔬菜。 **háizimen bù xǐhuan chī shūcài**
   The children don't like eating vegetables. (都 **dōu**)

2 他们没有去看京剧。 **tāmen méiyǒu qù kàn jīngjù**
   They didn't go to watch the Beijing Opera. (也 **yě**)
3 他吃饭前不洗手。 **tā chīfàn qián bù xǐ shǒu**
   He didn't wash his hands before meals. (常常 **chángcháng**)
4 我不抽烟。 **wǒ bù chōuyān**
   I don't smoke. (从来 **cónglái**)
5 她没喝茶。 **tā méi hē chá**
   She didn't drink any tea. (刚才 **gāngcái**)
6 他没看电视。 **tā méi kàn diànshì**
   He didn't watch TV. (今天 **jīntiān**)
7 她没吃蛋糕。 **tā méi chī dàngāo**
   She didn't eat any/touch the cake. (那天 **nà/nèi tiān**)
8 妹妹没坐过飞机。 **mèimei méi zuò guo fēijī**
   (My) younger sister has not flown in a plane before. (从来 **cónglái**)

Exercise 17.3

Indicate which of the Chinese sentences below is the correct translation of the English in each case:

1 I don't think the answer is correct.
   我认为那个答案不对。 **wǒ rènwéi nà/nèi gè dá'àn bù duì**
   我不认为那个答案对。 **wǒ bù rènwéi nà/nèi gè dá'àn duì**
2 I don't think it is worth considering any more.
   我不认为这值得多想。 **wǒ bù rènwéi zhè zhíde duō xiǎng**
   我认为这不值得多想。 **wǒ rènwéi zhè bù zhíde duō xiǎng**
3 I have never taken a liking to her.
   我从来没有喜欢过她。 **wǒ cónglái méiyǒu xǐhuan guo tā**
   我从来不喜欢过她。 **wǒ cónglái bù xǐhuan guo tā**
4 He was not wearing an overcoat.
   他没穿大衣。 **tā méi chuān dàyī**
   他没穿着大衣。 **tā méi chuān zhe dàyī**
   他不穿大衣。 **tā bù chuān dàyī**

Exercise 17.4

Insert an appropriate negator or negators in the right position in each of the following Chinese sentences to match the meaning of the English sentences:

1 他可以在那幢房子的墙上写标语。
   tā kěyǐ zài nà/nèi zhuàng fángzi de qiáng shang xiě biāoyǔ
   He is not supposed to write any slogans on the wall of that house.
2 你会包饺子吗？ **nǐ huì bāo jiǎozi ma**
   Can't you make Chinese dumplings?

3 经理愿意加陈先生的工资。 **jīnglǐ yuànyì jiā chén xiānsheng de gōngzī**
The manager was unwilling to give Mr Chen a pay rise.

4 我这个星期/礼拜能来吗？ **wǒ zhè/zhèi gè xīngqī/lǐbài néng lái ma**
Can I not come this week?

5 她来英国前见过松鼠。 **tā lái yīngguó qián jiàn guo sōngshǔ**
She had never seen squirrels before she came to Britain.

6 妹妹敢去邻居那儿借椅子。 **mèimei gǎn qù línjū nàr jiè yǐzi**
My younger sister dare not go and borrow chairs from our neighbour.

7 裤子太短。弟弟肯/愿意穿。 **kùzi tài duǎn | dìdi kěn/yuànyì chuān**
The trousers were too short and my younger brother was not willing to wear them.

8 水果很新鲜。大家都想吃。 **shuǐguǒ hěn xīnxiān | dàjiā dōu xiǎng chī**
The fruit were not fresh at all and nobody wanted to touch them.

9 昨天下大雨。我们去操场踢足球。
zuótiān xià dà yǔ | wǒmen qù cāochǎng tī zúqiú
There was heavy rain yesterday. We didn't go and play football on the sports field.

10 你应该告诉他们这件事。 **nǐ yīnggāi gàosu tāmen zhè/zhèi jiàn shì**
You shouldn't have told them about this.

11 这些花儿香。蜜蜂来采蜜。 **zhè/zhèi xiē huār xiāng | mìfēng lái cǎi mì**
These flowers aren't fragrant and the bees don't come to collect honey from them.

12 草莓比桃子好吃。 **cǎoméi bǐ táozi hǎochī**
Strawberries are not as delicious as peaches.

UNIT EIGHTEEN
Types of question (1)

A   General questions in Chinese can be formed by adding the particle 吗 **ma** to the end of a statement. Answers to such questions often employ the verb or adjective in the question with or without a negator as required by the meaning:

你是英国人吗？	**nǐ shì yīngguó rén ma**	Are you English?
是啊。	**shì a**	Yes. (*lit.* be)
不是，我是法国人。	**bù shì | wǒ shì fǎguó rén**	No (*lit.* not be), I am French.
你有笔吗？	**nǐ yǒu bǐ ma**	Have you got a pen?
有啊。	**yǒu a**	Yes. (*lit.* have)
对不起，我没有。	**duìbùqǐ | wǒ méi yǒu**	Sorry, I haven't.
你忙吗？	**nǐ máng ma**	Are you busy?
忙啊。	**máng a**	Yes. (*lit.* busy)
不忙。	**bù máng**	No, I'm not. (*lit.* not busy)
你去学校吗？	**nǐ qù xuéxiào ma**	Are you going to the school?
去啊。	**qù a**	Yes. (*lit.* go)
今天不去。	**jīntiān bù qù**	I'm not going today. (*lit.* today not go)

Note: 啊 **a** is a particle often placed at the end of an affirmative response to soften the tone.

In the answer to 吗 **ma** questions, it is also possible to use words or phrases indicating confirmation or denial, for example 是 **shì** or 是的 **shì de** 'yes' (*lit.* it is/does), 对 **duì** 'yes' (*lit.* right; correct), or 不 **bù** or 不是 **bù shì** 'no' (*lit.* it isn't/doesn't):

你的办公室很脏吗？ **nǐ de bàngōngshì hěn zāng ma**
Is your office very dirty?
是的，确实很脏。 **shì de \| quèshí hěn zāng**
Yes, it's really filthy.

不，一点儿也不脏。 **bù | yīdiǎnr yě bù zāng**
No, it's not at all dirty!

明天开会吗？ **míngtiān kāihuì ma**
Is the meeting tomorrow?
对，明天开会。 **duì | míngtiān kāihuì**
Yes, the meeting's tomorrow.
不，后天才开。 **bù | hòutiān cái kāi**
No, it's not till the day after tomorrow.
(才 **cái** is an adverb indicating 'not . . . until . . .'.)

你不喜欢吃鱼吗？	**nǐ bù xǐhuan chī yú ma**	Don't you like fish?
是的，我不喜欢吃鱼。	**shì de	wǒ bù xǐhuan chī yú**	No, I don't (like fish).
不，我很喜欢吃鱼。	**bù	wǒ hěn xǐhuan chī yú**	Yes, I do (like fish).
你身上没有钱吗？	**nǐ shēn shang méi yǒu qián ma**	Don't you have any money with you?
不，我身上有钱。	**bù	wǒ shēn shang yǒu qián**	Yes, I do.
对，我身上没有钱。	**duì	wǒ shēn shang méi yǒu qián**	No, I don't.

Note: From the last two examples you can observe that in answering a question couched in the negative, Chinese will agree or disagree with the proposition whereas English generally confirms the respondent's reaction putting 'yes' with an affirmative verb and 'no' with a negative verb.

B   General questions may also be expressed in an 'affirmative-negative' form by repeating the verb or adjective with the negator 不 **bù** or in the case of the verb 有 **yǒu** with the negator 没 **méi**. Answers to such 'affirmative-negative' questions likewise use the verb or adjective in the question with or without a negator:

你是不是王先生？ **nǐ *shì bù shì* wáng xiānsheng** Are you Mr Wang?
是。/不是。 **shì/bù shì** Yes./No. (*lit.* be/not be)

你买不买水果？ **nǐ *mǎi bù mǎi* shuǐguǒ** Are you going to buy any fruit?
买。/不买。 **mǎi/bù mǎi** Yes./No. (*lit.* buy/not buy)

你今晚有没有事儿？ **nǐ jīn wǎn *yǒu méi yǒu* shìr**
Have you got anything to do tonight?
有。/没有。 **yǒu/méi yǒu** Yes./No. (*lit.* have/not have)

昨天冷不冷？ **zuótiān *lěng bù lěng*** Was it cold yesterday?
冷啊。/不冷。 **lěng a/bù lěng** Yes./No. (*lit.* cold/not cold)

这个孩子乖不乖？ **zhè/zhèi gè háizi *guāi bù guāi***
Is this child disobedient?
这个孩子真乖。/这个孩子一点儿也不乖。
zhè/zhèi gè háizi zhēn guāi./zhè/zhèi gè háizi yīdiǎnr yě bù guāi
This child is really obedient./This child is not at all obedient.

你的行李重不重？ **nǐ de xíngli *zhòng bù zhòng*** Is your luggage heavy?
(我的行李)一点儿也不重。 **(wǒ de xíngli) yīdiǎnr yě bù zhòng**
My luggage isn't heavy at all.

Note: As we saw in Unit 10 it is not unusual for an adjectival predicative (as in the answers to the last three questions above) to incorporate some kind of modifier (e.g. 啊 **a**, 真 **zhēn** and, naturally, 不 **bù**).

C It must be pointed out that 没有 **méiyǒu**, when employed to negate a completed action or past experience (see Unit 17), follows two patterns in the formulation of affirmative-negative questions:

(i) 没有 **méiyǒu** is added to the positive statement with 了 **le** or 过 **guo**:

你吃了饭没有？	**nǐ chī le fàn méiyǒu**	Have you eaten yet?
吃了。/没有。	**chī le/méiyǒu**	Yes (I have)./No (I haven't).
小王来了没有？	**xiǎo wáng lái le méiyǒu**	Has Xiao Wang arrived yet?
来了。/还没有。	**lái le/hái méiyǒu**	Yes (he has)./No, not yet.
你去过中国没有？	**nǐ qù guo zhōngguó méiyǒu**	Have you ever been to China?
去过。/没(有)去过。	**qù guo/méi(yǒu) qù guo**	Yes (I have)./No (I haven't).

(ii) 有没有 **yǒu méiyǒu** is inserted before the verb (with 过 **guo** retained for past experience, but with 了 **le** omitted in the case of completed action questions):

你有没有买香蕉？ **nǐ yǒu méiyǒu mǎi xiāngjiāo**
Did you buy any bananas?
买了。/没有。 **mǎi le/méiyǒu**
Yes (I did)./No (I didn't).

昨晚你们有没有看电视？ **zuó wǎn nǐmen yǒu méiyǒu kàn diànshì**
Did you watch television yesterday?
看了。/没有。 **kàn le/méiyǒu**
Yes (I did)./No (I didn't).

你有没有谈过这个问题？ **nǐ yǒu méiyǒu tán guo zhè/zhèi gè wèntí**
Have you talked about this question?
谈过。/没有。 **tán guo/méiyǒu**
Yes (I have)./No (I haven't).

没有 **méiyǒu** may also be added to an adjectival predicative with 了 **le** which indicates a change of state (see *Intermediate Chinese*, Unit 1) to form the affirmative-negative question:

她的病好了没有？ **tā de bìng hǎo le méiyǒu**
Has she recovered from her illness? (*lit*. Her illness has got well or not?)
好了。/还没(有)好。 **hǎo le/hái méi(yǒu) hǎo**
Yes (she has)./No, not yet.

他醉了没有？ **tā zuì le méiyǒu**
Is he drunk?
醉了。/没(有)醉。 **zuì le/méi(yǒu) zuì**
Yes (he is)./No (he isn't).

树上的苹果熟了没有？ **shù shang de píngguǒ shú/shóu le méiyǒu**
Are the apples on the tree ripe? (*lit*. Have the apples on the tree ripened?)
熟了。/还没(有)熟。 **shú/shóu le/hái méi(yǒu) shú/shóu**
Yes (they are)./No, not yet.

D   If modal verbs are present, they form the affirmative-negative question:

你今晚能不能去跳舞？	**nǐ jīn wǎn néng bù néng qù tiàowǔ**	Can you go dancing tonight?
明天会不会下雪？	**míngtiān huì bù huì xià xuě**	Will it snow tomorrow?
你可(以)不可以帮帮我的忙？	**nǐ kě(yǐ) bù kěyǐ bāngbāng wǒ de máng**	Can you help me?
她愿(意)不愿意帮助你？	**tā yuàn(yì) bù yuànyì bāngzhù nǐ**	Is she willing to help you?

Note: With a disyllabic modal verb the affirmative part of the affirmative-negative sequence may often drop the second syllable, as the last two examples show.

E   Questions can, of course, be formulated with question words. In Chinese, the question word, whether it is an interrogative pronoun or adverb, is located in the sentence in the same position as the answer. That is to say, Chinese, unlike English, does not necessarily invert the order of a sentence when using a question word (see Units 4 and 9):

他是谁？	tā shì shéi	Who is he?
他是这儿的医生。	tā shì zhèr de yīshēng	He is the doctor here.
你去哪儿？	nǐ qù nǎr	Where are you going?
我去火车站。	wǒ qù huǒchēzhàn	I'm going to the railway station.
谁来了？	shéi lái le	Who has arrived?
张小姐来了。	zhāng xiǎojie lái le	Miss Zhang has arrived.
这是谁的包裹？	zhè shì shéi de bāoguǒ	Whose parcel is this?
这是那位先生的包裹。	zhè shì nà/nèi wèi xiānsheng de bāoguǒ	It is that gentleman's parcel.
你想喝点儿什么？	nǐ xiǎng hē diǎnr shénme	What would you like to drink?
我想喝点儿可乐。	wǒ xiǎng hē diǎnr kělè	I'd like (to have) some coke.
你在哪儿学习？	nǐ zài nǎr xuéxí	Where are you studying?
我在北京大学学习。	wǒ zài běijīng dàxué xuéxí	I am studying at Beijing University.
你要哪一个？	nǐ yào nǎ/něi yī gè	Which one do you want?
我要这个。	wǒ yào zhè/zhèi gè	I want this one.
哪辆车是你的？	nǎ liàng chē shì nǐ de	Which car is yours?
那辆黑车是我的。	nà/nèi liàng hēi chē shì wǒ de	That black one is mine.

F The particle 呢 **ne** is also used to formulate a variety of questions.

(i) It may be placed after a noun, noun phrase or pronoun when the speaker is expecting something (or someone) and queries this:

钥匙呢? **yàoshi ne**
Where are the keys? (Shouldn't they be here; you have not forgotten them, have you; etc.)

他呢? **tā ne**
Where is he? (Shouldn't he be here too/by now)

结果呢? **jiéguǒ ne**
And what was the result?/What happened then?

(ii) It also occurs after a noun, noun phrase or pronoun to ask about the condition of somebody or something, in response to a statement or suggestion, and it is usually translated as 'And how about . . . /And what about . . .?':

我很好，你呢？ **wǒ hěn hǎo | nǐ ne**
I'm very well. And you?

我的作业交了，你的呢？ **wǒ de zuòyè jiāo le | nǐ de ne**
I've handed in my course-work. How about you? (*lit.* how about yours?)

衬衫洗了，裤子呢？ **chènshēn xǐ le | kùzi ne**
The shirt has been washed but what about the trousers?

(iii) It can raise a question relating to a particular situation (couched in terms of a general statement) and is often roughly equivalent to English 'what if . . .':

他不同意呢？	**tā bù tóngyì ne**	What if he doesn't agree (to it)?
老师没空呢？	**lǎoshī méi kòng ne**	What if the teacher hasn't got time?
明天下雨呢？	**míngtiān xià yǔ ne**	What if it rains tomorrow?

(iv) It may be added to a question-word question or an affirmative-negative question to introduce a tone of surprise or impatience:

她是谁呢？	**tā shì shéi ne**	Who can she be?
小猫在哪儿呢？	**xiǎo māo zài nǎr ne**	Where can the kitten be?
他们忙不忙呢？	**tāmen máng bù máng ne**	Are they really busy?

Exercise 18.1

Change the statements below into two forms of questions using 吗 **ma** and the 'affirmative-negative' structure, providing answers in both the affirmative and the negative:

EXAMPLE
他抽烟。 **tā chōuyān**
He smokes.

他抽烟吗？ **tā chōuyān ma**/他抽(烟)不抽烟？ **tā chōu(yān) bù chōuyān**
Does he smoke?
抽。 **chōu**
Yes.
不抽。 **bù chōu**
No.

1 他们是农民。 **tāmen shì nóngmín**
  They are farmers.
2 他想打乒乓球。 **tā xiǎng dǎ pīngpāngqiú**
  He wants to play table-tennis.
3 他去过动物园。 **tā qù guo dòngwùyuán**
  He has been to the zoo.
4 那条街很干净。 **nà/nèi tiáo jiē hěn gānjìng**
  That street is very clean.
5 她明天会来。 **tā míngtiān huì lái**
  She will come tomorrow.
6 他有图书证。 **tā yǒu túshūzhèng**
  He's got a library card.
7 她带了钥匙。 **tā dài le yàoshi**
  She's brought her keys.
8 火很旺。 **huǒ hěn wàng**
  The fire was burning brightly.
9 你的朋友会哼那个曲子。 **nǐ de péngyou huì hēng nà/nèi gè qǔzi**
  Your friend can hum that tune.
10 他的弟弟喜欢穿牛仔裤。 **tā de dìdi xǐhuan chuān niúzǎikù**
  His younger brother likes wearing jeans.

Exercise 18.2

Convert the questions below into the aspect marker 了 **le** structure and translate the questions into English:

EXAMPLE
你有没有游泳？ **nǐ yǒu méiyǒu yóuyǒng**

你游了泳没有？ **nǐ yóu le yǒng méiyǒu**
Did you swim?/Did you go swimming?

1 你有没有洗衬衫？ **nǐ yǒu méiyǒu xǐ chènshān**
2 你昨天有没有读报？ **nǐ zuótiān yǒu méiyǒu dú bào**
3 上个月你有没有看电影？ **shàng gè yuè nǐ yǒu méiyǒu kàn diànyǐng**
4 昨晚你有没有写信？ **zuó wǎn nǐ yǒu méiyǒu xiě xìn**
5 你有没有买票？ **nǐ yǒu méiyǒu mǎi piào**
6 她有没有碰见张先生？ **tā yǒu méiyǒu pèngjiàn zhāng xiānsheng**
7 你们前天有没有上酒吧间？ **nǐmen qiántiān yǒu méiyǒu shàng jiǔbājiān**
8 你们那儿上星期有没有下雪？ **nǐmen nàr shàng xīngqī yǒu méiyǒu xià xuě**
9 他家去年夏天有没有去海边度假？
  tā jiā qùnián xiàtiān yǒu méiyǒu qù hǎi biān dùjià

10 这件事小黄有没有告诉你？
zhè/zhèi jiàn shì xiǎo huáng yǒu méiyǒu gàosu nǐ

Exercise 18.3

Translate the following sentences into Chinese, expressing the question in two ways in each case:

1 Have you ever been mountain-climbing?
2 Have you ever met your neighbour?
3 Have you ever blamed yourself?
4 Have you ever been to a soccer match?
5 Have you ever ridden a horse?
6 Have you ever been to the seaside?
7 Have you ever tried Chinese dumplings? (饺子 **jiǎozi** 'Chinese dumplings')
8 Have you ever seen a whale? (鲸鱼 **jīngyú** 'whale')
9 Have you ever kept a dog? (养 **yǎng** 'keep (a pet, etc.)')
10 Have you ever been to a pub?

Exercise 18.4

Translate the following sentences into Chinese:

1 Is it quiet in the library? (安静 **ānjìng** 'quiet')
2 Is it hot in Beijing?
3 Are your friends happy? (高兴 **gāoxìng** 'happy')
4 Are the dishes tasty?
5 Was that television programme interesting?
6 Was the soccer match exciting?
7 Is this chair comfortable? (舒服 **shūfu** 'comfortable')
8 Do the flowers smell nice? (香 **xiāng** 'sweet-smelling')
9 Was the cake sweet? (甜 **tián** 'sweet (to the taste)')
10 Is the table clean? (干净 **gānjìng** 'clean')
11 Is the room tidy? (整齐 **zhěngqí** 'tidy')
12 Was the manager generous? (慷慨 **kāngkǎi** 'generous')

Exercise 18.5

Translate these questions into Chinese using 呢 **ne**:

1 What if he gets drunk?
2 The trousers have been washed but what about the skirt?

 3 What if it rains tomorrow evening?
 4 What if I haven't got time?
 5 The coffee is nice but what do you think of the cake?
 6 I'm very busy. How about you?
 7 Where can she have gone?
 8 Whose computer is this then?
 9 Where are my keys?
10 Where can the kitten be?

UNIT NINETEEN
Types of question (2)

A   Tag questions, which are seeking agreement to, or approval of, a suggestion or proposal, are formed by attaching 好吗？/好不好？ **hǎo ma/hǎo bù hǎo**, 行吗？/行不行？ **xíng ma/xíng bù xíng** (*lit.* 'is this OK?'), 可以吗？/可(以)不可以？ **kěyǐ ma/kě(yǐ) bù kěyǐ** (*lit.* 'is that all right?'), etc. to the statement. Answers to such questions repeat the tag words 好 **hǎo**, 行 **xíng** or 可以 **kěyǐ**, sometimes with 啊 **a** in the affirmative, and with 不 **bù** in the negative:

咱们去散步，好吗？ 好啊。	**zánmen qù sànbù | hǎo ma** **hǎo a**	Shall we go for a walk? Fine/OK.
我想打个电话，行吗？ 行。	**wǒ xiǎng dǎ gè diànhuà** **| xíng ma** **xíng**	Is it all right if I make a phone call? Yes/All right.
我们今天早点儿回家，可以吗？ 不可以。	**wǒmen jīntiān zǎo** **diǎnr huí jiā | kěyǐ ma** **bù kěyǐ**	Can we go home earlier today? No, you can't.

B   吧 **ba** may be added to the end of a positive or negative statement to form a question implying surmise or supposition. Answers to these questions naturally invite the use of 是(的) **shì (de)** or 对 **duì** 'yes' or 不(是) **bù (shì)** or 不对 **bù duì** 'no' (see Unit 18), as a direct response to the surmise or supposition itself:

这个汉字不对吧？ **zhè/zhèi gè hànzì bù duì ba**
This Chinese character is wrong, isn't it? /Isn't this Chinese character wrong?
是，这个汉字不对。 **shì \| zhè/zhèi gè hànzì bù duì**
Yes, it is wrong.

那幅画儿是他画的吧？ **nà/nèi fú huàr shì tā huà de ba**
That picture was painted by him, wasn't it?
不，那幅画儿不是他画的。 **bù \| nà/nèi fú huàr bù shì tā huà de**
No, it wasn't painted by him.

他会骑摩托车吧？ **tā huì qí mótuōchē ba**
He can ride a motorbike, can't he?
是的，他会。 **shì dc | tā huì**
Yes, he can.

明天不会下雨吧？ **míngtiān bù huì xià yu ba**
It won't rain tomorrow, will it?
恐怕会下雨。 **kǒngpà huì xià yǔ**
I'm afraid it will.

Note: 吧 **ba** at the end of a statement can also express a suggestion or exhortation:

咱们走吧。 **zánmen zǒu ba** Let's go. (See Unit 20)

C An alternative question where the speaker presents two possibilities, e.g.
'Are you English or French?', is formed by placing 还是 **háishi** 'or' between the
two possibilities:

你是中国人还是日本人？ **nǐ shì zhōngguó rén háishi rìběn rén**
Are you Chinese or Japanese?
我是中国人。 **wǒ shì zhōngguó rén**
I am Chinese.

你喜欢看电影还是听音乐？ **nǐ xǐhuan kàn diànyǐng háishi tīng yīnyuè**
Do you like watching films or listening to music?
我喜欢看电影。 **wǒ xǐhuan kàn diànyǐng**
I like watching films.

你回家还是去银行？ **nǐ huí jiā háishi qù yínháng**
Are you going home or going to the bank?
我去银行。 **wǒ qù yínháng**
I am going to the bank.

Note 1: The two posed alternatives must be of similar structure, i.e. 中国人 **zhōngguó rén** . . . or
日本人 **rìběn rén** . . . (nouns); 看电影 **kàn diànyǐng** . . . or 听音乐 **tīng yīnyuè** . . . (verb + object), etc.

Note 2: Also, 还是 **háishi** meaning 'or' is used only in questions. In statements 'or' is 或者 **huòzhě**.

D In Unit 11, it was explained that to emphasize the initiator, target, time, place,
means, purpose, etc. of a past action the 是 **shì** . . . 的 **de** construction is used:

客人是昨天到的。 **kèren shì zuótiān dào de**   (time)
The guests arrived *yesterday*.
他们是坐飞机去的。 **tāmen shì zuò fēijī qù de**   (means)
They went *by plane*.

她是来找的经理。 **tā shì lái zhǎo de jīnglǐ**   (target)
She came to see *the manager*.

For present and future action 是 **shì** is employed without 的 **de**:

客人是明天到。 **kèren shì míngtiān dào**   The guests are arriving
tomorrow.

他们是坐飞机去。 **tāmen shì zuò fēijī qù**   They are going *by plane*.
她是来找经理(的)。 **tā shì lái zhǎo jīnglǐ (de)**   She is coming to see *the
manager*.

Note: In the last example, 的 **de** is optional. If it is present, it must be positioned at the end of the
sentence following the object. This position signals future action and contrasts with past action (as in
the earlier example) when the 的 **de** comes before the object.

These sentences of emphasis with 是 **shì** or 是 **shì** . . . 的 **de** can be formulated
into various forms of question, with 是 **shì** being the verb element in affirmative-
negative questions:

(i) past actions:

客人是什么时候到的？ **kèren shì shénme shíhou dào de**
When did the guests arrive?

客人是昨天到的吗？ **kèren shì zuótiān dào de ma**
客人是不是昨天到的？ **kèren shì bù shì zuótiān dào de**
Did the guests arrive *yesterday*?

客人是昨天到的，还是前天到的？
kèren shì zuótiān dào de | háishi qiántiān dào de
Did the guests arrive yesterday or the day before yesterday?

他们是怎么去的？ **tāmen shì zěnme qù de**
How did they travel?

他们是坐飞机去的吗？ **tāmen shì zuò fēijī qù de ma**
他们是不是坐飞机去的？ **tāmen shì bù shì zuò fēijī qù de**
Did they go *by plane*?

他们是坐飞机去的，还是坐船去的？
tāmen shì zuò fēijī qù de | háishi zuò chuán qù de
Did they go by plane or by boat?

她是来找的谁？ **tā shì lái zhǎo de shéi/shuí**
Who(m) did she come to see?

她是来找的经理吗？ **tā shì lái zhǎo de jīnglǐ ma**
她是不是来找的经理？ **tā shì bù shì lái zhǎo de jīnglǐ**
Did she come to see *the manager*?

她是来找的经理，还是来找的会计？
tā shì lái zhǎo de jīnglǐ | háishi lái zhǎo de kuàijì
Did she come to see the manager or the accountant?

(ii) present or future actions:

客人是什么时候到？ **kèren shì shénme shíhou dào**
When are the guests arriving?

客人是明天到吗？ **kèren shì míngtiān dào ma**
客人是不是明天到？ **kèren shì bù shì míngtiān dào**
Are the guests arriving *tomorrow*?

客人是明天到，还是后天到？
kèren shì míngtiān dào | háishi hòutiān dào
Are the guests arriving tomorrow or the day after tomorrow?

他们是怎么去？ **tāmen shì zěnme qù**
How are they travelling?

他们是坐飞机去吗？ **tāmen shì zuò fēijī qù ma**
他们是不是坐飞机去？ **tāmen shì bù shì zuò fēijī qù**
Are they going *by plane*?

他们是坐飞机去，还是坐船去？
tāmen shì zuò fēijī qù | háishi zuò chuán qù
Are they going by plane or by boat?

她是来找谁？ **tā shì lái zhǎo shéi/shuí**
Who(m) is she coming to see?

她是来找经理(的)吗？ **tā shì lái zhǎo jīnglǐ (de) ma**
她是不是来找经理(的)？ **tā shì bù shì lái zhǎo jīnglǐ (de)**
Is she coming to see *the manager*?

她是来找经理，还是来找会计？
tā shì lài zhǎo jīnglǐ | háishi lái zhǎo kuàijì
Is she coming to see the manager or the accountant?

The answer to all general, affirmative-negative questions is either 是(的) **shì (de)** 'yes' or 不是 **bù shì** 'no':

是你去找的她吗？ **shì nǐ qù zhǎo de tā ma**
是不是你去找的她？ **shì bù shì nǐ qù zhǎo de tā**
Was it you who went to see her?/Did *you* go to see her?
是的，是我。 **shì de | shì wǒ**
Yes, it was me.

你是去看电影吗？ **nǐ shì qù kàn diànyǐng ma**
你是不是去看电影？ **nǐ shì bù shì qù kàn diànyǐng**
Are you going to see a film?
不，我不是去看电影，我是去跳舞。
bù | wǒ bù shì qù kàn diànyǐng | wǒ shì qù tiàowǔ
No, I'm not going to see a film, I'm going dancing.

Exercise 19.1

Translate the following questions into Chinese using the tags 好吗 **hǎo ma**, 行吗 **xíng ma** or 可以吗 **kěyǐ ma**:

EXAMPLE
Could you shut the door, please?
请你关上门，好吗？ **qǐng nǐ guān shàng mén | hǎo ma**

 1 Could you close the window, please?
 2 Could you please speak Chinese?
 3 May I use the phone?
 4 Shall we go to the cinema?
 5 May I borrow a pen? (借 **jiè** 'to borrow')
 6 Can I sleep in tomorrow? (睡懒觉 **shuì lǎn jiào** 'to sleep in')
 7 May I sit here?
 8 May I make a suggestion? (提 **tí** 'to put forward')
 9 Could you tell us a story, please?
10 Could we go dancing tonight?

Exercise 19.2

Formulate questions, using 是不是 **shì bù shì** and where necessary 的 **de** on the basis of the statements below to elicit the required information:

EXAMPLE
周先生坐飞机去英国。 **zhōu xiānsheng zuò fēijī qù yīngguó**
Mr Zhou went to England by plane.

(i) Did *Mr Zhou* go to England/Was it Mr Zhou who went to England?

是不是周先生去的英国？ **shì bù shì zhōu xiānsheng qù de yīngguó**

(ii) Did Mr Zhou *travel by plane*?

周先生是不是坐飞机去的？ **zhōu xiānsheng shì bù shì zuò fēijī qù de**

(iii) Did Mr Zhou *go to England*/Was it England Mr Zhou went to?

周先生是不是去的英国？ **zhōu xiānsheng shì bù shì qù de yīngguó**

1 小李骑自行车去运动场。 **xiǎo lǐ qí zìxíngchē qù yùndòngchǎng**

Xiao Li went to the sports field on his bike.

  (i) Is *Xiao Li* going to the sports field/Is it Xiao Li who is going to the sports field?

 (ii) Is Xiao Li going *to the sports field*/ Is it the sports field that Xiao Li is going to?

(iii) Is Xiao Li *going on his bike* to the sports field?

2 王小姐刚才去邮局。 **wáng xiǎojie gāngcái qù yóujú**

Miss Wang went to the post office just now.

  (i) Did *Miss Wang* go to the post office/Was it Miss Wang who went to the post office?

 (ii) Did Miss Wang go *just now*/Was it just now that Miss Wang went?

(iii) Did Miss Wang go to the *post office*/Was it the post office Miss Wang went to?

Exercise 19.3

Make questions using 还是 **háishi** which might be answered by the statements below. (Note that in some cases the pronoun may have to be changed.):

1 我是老师，不是学生。 **wǒ shì lǎoshī | bù shì xuésheng**

I'm a teacher, not a student.

2 他喜欢看小说，不喜欢看电视。

tā xǐhuan kàn xiǎoshuō | bù xǐhuan kàn diànshì

He likes reading fiction, but he doesn't like watching television.

3 他不是昨天去的中国，是前天去的。

tā bù shì zuótiān qù de zhōngguó | shì qiántiān qù de

He didn't go to China yesterday, he went the day before.

4 我是坐火车去上班，不是坐汽车。

wǒ shì zuò huǒchē qù shàngbān | bù shì zuò qìchē

I go to work by train, not by bus.

5 我是去电影院，不是去饭馆。 **wǒ shì qù diànyǐngyuàn | bù shì qù fànguǎn**

I'm going to the cinema, not to the restaurant.

6 这是医院，不是大学。 **zhè shì yīyuàn | bù shì dàxué**
This is a hospital, not a university.
7 她那天是穿的裙子，不是裤子。
tā nà/nèi tiān shì chuān de qúnzi | bù shì kùzi
What she wore that day was a skirt, not a pair of trousers.
8 我前天是碰见的老王，不是小张。
wǒ qiántiān shì pèng jiàn de lǎo wáng | bù shì xiǎo zhāng
I bumped into Lao Wang, not Xiao Zhang, the day before yesterday.

Exercise 19.4

Change the following Chinese sentences into questions using 吧 **ba**, and then (1) provide English translations of the questions and (2) give positive and negative answers to the questions in Chinese and English. (Note again that in some cases the pronoun may need to be changed.)

EXAMPLE
夏天太阳五点半就出来了。 **xiàtiān tàiyáng wǔ diǎn bàn jiù chū lái le**
The sun rises at five thirty in the summer.

夏天太阳五点半就出来了吧？ **xiàtiān tàiyáng wǔ diǎn bàn jiù chū lái le ba**
The sun rises at half past five in the summer, doesn't it?
对。/是(的)。 **duì | shì (de)**
Yes.
不对。/不是(的)。 **bù duì | bù shì (de)**
No.

1 这本书是我写的。 **zhè/zhèi běn shū shì wǒ xiě de**
This book was written by me.
2 伦敦离北京很远。 **lúndūn lí běijīng hěn yuǎn**
London is a long way from Beijing.
3 火车已经开走了。 **huǒchē yǐjing kāi zǒu le**
The train has already gone.
4 那条裙子太长了。 **nà/nèi tiáo qúnzi tài cháng le**
That skirt is too long.
5 我每天都剃/刮胡子。 **wǒ měitiān dōu tì/guā húzi**
I shave every day.
6 我爸爸、妈妈下个月去度假。 **wǒ bàba | māma xià gè yuè qù dùjià**
My parents will go away on holiday next month.
7 我不喜欢喝中国茶。 **wǒ bù xǐhuan hē zhōngguó chá**
I don't like Chinese tea.
8 我妻子不吃牛肉。 **wǒ qīzi bù chī niúròu**
My wife does not eat beef.

Exercise 19.5

Translate the following sentences into Chinese, giving emphasis to the expressions underlined and paying particular attention to whether or not 的 **de** must be included to indicate past or future events:

1 Are you going to China *next month*?
2 Did you go to China *last year*?
3 Are you going *by plane* or *by boat*?
4 Did you go *by car* or *on a bike*?
5 *Where* did you learn your Chinese?
6 *Where* are you going to learn your Chinese?
7 *Who* washed the bowls last night?
8 *Who* is going to wash the bowls tonight?

UNIT TWENTY
Imperatives and exclamations

A   Imperatives, as commands or requests directed at the listener in given contexts, do not usually need a subject (unless the speaker wants to single out a particular person from a group):

进来!	**jìn lái**	Come in!
出去!	**chū qù**	Get out!
站起来!	**zhàn qǐlái**	Stand up!
坐下!	**zuò xià**	Sit down!
安静点儿!	**ānjìng diǎnr**	Quieten down! (*lit.* a bit quieter)
严肃点儿!	**yánsù diǎnr**	Be serious! (*lit.* a bit serious)

你去浇水，你去割草，你去剪树篱!
nǐ qù jiāo shuǐ, nǐ qù gē cǎo, nǐ qù jiǎn shùlí
You, water the plants! You, mow the grass! And you, clip the hedge!

B   To soften the tone of an imperative to the level of a request, 请 **qǐng** 'please' is placed at the beginning of the imperative:

请进来!	**qǐng jìn lái**	Come in, please!
请坐下!	**qǐng zuò xià**	Please take a seat!
请大家安静点儿!	**qǐng dàjiā ānjìng diǎnr**	Would everybody be quiet, please!

To soften the tone still further, the sentence particle 吧 **ba** can be used:

请进来吧!	**qǐng jìn lái ba**	Won't you please come in!
请坐吧!	**qǐng zuò ba**	Won't you please sit down!

吧 **ba** occurs without 请 **qǐng** and carries a casual tone:

坐吧!	**zuò ba**	Sit down then!/Okay, take a seat!/Why don't you take a seat!
进来吧!	**jìn lái ba**	Come in then!/Okay, you can come in now.

C   Commands and requests usually call for actions on the part of the listener. If they involve a third party, verbs like 让 **ràng** 'to let; to allow; to permit', 叫 **jiào** 'to order', etc. are usually placed before the third-person pronoun:

让他走吧!	**ràng tā zǒu ba**	Let him go!
叫他来见我!	**jiào tā lái jiàn wǒ**	Tell him to come and see me!
让他去!	**ràng tā qù**	Leave him alone! (*lit.* Let him go.)

Note: Observe the idiomatic use of the verb 去 **qù** 'to go' in the third example.

让 **ràng** is, of course, also used by the speaker in relation to him- or herself:

让我帮你的忙!	**ràng wǒ bāng nǐ de máng**	Let me give you a hand!
让我看一看!	**ràng wǒ kàn yī kàn**	Let me have a look!
让我想一下!	**ràng wǒ xiǎng yīxià**	Let me think about it!

D   In the case of an imperative involving the action of the speaker and the listener, the pronoun 咱们 **zánmen** 'we/us' is used together with the particle 吧 **ba**:

咱们走吧!	**zánmen zǒu ba**	Let's go!
咱们喝一杯吧!	**zánmen hē yī bēi ba**	Let's have a drink!

E   Commands or requests may also be concerned with the manner in which actions are carried out. Under such circumstances, the relevant adverbials are placed before the imperative verb:

快走!	**kuài zǒu**	Hurry up!
慢慢来!	**mànmàn lái**	Take it easy!/Take your time!
多吃点儿!	**duǒ chī diǎnr**	Have some more (food)!

F   Negative imperatives (or prohibitions) are expressed by 不要 **bù yào** 'don't' or its short form 别 **bié**:

等一等! 别走!	**děng yī děng | bié zǒu**	Wait a minute!/Hang on! Don't go (yet)!
别说话!	**bié shuōhuà**	Keep quiet! (*lit.* don't speak)
别客气!	**bié kèqi**	Make yourself at home! (*lit.* don't be polite)
不要抽烟!	**bù yào chōuyān**	Don't smoke!
不要开玩笑!	**bù yào kāi wánxiào**	Don't (treat it as a) joke.

G   Sentence particle 了 **le** (sometimes in combination with 啊 **a** and pronounced 啦 **la**) is added to introduce a note of urgency:

| 别说话了! | **bié shuōhuà le** | Silence, please!/Stop talking! |
| 起床啦! | **qǐchuáng la** | It's time to get up./Up you get! |

H More formal prohibitions which appear on public notices are expressed by 不准 **bù zhǔn** 'not allowed', 不许 **bù xǔ** 'not permitted' and 不得 **bù děi** 'must not':

不准抽烟!	**bù zhǔn chōuyān**	No smoking!
不得入内!	**bù děi rù nèi**	No entry!
不许在此乱丢垃圾!	**bù xǔ zài cǐ luàn diū lājī**	No litter on the premises!

I Exclamations are formed by placing a degree adverb like 多(么) **duō(me)** 'how', 真 **zhēn** 'really/truly' before the adjective, which is often followed by 啊 **a**:

伦敦的街道多么繁忙啊! **lúndūn de jiēdào duōme fánmáng a**
How busy the streets in London are!

瞧，他跑得真快啊! **qiáo | tā pǎo de zhēn kuài a**
Look, he can run really fast!

你真逗! **nǐ zhēn dòu**
You are really funny/witty!

J There is a tendency for the particle 啊 **a** to be affected by the vowel or consonant ending of the word that precedes it. This leads to possible variants including the following:

Endings	*Variant*
-i	呀 **ya**
-u, -ao	哇 **wa**
-n	哪 **na**

了 **le** and 啊 **a** (see G above) fuse to become 啦 **la**.

Examples

天哪! **tiān na** Heavens!

这道题目真难哪! **zhè/zhèi dào tímù zhēn nán na**
This question is really difficult!

这种药多么苦哇! **zhè/zhèi zhǒng yào duōme kǔ wa**
This medicine is so bitter/really awful/nasty!

不是这回事呀! **bù shì zhè/zhèi huí shì ya**
It is certainly not the case!

汽车修好啦! **qìchē xiū hǎo la**
The car has been repaired at last!

一只多么美丽的小鸟吐! **yī zhī duōme měilì de xiǎo niǎo wa**
What a beautiful little bird!

这头熊猫多可爱呀! **zhè/zhèi tóu xióngmāo duō kě'ài ya**
Isn't this panda sweet!

这场球赛多么精彩呀! **zhè/zhèi chǎng qiúsài duōme jīngcǎi ya**
This football match is so exciting!

Note: The above are not rigid rules and it is possible for individual speakers simply to use 啊 **a** or 呀 **ya** in many cases.

Exercise 20.1

Translate the following imperatives into Chinese:

1 Come in!
2 Stand up!
3 Get out!
4 Sit down!
5 Get up!
6 Be quick!
7 Come back early!
8 Close the door!
9 Be serious!
10 Don't switch off the light!

Exercise 20.2

Translate the following imperatives into Chinese, using 请 **qǐng** and/or 吧 **ba**, 让 **ràng**, 叫 **jiào** where appropriate:

1 Do have some more (food)!
2 Let's get off (the bus) here.
3 Leave him alone.
4 Hurry up!
5 Please queue up here! (排队 **páiduì** 'to queue')
6 Switch on the light, please!
7 Come in, please!

8 Let's have a little rest!
9 Listen! Who is it?
10 Please open the door.

Exercise 20.3

Rephrase the imperative sentences below as negatives:

1 关窗!	**guān chuāng**	Close the window!
2 关灯!	**guān dēng**	Turn off the light!
3 晾衣服!	**liàng yīfu**	Hang the clothes out to dry!
4 上车!	**shàng chē**	Get on the bus!/Get into the car!
5 过来!	**guò lái**	Come here!
6 穿这双鞋!	**chuān zhè/zhèi shuāng xié**	Wear this pair of shoes!
7 开车!	**kāichē**	(in a car) Let's go!
8 让他走!	**ràng tā zǒu**	Let him go.
9 叫她回来!	**jiào tā huí lái**	Tell her to come back.
10 请大家带伞!	**qǐng dàjiā dài sǎn**	Would everyone please bring umbrellas.

Exercise 20.4

Translate into Chinese the two imperative sentences (i) and (ii) in each of the following cases, building on the basic imperative provided:

1 进去! **jìn qù** Go in!

(i) Let's go in!
(ii) Okay, you may go in now!

2 去割草! **qù gē cǎo** Go and cut the grass!

(i) Would you please go and mow the grass!
(ii) Go and mow the grass now please! (It's time for you to go and mow the grass now.)

3 下车! **xià chē** Get off the bus!

(i) Let's get off the bus!
(ii) Come on, we're getting off here!

4 喝一杯! **hē yī bēi** Have a drink!

(i) Let's have a drink!
(ii) It's okay, you may have a drink!

Exercise 20.5

Complete the following sentences with a likely exclamatory particle in each case, such as 啊 **a**, 呀 **ya**, 哇 **wa**, 哪 **na** or 啦 **la**, remembering that with 啦 **la** an element must be replaced:

1 这块石头多重 _____! **zhè/zhèi kuài shítou dōu zhòng** _____
  This stone is so heavy!
2 那幢大楼真高 _____! **nà/nèi zhuàng dàlóu zhēn gāo** _____
  That building is really tall!
3 外面多冷 _____! **wàimian duō lěng** _____
  How cold it is outside!
4 我饿死了 _____! **wǒ è sǐ le** _____
  I am so hungry!
5 他来得真早 _____! **tā lái de zhēn zǎo** _____
  He's here really early!
6 你看地板都湿了 _____! **nǐ kàn dìbǎn dōu shī le** _____
  Look, the floor is all wet!
7 今天的天气多么好 _____! **jīntiān de tiānqì duōme hǎo** _____
  What a nice day it is today!
8 这道题真难 _____! **zhè/zhèi dào tí zhēn nán** _____
  This question is really difficult!
9 这是一条多么漂亮的裙子 _____!
  zhè shì yī tiáo duōme piàoliang de qúnzi _____
  What a pretty skirt this is!
10 图书馆里真安静 _____! **túshūguǎn li zhēn ānjìng** _____
  How quiet it is in the library!
11 这个孩子多可爱 _____! **zhè/zhèi gè háizi duō kě'ài** _____
  How lovely this child is!
12 多么可爱的一只小猫 _____! **duōme kě'ài de yī zhī xiǎo māo** _____
  What a lovely kitten!

UNIT TWENTY-ONE
Complements of direction and location (or destination)

Complements are those elements in a sentence which follow the verb (or adjective), apart from the object. They usually signify such meaning categories as direction, location, duration, result, manner, possibility, degree, etc. In this unit we are concerned with complements of direction and location.

A   The verbs 来 **lái** 'to come' and 去 **qù** 'to go' form the two basic complements of direction which are used after verbs of movement or action to indicate a direction 'towards' or 'away from' the speaker:

(a) after verbs of movement

跑来	**pǎo lái**	run over (here)
跑去	**pǎo qù**	run over (there)
飞来	**fēi lái**	fly over (towards the speaker)
飞去	**fēi qù**	fly away (from the speaker)

(b) after verbs of action

拿来	**ná lái**	bring
拿去	**ná qù**	take
带来	**dài lái**	bring with one
带去	**dài qù**	take with one

广场上飞来了不少鸽子。 **guǎngchǎng shang fēi lái le bù shǎo gézi**
Quite a number of pigeons flew over/came flying to the square.

钱已经汇去了。 **qián yǐjing huì qù le**
The money was already remitted [to someone].

叔叔寄来了很多圣诞礼物。 **shūshu jì lái le hěn duō shèngdàn lǐwù**
Uncle sent [us] (by post) a lot of Christmas presents.

昨天传来了舅舅出国的消息。 **zuótiān chuán lái le jiùjiu chū guó de xiāoxi**
The news of uncle's going abroad came yesterday.

B   来 **lái** or 去 **qù** may be linked, in particular, to the following group of verbs to form a set of common disyllabic verbs of movement. These disyllabic verbs also function themselves as directional complements with either verbs of movement or verbs of action:

			来	**lái**	'come'	去	**qù**	'go'
				(*towards the speaker*)			(*away from the speaker*)	
进	**jìn**	'enter'	进来	**jìn lái**	come in	进去	**jìn qù**	go in
出	**chū**	'exit'	出来	**chū lái**	come out	出去	**chū qù**	go out
上	**shàng**	'ascend'	上来	**shàng lái**	come up	上去	**shàng qù**	go up
下	**xià**	'descend'	下来	**xià lái**	come down	下去	**xià qù**	go down
回	**huí**	'return'	回来	**huí lái**	come back	回去	**huí qù**	go back
过	**guò**	'cross'	过来	**guò lái**	come over/ across	过去	**guò qù**	go over/ across
起	**qǐ**	'rise'	起来	**qǐ lái**	rise (from a lower position to a higher position)	*起去	**qǐ qù**	is no longer used

Examples:

(a) as independent verbs of movement

他进来了。	**tā jìn lái le**	He came in(to the room).
请上来!	**qǐng shàng lái**	Please come up!
他出去了。	**tā chū qù le**	He's out.
他们回去了。	**tāmen huí qù le**	They have gone back.
太阳出来了。	**tàiyáng chū lái le**	The sun came out.
我不敢下去。	**wǒ bù gǎn xià qù**	I dare not go down.
他起来了。	**tā qǐ lái le**	He's got up.

(b) as complements of direction following verbs of movement

他们赶回去了。	**tāmen gǎn huíqù le**	They hurried back (to where they had come from).
她不敢跳下去。	**tā bù gǎn tiào xiàqù**	She did not dare to jump down.
画儿掉下来了。	**huàr diào xiàlái le**	The picture fell down.
车开过去了。	**chē kāi guòqù le**	The car went past.
太阳升起来了。	**tàiyáng shēng qǐlái le**	The sun rose.

(c) as complements of direction following verbs of action

书放回去了。	**shū fàng huíqù le**	The books have been put back (where they were).
菜端进来了。	**cài duān jìnlái le**	The dishes were brought in.
圣诞卡寄出去了。	**shèngdànkǎ jì chūqù le**	The Christmas cards have been sent (by post).
画儿挂起来了。	**huàr guà qǐlái le**	The pictures were hung up.
作业交上去了。	**zuòyè jiāo shàngqù le**	The coursework has been handed in.
借出去的钱还回来了。	**jiè chūqù de qián huán huílái le**	The money which had been lent was returned.

Note: 起来 **qǐlái**, 下去 **xiàqù** and 下来 **xiàlái** as we have seen may also be used as aspect markers (see Unit 15):

他唱起来了。	**tā chàng qǐlái le**	He started singing.
你可以在这儿住下去。	**nǐ kěyǐ zài zhèr zhù xiàqù**	You can stay on here.
车停下来了。	**chē tíng xiàlái le**	The car came to a stop.

C   When the verb takes a location object, it is placed between the verb and its directional complement 来 **lái** or 去 **qù** or between the two elements of a disyllabic complement of direction:

(a) between the verb and 来 **lái** or 去 **qù**

她进办公室来了。	**tā jìn bàngōngshì lái le**	She came into the office.
哥哥出门去了。	**gēge chūmén qù le**	My elder brother is away. (*lit.* Elder brother went out of the door.)
小李上台去了。	**xiǎo lǐ shàng tái qù le**	Xiao Li went onto the stage.
妈妈下楼来了。	**māma xià lóu lái le**	Mum came downstairs.

Note: 出门 **chūmén** 'be away' is a verb with an inbuilt object.

(b) between the two elements of a disyllabic directional complement

   (i)   following a verb of movement

妈妈跑下楼来。	**māma pǎo xià lóu lái**	Mum came running downstairs.

公共汽车开过桥去。	**gōnggòng qìchē kāi guò qiáo qù**	The bus went across the bridge.
叔叔跑回家去了。	**shūshu pǎo huí jiā qù le**	(My) uncle has gone home.
姑姑走进屋子来了。	**gūgu zǒu jìn wūzi lái le**	(My) aunt walked into the room.
松鼠爬上树去了。	**sōngshǔ pá shàng shù qù le**	The squirrel climbed up the tree.
救生员跳进水里去了。	**jiùshēngyuán tiào jìn shuǐ li qù le**	The life-guard jumped into the water.

(ii) following a verb of action

钥匙放回抽屉里去了。 **yàoshi fàng huí chōuti li qù le**
The keys have been put back into the drawer.
钱存进银行去了。 **qián cún jìn yínháng qù le**
The money has been deposited in the bank.

One cannot, for instance, say:

| *她进来办公室了。 | **tā jìn lái bàngōngshì le** | (*lit.* She came into the office.) |
| *松鼠爬上去树了。 | **sōngshǔ pá shàngqù shù le** | (*lit.* The squirrel climbed up the tree.) |

If the object is not a location, it may precede or follow a monosyllabic directional complement:

舅舅带了一瓶酒来。   **jiùjiu dài le yī píng jiǔ lái**
舅舅带来了一瓶酒。   **jiùjiu dài lái le yī píng jiǔ**
(My) uncle brought a bottle of wine.

嫂嫂借了两把椅子去。   **sǎosao jiè le liǎng bǎ yǐzi qù**
嫂嫂借去了两把椅子。   **sǎosao jiè qù le liǎng bǎ yǐzi**
(My) Elder brother's wife has borrowed two chairs from us.

With a disyllabic directional complement, a non-location object may precede it, follow it or go between its two syllables:

爸爸租了一辆小面包车回来。   **bàba zū le yī liàng xiǎo miànbāochē huílái**
爸爸租回来了一辆小面包车。   **bàba zū huílái le yī liàng xiǎo miànbāochē**
爸爸租回一辆小面包车来。   **bàba zū huí yī liàng xiǎo miànbāochē lái**
Father has hired a mini-van.

Note: In the last instance, the aspect marker 了 **le** has to be dropped as it cannot go between 回 **huí** and 来 **lái**.

D Location (or destination) complements are usually formed by the verb 在 **zài** 'to be in/at' or 到 **dào** 'to arrive in/at' followed by a location phrase:

(a) location

爷爷住在城里。	**yéye zhù zài chéng li**	Grandpa lives in town.
有很多人坐在草地上。	**yǒu hěn duō rén zuò zài cǎodì shang**	There are a lot of people sitting on the grass.
衣服挂在衣架上。	**yīfu guà zài yījià shang**	The clothes were hung on the coat-hangers.

(b) destination

公共汽车开到桥边。	**gōnggòng qìchē kāi dào qiáo biān**	The bus went as far as the bridge.
我们赶到火车站。	**wǒmen gǎn dào huǒchēzhàn**	We hurried to the station.
我家搬到公园附近。	**wǒ jiā bān dào gōngyuán fùjìn**	We moved (home) to a place by the park.
青蛙跳到水里去了。	**qīngwā tiào dào shuǐ li qù le**	The frog jumped into the water.

Note: In the last example above, we can see that 去 **qù** (and therefore also 来 **lái**) may also be integrated into a destination complement begun with 到 **dào**, when a location object is present.

Exercise 21.1

Translate the following phrases into Chinese using directional complements:

1	go back	13	come back home
2	come over here	14	drive over the bridge (to the other side)
3	go up	15	climb up the tree
4	come down	16	come down the hill
5	bring here	17	bring to the classroom
6	go out	18	go out of the house
7	come back	19	run back to the office
8	take to	20	take back to the hospital
9	get up	21	jump into the swimming-pool
10	go in	22	go into the post-office
11	go across	23	go across the street
12	come out	24	come out of the room

Exercise 21.2

Complete the Chinese translations with disyllabic directional complements:

1 The children have gone out.
孩子们跑 _____ _____ 了。 **háizimen pǎo** _____ **le**
2 The clothes have fallen off the clothes-line.
晾衣绳上的衣服掉 _____ _____ 了。
liàngyīshéng shang de yīfu diào _____ **le**
3 He lay down on the grass.
他在草地上躺 _____ _____ 。 **tā zài cǎodì shang tǎng** _____
4 The doctor has come in.
医生走 _____ _____ 了。 **yīshēng zǒu** _____ **le**
5 She just went past.
她刚刚走 _____ _____ 。 **tā gānggāng zǒu** _____
6 Don't throw it out of the window.
不要扔 _____ 窗外 _____! **bù yào rēng** _____**chuāng wài** _____
7 The cups have been put back in the cupboard.
杯子放 _____ 碗柜里 _____ 了。 **bēizi fàng** _____ **wǎnguì li** _____ **le**
8 The teacher has gone back to the school.
老师跑 _____ 学校 _____ 了。 **lǎoshī pǎo** _____ **xuéxiào** _____ **le**
9 The kitten has jumped onto the bed.
小猫跳 _ _____ 床 _____ 了。 **xiǎo māo tiào** _____ **chuáng** _____ **le**
10 The dog jumped over the wall.
狗跳 _____ 墙 _____ 了。 **gǒu tiào** _____ **qiáng** _____ **le**
11 The letter has been dropped into the pillar-box.
信已经扔 _ _ 邮筒 _ _ 了。
xìn yǐjing rēng _____ **yóutǒng** _____ **le**
12 The ball did not go into the goal.
球没有踢 _____ 球门 _____ 。 **qiú méiyǒu tī** _____ **qiúmén** _____

Exercise 21.3

Rephrase the following Chinese sentences, adding the location words shown in the brackets (Note: in some cases a postposition may be needed), and then translate the rephrased sentences into English:

EXAMPLE
小李回来了。 **xiǎo lǐ huí lái le** (家 **jiā**)

小李回家来了。 **xiǎo lǐ huí jiā lái le**
Xiao Li came home.

1 老师走进去了。	**lǎoshī zǒu jìnqù le**	(图书馆 **túshūguǎn** the library)
2 飞机飞过去了。	**fēijī fēi guòqù le**	(山 **shān** the mountains)
3 我爬上去。	**wǒ pá shàngqù**	(山坡 **shānpō** the hillside)
4 孩子们跑过去了。	**háizimen pǎo guòqù le**	(马路 **mǎlù** the road)
5 他们走出去了。	**tāmen zǒu chūqù le**	(教堂 **jiàotáng** the church)
6 医生回去了。	**yīshēng huí qù le**	(医院 **yīyuàn** the hospital)
7 青蛙跳下去了。	**qīngwā tiào xiàqù le**	(水 **shuǐ** the water)
8 车开过来了。	**chē kāi guòlái le**	(桥 **qiáo** the bridge)
9 小鸡钻出来了。	**xiǎo jī zuān chūlái le**	(蛋壳 **dànké** the shell)
10 小猫爬上去了。	**xiǎo māo pá shàngqù le**	(树 **shù** the tree)
11 鸟儿飞出去了。	**niǎor fēi chūqù le**	(笼子 **lóngzi** the cage)
12 学生走进来了。	**xuésheng zǒu jìnlái le**	(教室 **jiàoshì** the classroom)
13 老鼠钻回去了。	**lǎoshǔ zuān huíqù le**	(洞 **dòng** hole)
14 渡船开过去了。	**dùchuán kāi guòqù le**	(河 **hé** river)

Exercise 21.4

Fill in the blanks with an appropriate location or destination phrase in accordance with the English version provided, making use of the words given in the following list:

银行	**yínháng**	bank
垃圾桶	**lājītǒng**	garbage bin
晾衣绳	**liàngyīshéng**	clothes-line
箱子	**xiāngzi**	box/trunk
冰箱	**bīngxiáng**	refrigerator
保险柜	**bǎoxiǎnguì**	strongbox/safe
行李架	**xínglijià**	luggage rack
海边	**hǎi biān**	the seaside
天上	**tiān shang**	the sky
城外	**chéng wài**	out-of-town areas
湖上	**hú shang**	surface of the lake
屋顶上	**wūdǐng shang**	top of the roof

1 衣服都装 _____ _____ _____ _____ 去了。 **yīfu dōu zhuāng . . . qù le**
   All the clothes have been packed into the box.
2 钱都存 _____ _____ _____ _____ 了。 **qián dōu cún . . . le**
   All the money has been deposited in the bank.
3 垃圾都倒 _____ _____ _____ _____ _____ 去了。
   lājī dōu dào . . . qù le
   All the rubbish has been tipped into the garbage bin.

4 你的行李都放 —— —— —— —— —— 了。
nǐ de xíngli dōu fàng . . . le
All your luggage was put on the luggage rack.

5 洗好的衣服都晾 —— —— —— —— —— (——)了。
xǐ hǎo de yīfu dōu liàng . . . le
All the washing has been hung on the clothes-line [to dry].

6 煮好的菜都搁 —— —— —— —— 了。
zhǔ hǎo de cài dōu gē . . . le
All the cooked dishes were left in the fridge.

7 首饰都放 —— —— —— —— ——。 **shǒushi dōu fàng . . .**
All the jewels are in the safe.

8 他们搬 —— —— —— 来了。 **tāmen bān . . . lái le**
They have moved into the town.

9 汽车一直开 —— —— ——。 **qìchē yīzhí kāi . . .**
The car went straight to the seaside.

10 气球一直升 —— —— —— 去了。 **qìqiú yīzhí shēng . . . qù le**
The balloon rose straight into the sky.

11 乌鸦飞 —— —— —— —— 去了。 **wūyā fēi . . . qù le**
The crow flew to the top of the roof.

12 我的帽子让风给吹 —— —— —— 去了。
wǒ de màozi ràng fēng gěi chuī . . . qù le
My hat was blown into the lake by the wind.

UNIT TWENTY-TWO
Complements of result and manner

This unit deals with complements of result and what are generally called complements of manner. These complements, like those of direction and location or destination, are invariably positioned after verbs.

A Complements of *result* can be either adjectives or verbs and they imply that a result of the action of the verb has been achieved:

(a) Adjectives

大家都坐好了。	**dàjiā dōu zuò *hǎo* le**	Everybody has sat/settled down.
你猜错了。	**nǐ cāi *cuò* le**	You have guessed wrongly.
你们听清楚了吗?	**nǐmen tīng *qīngchu* le ma**	Did you hear that clearly?

(b) Verbs

他们都站住了。	**tāmen dōu zhàn *zhù* le**	They all stood still.
你看见她了吗?	**nǐ kàn *jiàn* tā le ma**	Did you see her?
我学会开车了。	**wǒ xué *huì* kāichē le**	I have learnt to drive.
你听懂了吗?	**nǐ tīng *dǒng* le ma**	Did you understand (what was said)?

B The objects of verbs with complements are regularly shifted to a preverbal position where they have definite reference:

文章我写完了。	**wénzhāng wǒ xiě *wán* le**	I have finished writing the essay.
桌子擦干净了。	**zhuōzi cā *gānjìng* le**	The table has been wiped (clean).
工作做完了。	**gōngzuò zuò *wán* le**	The work was done.

那个问题你想清楚了没有？ **nà/nèi gè wèntí nǐ xiǎng *qīngchu* le méiyǒu**
Have you thought out that question thoroughly?

他的话我都听明白了。 **tā de huà wǒ dōu tīng *míngbai* le**
I understood every word he said.

C   Complements of result by definition imply completed action and/or change of circumstances and therefore naturally occur with 了 **le**. (For discussion of 了 **le** as completed action, see Unit 15; for a detailed analysis of 了 **le** as a 'change-of-state' sentence particle, see *Intermediate Chinese*, Unit 1.) For example,

他喝醉了。	**tā hē *zuì* le**	He's drunk.
衣服晒干了。	**yīfu shài *gān* le**	The clothes are dry.
信寄走了。	**xìn jì *zǒu* le**	The letter has been sent.

It follows that the negation of these statements will involve the use of 没(有) **méi(yǒu)** without 了 **le** since the action has never been completed or the state achieved:

他没喝醉。	**tā méi hē *zuì***	He isn't drunk.
衣服没晒干。	**yīfu méi shài *gān***	The clothes are not dry.
信还没寄走。	**xìn hái méi jì *zǒu***	The letter has not been sent yet.

D   The complement of *manner* in its simple form consists of 得 **de** followed by an adjective, usually with a degree adverb or negator:

他学得很好。	**tā xué de hěn hǎo**	He studies very well.
她跑得非常快。	**tā pǎo de fēicháng kuài**	She runs/ran extremely fast.
你说得很对。	**nǐ shuō de hěn duì**	You are/were quite right (in what you said).
他睡得太晚。	**tā shuì de tài wǎn**	He goes/went to bed too late.
谁来得最早？	**shéi/shuí lái de zuì zǎo**	Who arrived earliest?
他写得不好。	**tā xiě de bù hǎo**	He writes/wrote badly.
她讲得不太清楚。	**tā jiǎng de bù tài qīngchu**	She does/did not put it too clearly.

Note: In these cases a degree adverb is almost indispensable and that, as a state or situation is being described with no reference to a previous situation, sentence 了 **le** is not generally used.

E   More complex forms of the complement of *manner* entail the placing of a verb phrase or a clause after the 得 **de**. These complements in fact normally convey a sense of resultant state. The verb phrase usually follows an adjectival predicate, but the clause can come after an adjectival or verb predicate:

(a) Verb phrases

他高兴得跳起来。 **tā gāoxìng de tiào qǐlái**
He jumped for joy.
(*lit.* he was [so] pleased that he jumped up)

她疼得倒下去了。 **tā téng de dǎo xiàqù le**
She collapsed with the pain./She was in such great pain she collapsed.

妈妈急得哭起来了。 **māma jí de kū qǐlái le**
Mother was so anxious she started to cry.

(b) Clauses

太阳照得我眼也花了。 **tàiyáng zhào de wǒ yǎn yě huā le**   (verb)
The sun was so bright it dazzled my eyes.
(*lit.* the sun shone [so that] my eyes were dazzled)

他高得手能碰到天花板。
tā gāo de shǒu néng pèng dào tiānhuābǎn   (adjective)
He is so tall he can touch the ceiling with his hands.

她站得腿都酸了。 **tā zhàn de tuǐ dōu suān le**   (verb)
She stood there for so long her legs began to ache.

他们唱得嗓子都哑了。 **tāmen chàng de sǎngzi dōu yǎ le**   (verb)
They sang until they were hoarse.

Note: The above structures often imply a change of situation, and 了 **le** is therefore regularly present.

F   If the verb in a sentence with a complement of manner, is of a 'verb + object' form (e.g. 游泳 **yóuyǒng** 'swim'; 唱歌 **chàng gē** 'sing'; 聊天儿 **liáotiānr** 'chat'), the verb is repeated before the complement is added:

她唱歌唱得嗓子都哑了。 **tā chàng gē chàng de sǎngzi dōu yǎ le**
She sang until she was hoarse.

他游泳游得很慢。 **tā yóuyǒng yóu de hěn màn**
He swims very slowly./He is a slow swimmer.

One cannot say:

*她唱歌得嗓子都哑了。 **tā chàng gē de sǎngzi dǒu yǎ le**

Exercise 22.1

Complete each of the following Chinese sentences with an appropriate complement of result or manner to match the English sentence:

1 The dog ran very fast.
   小狗跑 _____ _____ _____。 **xiǎo gǒu pǎo** _____ _____ _____

2 The clothes have been washed (clean).
   衣服洗 _____ _____ 了。 **yīfu xǐ** _____ **le**

3 I have understood this article.
   这篇文章我看 _____ 了。 **zhè/zhèi piān wénzhāng wǒ kàn** _____ **le**

4 Who writes Chinese the best?
   谁汉字写 _____ _____ _____?
   shéi/shuí hànzì xiě _____ _____ _____

5 The rice is cooked.
   饭煮 _____ 了。 **fàn zhǔ** _____ **le**

6 Xiao Wang can speak English very fluently.
   小王英语说 _____ _____ _____ _____。
   xiǎo wáng yīngyǔ shuō _____ _____ _____

7 All the children have sat down.
   孩子们都坐 _____ 了。 **háizimen dōu zuò** _____ **le**

8 My daughter has learned how to play the piano.
   我女儿学 _____ 弹钢琴了。 **wǒ nǚ'ér xué** _____ **tán gāngqín le**

9 I managed to buy a good book.
   我买 _____ 了一本好书。 **wǒ mǎi** _____ **le yī běn hǎo shū**

10 The grass dried (in the sun).
   草晒 _____ 了。 **cǎo shài** _____ **le**

11 Mother went to bed very late.
   妈妈睡 _____ _____ _____。 **māma shuì** _____ _____ _____

12 Did you see him?
   你看 _____ 他了吗? **nǐ kàn** _____ **tā le ma**

13 The kitten jumped really high.
   小猫跳 _____ _____ _____。 **xiǎo māo tiào** _____ _____ _____

14 The teacher has explained this problem extremely clearly.
   这个问题老师说 _____ _____ _____ _____。
   zhè/zhèi gè wèntí lǎoshī shuō _____ _____ _____ _____

15 You are perfectly correct.
   你说 _____ _____ _____。 **nǐ shuō** _____ _____ _____

16 The car stopped.
   车子停 _____ 了。 **chēzi tíng** _____ **le**

Exercise 22.2

Form sentences by matching an appropriate clause complement of manner (or
resultant state) from the list on the right with a main clause from the list on the

left. Naturally 得 **de** will be needed at the beginning of the complement. Remember that with 'verb + object' constructions, the verb needs to be repeated before it can be followed by a complement. When you have constructed the sentences, translate them into English:

1	我嗓子疼	**wǒ sǎngzi téng**	腿都酸了	**tuǐ dōu suān le**
2	他游泳	**tā yóuyǒng**	嗓子都哑了	**sǎngzi dōu yǎ le**
3	她跑路	**tā pǎo lù**	饭也吃不下了	**fàn yě chī bu xià le**
4	老师说话	**lǎoshī shuōhuà**	谁也不认识了	**shéi/shuí yě bù rènshi le**
5	我眼睛花	**wǒ yǎnjing huā**	大家都笑起来了	**dàjiā dōu xiào qǐlái le**
6	我高兴	**wǒ gāoxìng**	话也说不出来了	**huà yě shuō bu chūlái le**
7	哥哥醉	**gēge zuì**	气也喘不过来了	**qì yě chuǎn bu guòlái le**
8	学生写字	**xuésheng xiě zì**	什么也看不清楚了	**shénme yě kàn bu qīngchu le**
9	妹妹哭	**mèimei kū**	手也酸了	**shǒu yě suān le**
10	她开玩笑	**tā kāi wánxiào**	眼睛都红了	**yǎnjing dōu hóng le**

Exercise 22.3

Complete the following Chinese sentences by choosing the appropriate verb or adjective from the list given (Note: in some cases some form of modification is needed) to complete the translations of the English sentences:

漂亮	**piàoliang**	饱	**bǎo**	好	**hǎo**
醉	**zuì**	倒	**dǎo**	干净	**gānjìng**
到	**dào**	破	**pò**	早	**zǎo**
对	**duì**	明白	**míngbai**	晚	**wǎn**

1 你没猜 _____。 **nǐ méi cāi** _____
   You didn't guess it right.
2 那本书我没买 _____。 **nà/nèi běn shū wǒ méi mǎi** _____
   I did not manage to obtain that book.
3 那天大家都喝 _____ 了。 **nà/nèi tiān dàjiā dōu hē** _____ **le**
   Everybody got drunk that day.
4 那天大家都穿 _____ _____ _____ _____。
   nà/nèi tiān dàjiā dōu chuān _____ _____ _____
   That day everyone was dressed up beautifully.
5 他还没吃 _____。 **tā hái méi chī** _____
   He has not eaten his fill yet.
6 电视机也修 _____ 了。 **diànshìjī yě xiū** _____ **le**
   The television set has also been repaired.

7 她碰 ———— 了窗台上的花瓶。
  tā pèng — — le chuāngtái shang de huāpíng
  She knocked over the vase on the window sill.

8 隔壁的孩子弄 ———— 了我孩子的玩具。
  gébì de háizi nòng   — le wǒ háizi de wánjù
  Next door's child broke my child's toy.

9 窗户我都擦 ———— ———— 了。 **chuānghu wǒ dōu cā ———— le**
  I have wiped all the windows (clean).

10 这个问题你弄 ———— ———— 了没有？
  zhè/zhèi ge wèntí nǐ nòng ———— le méiyǒu
  Have you thrashed out this problem?

11 妈妈今早起来 ———— ———— ————。
  māma jīn zǎo qǐ lái ———— ———— ————
  Mother got up very early this morning.

12 爸爸昨晚睡 ———— ———— ————。
  bàba zuó wǎn shuì ———— ———— ————
  Father went to bed very late last night.

Exercise 22.4

Translate the following into Chinese:

1 They danced beautifully.
2 The life-guard swam extremely fast.
3 The student read slowly.
4 The child ate a lot.
5 Everybody slept soundly.
6 The actor sang very badly.
7 We ran till we were too tired./We ran so much we were really tired.
8 The athlete jumped really high.
9 (My) Elder brother didn't drink much.
10 My coursemate didn't speak fluently.

UNIT TWENTY-THREE
Potential complements

A Complements of direction and result (see Units 21 and 22) may be extended to indicate whether the said direction or result is likely or unlikely to happen or be attained. These potential complements, which are distinct from the modal verbs 能 **néng** 'can' and 可以 **kěyǐ** 'may' seen in Unit 16, are formed by placing 得 **de** or 不 **bù** between the verb and the complement to convey positive or negative potential:

(a) potential complements of result

> 黑板上的字你看得清楚吗？ **hēibǎn shang de zì nǐ kàn de qīngchu ma**
> Can you see the words on the blackboard clearly?

> 他说的话你听得懂吗？ **tā shuō de huà nǐ tīng de dǒng ma**
> Can you understand what he said?

> 我昨天晚上睡不着。 **wǒ zuótiān wǎnshang shuì bu zháo**
> I could not sleep last night.

Note: In the last example the pronunciation of 着 **zháo** which is here used as a verb meaning 'to achieve a desirable result'.

Virtually all complements of result, whether verbal or adjectival, can be used in the potential form:

看得见	**kàn de jiàn**	can see
看不见	**kàn bu jiàn**	cannot see
做得完	**zuò de wán**	can finish (the job)
做不完	**zuò bu wán**	cannot finish (the job)
办得到	**bàn de dào**	can be managed
办不到	**bàn bu dào**	cannot be managed
修得好	**xiū de hǎo**	can be repaired
修不好	**xiū bu hǎo**	cannot be repaired

说得明白	**shuō de míngbai**	can be explained clearly
说不明白	**shuō bu míngbai**	cannot be explained clearly
洗得干净	**xǐ de gānjìng**	can be washed (clean)
洗不干净	**xǐ bu gānjìng**	cannot be washed (clean)

(b) potential complements of direction (in terms of space or time)

你还吃得下吗？ **nǐ hái chī de xià ma**
Can you eat any more?

我真的吃不下了。 **wǒ zhēn de chī bu xià le**
Honestly, I can't eat any more.

我站不起来。 **wǒ zhàn bu qǐlái**
I could not stand up.

里面人太多，我们进不去。 **lǐmiàn rén tài duō | wǒmen jìn bu qù**
There were so many people inside. We [simply] could not get in.

这儿有条沟，你跳得过来吗？ **zhèr yǒu tiáo gōu | nǐ tiào de guòlái ma**
There's a ditch here. Can you jump over (here)?

箱子关不上了。 **xiāngzi guān bu shàng le**
The box cannot be closed. (e.g. too full; the lock is broken; etc.)

他待(呆)不下来。 **tā dāi bu xiàlái**
He cannot stay on. (e.g. He has been called away on business; always
wants to be on the move; etc.)

When directional complements are used in a potential form with 得 **de** and
不 **bù**, they often acquire a metaphorical meaning beyond their original
sense of physical direction:

她说不下去了。 **tā shuō bu xiàqù le**
She could not carry on (speaking).
(e.g. She was choked by emotion; forgot what to say; etc.)

太贵了，我买不起。 **tài guì le | wǒ mǎi bu qǐ**
[It's] too expensive. I [just] can't afford [it].

B Some complements of result or direction exist *only* in the potential form (as
can be seen from the last example cited immediately above). Other examples
are:

positive

走得动	**zǒu de dòng**	can walk on
来得及	**lái de jí**	be in time for
去得成	**qù de chéng**	can (ultimately) go
行得通	**xíng de tōng**	will do/work
谈得上	**tán de shàng**	can be regarded as
看得起	**kàn de qǐ**	think highly of
合得来	**hé de lái**	can get along with
说得过去	**shuō de guòqù**	be justifiable
坐得下	**zuò de xià**	can seat/have room for
解决得了	**jiějué de liǎo**	can be resolved

negative

走不动	**zǒu bu dòng**	cannot walk (any more)
来不及	**lái bu jí**	be too late for
去不成	**qù bu chéng**	cannot (ultimately) go
行不通	**xíng bu tōng**	won't do/work
谈不上	**tán bu shàng**	can't be regarded as
看不起	**kàn bu qǐ**	look down upon
合不来	**hé bu lái**	cannot get along with
说不过去	**shuō bu guòqù**	cannot be justified
坐不下	**zuò bu xià**	does not have room for
解决不了	**jiějué bu liǎo**	cannot be resolved

Note: In the last two examples 下 **xià** does not mean the same as in the non-potential form 坐下 **zuò xià** 'sit down' and that 了, pronounced as **liǎo**, which is widely used as a complement, only exists as a potential complement meaning 'to do something successfully'.

Sentence examples:

他这个坏习惯改得了吗？ **tā zhè/zhèi gè huài xíguàn gǎi de liǎo ma**
Can this bad habit of his be changed/corrected?

他们两个人合不来。 **tāmen liǎng gè rén hé bu lái**
They too do not get on with each other.

你别看不起他。 **nǐ bié kàn bu qǐ tā**
Don't you look down upon him.

我赶不上她。 **wǒ gǎn bu shàng tā**
I can't catch up with her.

In some cases, there are only negative potentials:

巴不得	**bā bu de**	be more than willing/be only too anxious to
怪不得	**guài bu de**	no wonder

禁不住	**jīn bu zhù**	cannot help but
免不了	**miǎn bu liǎo**	can do nothing but/cannot avoid
大不了	**dà bu liǎo**	if the worst comes to the worst (*lit.* it can't be worse than)

These negative potentials are usually followed by verbal or clausal objects.

大家禁不住笑起来了。 **dàjiā jīn bu zhù xiào qǐlái le**
Everybody could not help laughing.

他巴不得大家都选他。 **tā bā bu de dàjiā dōu xuǎn tā**
He longed for everybody to vote for him.

大不了她不同意。 **dà bu liǎo tā bù tóngyì**
At the worst, she will disagree. [That's all.]

C   Potential complements, as can be seen from above, may take objects:

你听得懂俄语吗？ **nǐ tīng de dǒng éyǔ ma**
Do you understand Russian (when you listen to it being spoken)?

我想不起那件事儿来。 **wǒ xiǎng bu qǐ nà/nèi jiàn shìr lái**
I could not/cannot recall that (matter).

我们赶得上那班火车吗？ **wǒmen gǎn de shàng nà/nèi bān huǒchē ma**
Can we catch that train?

这儿住得下五个人吗？ **zhèr zhù de xià wǔ gè rén ma**
Can five people be housed here?

D   The distinction between the potential complements and the modal verbs 能 **néng** and 可以 **kěyǐ** is that the modal verbs imply some degree of subjective influence while the potential complements indicate that external circumstances are the deciding factor.

Compare:

我不能去。 **wǒ bù néng qù**
I can't go [because I don't want to/I don't think it would be appropriate].

我去不了。 **wǒ qù bu liǎo**
I can't go [because I am ill/the last train has gone etc.].

Exercise 23.1

Complete the following sentences with the appropriate potential complements:

1 你还走得 _____ 吗？ **nǐ hái zǒu de _____ ma**
   Can you walk on?
2 这条沟这么宽，我跳不 _____ _____。
   zhè/zhèi tiáo gōu zhème kuān | wǒ tiào bu _____ _____
   This ditch is too wide for me to jump over.
3 这件事儿你还想得 _____ _____吗？
   zhè/zhèi jiàn shìr nǐ hái xiǎng de _____ ma
   Do you still remember that?
4 昨晚我睡不 _____。 **zuó wǎn wǒ shuì bu _____**
   I couldn't sleep last night.
5 你还吃得 _____ 吗？ **nǐ hái chī de _____ ma**
   Can you eat any more?
6 这个坏习惯你改得 _____ 吗？
   zhè/zhèi gè huài xíguàn nǐ gǎi de _____ ma
   Can you do something about (change) this bad habit of yours?
7 这么贵，我买不 _____。 **zhème guì | wǒ mǎi bu _____**
   It's so expensive, I can't afford it.
8 我找不 _____ 我的钥匙了。 **wǒ zhǎo bu _____ wǒ de yàoshi le**
   I can't find my keys.
9 现在还来得 _____ 赶那班火车吗？
   xiànzài hái lái de _____ gǎn nà/nèi bān huǒchē ma
   Have we got enough time to catch the train?
10 这个工作我们今天做得 _____ 吗？
   zhè/zhèi gè gōngzuò wǒmen jīntiān zuò de _____ ma
   Will we be able to finish this job today?

Exercise 23.2

Translate the phrases below into Chinese using potential complements:

1 can eat one's fill
2 can't stand up
3 can't drink any more
4 can't be washed (clean)
5 can sit comfortably
6 be too high to reach
7 can't see clearly
8 can memorize (it)
9 can get on with (someone)
10 can get by (survive)

Exercise 23.3

Provide appropriate potential complements in each of the following sentences:

1 门 _____ _____ 了。 **mén** _____ _____ _____ **le**
The door can't be closed.

2 今天天阴。衣服 _____ _____ _____ 吗？
jīntiān tiān yīn | yīfu _____ _____ _____ **ma**
It's cloudy today. Will the washing get dry?

3 我们人这么多。屋子里 _____ _____ _____ 吗？
wǒmen rén zhème duō | wūzi li _____ _____ _____ **ma**
There are so many of us. Can the room seat us all?

4 我很累，真的 _____ _____ _____ 了。
wǒ hěn lèi | zhēn de _____ _____ _____ **le**
I'm very tired. Honestly I can't go on.

5 我们还 _____ _____ _____ 那班汽车吗？
wǒmen hái _____ _____ _____ **nà/nèi bān qìchē ma**
Are we still in time to catch that coach?

6 我认为这种做法 _____ _____ _____ 。
wǒ rènwéi zhè/zhèi zhǒng zuòfǎ _____ _____ _____
I don't think this method will work.

7 他们两个人 _____ _____ _____ _____ _____ _____ ？
tāmen liǎng gè rén _____ _____ _____ _____ _____ _____
Can the two of them get along with each other?

8 你 _____ _____ _____ 那件事儿吗？
nǐ _____ _____ _____ **nà/nèi jiàn shìr ma**
Can you recall that incident?

9 我 _____ _____ _____ 看了他一眼。
wǒ _____ _____ _____ **kàn le tā yī yǎn**
I could not help casting him a glance.

10 我的话你 _____ _____ _____ 吗？
wǒ de huà nǐ _____ _____ _____ **ma**
Can you understand what I'm saying?

Exercise 23.4

Translate the following sentences into Chinese, using a potential complement or a modal verb as appropriate. Do not translate the phrases in brackets.

1 I can't go to bed yet (as I've get some more work to do).
2 I couldn't sleep (because I was worried).
3 I can't buy it today (because I can't carry it).
4 I can't afford it.

5 I can't tell you (because it's confidential).
6 I can't tell you (because I've forgotten).
7 I can't do it (because I haven't the ability to).
8 I can't do it (because I don't think it's right).
9 I couldn't go on (talking – because I was choked by emotion).
10 I couldn't go on (talking – because I was disturbing other people).

UNIT TWENTY-FOUR
Coverbal phrases

A A coverb (or preposition) with its attendant noun precedes the main verb or adjective of the sentence, setting the scene for the action or situation. That is to say it indicates to whom, for whom, the means by which, the purpose for which, the direction in which etc. something is to be done or happens. The term coverb is perhaps preferable to preposition as the words in this category have a verb basis and can be used separately as verbs. The 在 **zài** location phrases discussed in Unit 13 are, in fact, coverbal phrases; as are the comparison phrases with 比 **bǐ** in Unit 12.

他在图书馆看书。
tā zài túshūguǎn kàn shū (在图书馆 **zài túshūguǎn** coverbal phrase)
He is reading in the library.

她比她朋友大三岁。
ta bǐ tā péngyou dà sān suì (比她朋友 **bǐ tā péngyou** coverbal phrase)
She is three years older than her friend.

Adverbs of time, negators, etc. are generally placed before the coverb:

他一贯对我很好。
tā yīguàn duì wǒ hěn hǎo (对我 **duì wǒ** coverbal phrase)
He has all along been very good (kind/respectful) to me./He always treats me very well.

她没给我来信。 **tā méi gěi wǒ lái xìn** (给我 **gěi wǒ** coverbal phrase)
She didn't write to me.

The main coverbs are:

B 和 **hé**/跟 **gēn**/与 **yǔ**/同 **tóng** 'with':

我跟你谈谈这个问题。 **wǒ gēn nǐ tántán zhè/zhèi gè wèntí**
I'll discuss this matter with you.

她同你很好。 **tā tóng nǐ hěn hǎo**
She gets on very well with you.

These four coverbs are often used with 一起 **yīqǐ** to emphasize the notion of 'together with':

你跟我一起去看电影吗？ **nǐ gēn wǒ yīqǐ qù kàn diànyǐng ma**
Are you going to the cinema with me?

老张和小李一起做实验。 **lǎo zhāng hé xiǎo lǐ yīqǐ zuò shíyàn**
Old Zhang and Little Li did the experiment together.

As we have seen (Unit 12), these coverbs may also be used with 一样 **yīyàng** to express similarity:

这个手表同那个手表一样准。
zhè/zhèi gè shǒubiǎo tóng nà/nèi gè shǒubiǎo yīyàng zhǔn
This watch is as accurate as that one.

哥哥与弟弟一样聪明。 **gēge yǔ dìdi yīyàng cōngming**
The elder brother is as clever as the younger brother.

C   给 **gěi**/为 **wèi**/替 **tì** 'for/to' all in the sense of 'rendering a service to':

(i) 给 **gěi** 'for/to'

我今晚给你打电话。 **wǒ jīn wǎn gěi nǐ dǎ diànhuà**
I'll ring you this evening.

她没有给我写信。 **tā méiyǒu gěi wǒ xiě xìn**
She didn't write to me.

我给女儿买了一台电脑。 **wǒ gěi nǚ'ér mǎi le yī tái diànnǎo**
I bought a computer for my daughter.

(ii) 为 **wèi** 'for' implying 'for someone's benefit; in someone's interest'

他为我开了一个茶会/酒会。 **tā wèi wǒ kāi le yī gè cháhuì/jiǔhuì**
He held a party for me.

妈妈为儿子操心。 **māma wèi érzi cāoxīn**
The mother is worried about her son.

(iii) 替 **tì** 'for/on behalf of'

他替她回了很多信。 **tā tì tā huí le hěn duō xìn**
He replied to a lot of letters on her behalf.

我替邻居割草。 **wǒ tì línjū gē cǎo**
I mowed the lawn for my neighbour.

D (i) 对 **duì** 'to/at', implying the idea 'face to face', is often used in conjunction with verbs such as 说 **shuō** 'say' 笑 **xiào** 'smile':

她对我说："..."。 **tā duì wǒ shuō ...**
"..." she said (to me).

他对我笑了(一)笑。 **tā duì wǒ xiào le (yī) xiào**
He gave me a smile./He smiled at me.

(ii) 对 **duì** meaning 'to(wards)' is also often linked with adjectives expressing 'attitude or frame of mind towards something or someone' such as 友好 **yǒuhǎo** 'friendly', 热情 **rèqíng** 'warmhearted; kind', 负责 **fùzé** 'responsible':

他对工作很负责。 **tā duì gōngzuò hěn fùzé**
He is very responsible about his work.

王先生对学生很热情。 **wáng xiānsheng duì xuésheng hěn rèqíng**
Mr Wang is very kind to his students.

姐姐对人很友好。 **jiějie duì rén hěn yǒuhǎo**
My elder sister is very friendly towards people.

E (i) 往 **wàng**/向 **xiàng**/朝 **cháo** 'towards/in the direction of':

车子向机场开去。 **chēzi xiàng jīchǎng kāi qù**
The car headed for the airport.

小李往教室跑去。 **xiǎo lǐ wàng jiàoshì pǎo qù**
Xiao Li hurried towards the classroom.

他们朝教堂走来。 **tāmen cháo jiàotáng zǒu lái**
They came towards the church.

(ii) 朝 **cháo**/向 **xiàng** can also mean 'at/to' in the sense of 'facing somebody or something'. 朝 **cháo** is used with either static or dynamic action whereas 向 **xiàng** is usually employed only when the action is dynamic:

小孩朝天空望着。 **xiǎohái cháo tiānkōng wàng zhe**
The child gazed at the sky.

他朝我点点头。 **tā cháo wǒ diǎndiǎn tóu**
He nodded to me.

她向我招手。 **tā xiàng wǒ zhāo shǒu**
She beckoned to me.

One does not say:

*他向南站着。 **tā xiàng nán zhàn zhe**
(*lit*. He is standing facing south.)

往 **wàng**, on the other hand, must involve movement:

她往医院走来。 **tā wàng yīyuàn zǒu lái**
She came towards the hospital.

One cannot say:

*她往医院望着。 **tā wàng yīyuàn wàng zhe**
(*lit*. She is looking in the direction of the hospital.)

F　到 **dào** 'to' is used with objects indicating destination (see Unit 21):

老张到医院去看病。 **lǎo zhāng dào yīyuàn qù kànbìng**
Lao Zhang went to the hospital to see the doctor.

我们到中国去访问。 **wǒmen dào zhōngguó qù fǎngwèn**
We went on a visit to China.

他们到博物馆来参观。 **tāmen dào bówùguǎn lái cānguān**
They came to the museum for a visit.

Note: As can be seen in the above examples, the coverb 到 **dào** 'to' often occurs with the directional verbs 来 **lái** or 去 **qù** followed by another verb indicating purpose.

到 **dào** may also be used with time expressions to mean 'up to; until':

他到现在还没来。 **tā dào xiànzài hái méi lái**
Up till now he has not turned up./He has not turned up yet.

经理到昨天才回来。 **jīnglǐ dào zuótiān cái huí lái**
The manager did not come back till yesterday.

我们到下个月就可以完成这个任务了。
wǒmen dào xià gè yuè jiù kěyǐ wánchéng zhè/zhèi gè rènwu le
We shall be able to accomplish this task by next month.

G 从 **cóng 'from (place); since (time)'**

(i) 从 **cóng** 'from (place)' is used either with verbs of movement (e.g. 去 **qù** 'go'; 来 **lái** 'come'; 出发 **chūfā** 'set off/set out'; 起程 **qǐchéng** 'depart') or with verbs which incorporate a directional complement:

他从中国来。 **tā cóng zhōngguó lái**
He came from China.

我从伦敦出发。 **wǒ cóng lúndūn chūfā**
I set out from London.

我从衣柜里拿出一件大衣来。 **wǒ cóng yīguì li ná chū yī jiàn dàyī lái**
I took a coat out of the wardrobe.

她从口袋里掏出一镑钱。 **tā cóng kǒudài li tāo chū yī bàng qián**
She took a pound from her pocket.

(ii) 从 **cóng** 'since (time)' often occurs together with 起 **qǐ** or 开始 **kāishǐ** 'start', and also in conjunction with 到 **dào** 'till/to':

我从去年起就在这个学校教书了。
wǒ cóng qùnián qǐ jiù zài zhè/zhèi gè xuéxiào jiāoshū le
I have been teaching at this school since last year.

她从上个星期开始吃素了。 **tā cóng shàng gè xīngqī kāishǐ chīsù lc**
She became a vegetarian last week.
(*lit.* Beginning from last week she started eating vegetarian food.)

我从上午到现在没吃过东西。
wǒ cóng shàngwǔ dào xiànzài méi chī guo dōngxi
I haven't eaten anything since this morning.
(*lit.* from morning till/to now)

H 离 **lí** expresses the idea of 'distance from (a place)'. (Note that 从 **cóng** cannot mean 'distance from'.)

我家离大学不远。 **wǒ jiā lí dàxué bù yuǎn**
My house is not far from the university.

曼城离利兹很近。 **mànchéng lí lìzī hěn jìn**
Manchester is close to Leeds.

伦敦离这儿有二百多英里(路)。 **lúndūn lí zhèr yǒu èr bǎi duō yīnglǐ (lù)**
London is over two hundred miles from here.

I 由 **yóu** 'up to/by' conveys the idea of 'responsibility':

这件事由我负责。 **zhè/zhèi jiàn shì yóu wǒ fùzé**
I'll be responsible for this.

那项工作由他去办。 **nà/nèi xiàng gōngzuò yóu tā qù bàn**
That piece of work is up to him to handle/deal with.

由 **yóu**, like 从 **cóng**, may also be used to mean 'from (a place/time)':

我们由伦敦出发。 **wǒmen yóu lúndūn chūfā**
We set off from London.

英国夏令时间由上个星期结束。
yīngguó xiàlìng shíjiān yóu shàng gè xīngqī jiéshù
British Summer Time ended last week.

Note: 由 **yóu**, however, cannot be used with postpositional phrases. For example,

One cannot say:

*松鼠由大树下钻出来。 **sōngshǔ yóu dà shù xià zuān chūlái**
(*lit.* The squirrel came burrowing out from under a big tree.)

由 **yóu**, like 从 **cóng** 'from' can be used in conjunction with 到 **dào** to specify a
period of time:

商店由上午九点到下午五点营业。
shāngdiàn yóu shàngwǔ jiǔ diǎn dào xiàwǔ wǔ diǎn yíngyè
The shop is open from 9 a.m. to 5 p.m.

由 **yóu** can also mean 'by; out of' to identify members of a group or components
of a unit:

足球队由十一个队员组成。 **zúqiúduì yóu shí yī gè duìyuán zǔchéng**
The football team consists of 11 players.

水由氢和氧合成。 **shuǐ yóu qīng hé yǎng héchéng**
Water is composed of hydrogen and oxygen.

J   于 **yú** 'in; on; at' is generally used with years or dates:

他于一九九五年毕业。 **tā yú yī jiǔ jiǔ wǔ nián bìyè**
He graduated in 1995.

通知已于今天上午发出。 **tōngzhī yǐ yú jīntiān shàngwǔ fā chū**
The circular was issued this morning.

火车于十三点零五分到达。 **huǒchē yú shí sān diǎn líng wǔ fēn dàodá**
The train arrives at 1:05 (five past one).

K 沿 **yán** 'along(side)', is used with monosyllabic nouns to describe a location:

沿岸都是树木。 **yán àn dōu shì shùmù**
There are trees all along the river.

沿街都是商店。 **yán jiē dōu shì shāngdiàn**
There are shops all along the street.

沿着 **yán zhe** 'along', is employed when movement is involved:

| 她沿着河边散步。 | **tā yán zhe hé biān sànbù** | She went for a walk along the river. |
| 汽车沿着大路行驶。 | **qìchē yán zhe dàlù xíngshǐ** | The car was going along the main road. |

Exercise 24.1

Complete the following Chinese sentences with 和 **hé**/跟 **gēn**, 向 **xiàng**/朝 **cháo**/往 **wàng** or 对 **duì** to match the English:

1 大家 _____ 他的建议表示赞同。 **dàjiā _____ tā de jiànyì biǎoshì zàntóng**
Everybody agreed to his suggestion.
2 她 _____ 以前一样聪明。 **tā _____ yǐqián yīyàng cōngming**
She is as clever as she always was.
3 你每天 _____ 谁一起学习？ **nǐ měi tiān _____ shéi yīqǐ xuéxí**
Who do you study with every day?
4 汽车 _____ 电影院开去。 **qìchē _____ diànyǐngyuàn kāi qù**
The car headed in the direction of the cinema.
5 小李 _____ 北京很熟悉。 **xiǎo lǐ _____ běijīng hěn shúxī/shóuxī**
Xiao Li knows Beijing very well.
6 学生 _____ 图书馆走去。 **xuésheng _____ túshūguǎn zǒu qù**
The students walked towards the library.
7 他 _____ 窗外看了一下。 **tā _____ chuāng wài kàn le yīxià**
He glanced out of the window.
8 她 _____ 爸爸一起住。 **tā _____ bàba yīqǐ zhù**
She lived with her father.

Exercise 24.2

Complete the Chinese sentences below with 为 **wèi**, 替 **tì** or 给 **gěi** as appropriate:

1 我们都 _____ 你的喜事高兴。 **wǒmen dōu _____ nǐ de xǐshì gāoxìng**
   We congratulate you on this happy occasion.
2 你 _____ 我 _____ 小李打个电话，好吗？
   nǐ _____ wǒ _____ xiǎo lǐ dǎ ge diànhuà | hǎo ma
   Could you phone Xiao Li for me please?
3 他每两个星期 _____ 儿子写一封信。
   tā měi liǎng gè xīngqī _____ érzi xiě yī fēng xìn
   He writes a letter to his son every two weeks.
4 保姆 _____ 她看孩子。 **bǎomǔ _____ tā kān háizi**
   The nanny looked after her children.
5 他 _____ 女朋友买了一台音响。
   tā _____ nǚ péngyou mǎi le yī tái yīnxiǎng
   He bought a hi-fi for his girlfriend.
6 她 _____ 这个问题睡不着觉。
   tā _____ zhè/zhèi gè wèntí shuì bu zháo jiào
   She could not sleep because of this problem.
7 她 _____ 朋友洗衣服。 **tā _____ péngyou xǐ yīfu**
   She did the washing for her friend.
8 小李 _____ 她父亲担心。 **xiǎo lǐ _____ tā fùqīn dānxīn**
   Xiao Li was worried about her father.

Exercise 24.3

Identify in the examples below which of the sentences in Chinese is the correct translation of the English:

1 In which direction shall we go?
   我们对哪个方向走？ **wǒmen duì nǎ/něi gè fāngxiàng zǒu**
   我们朝哪个方向走？ **wǒmen cháo nǎ/něi gè fāngxiàng zǒu**

2 She is very responsible about her work.
   她替工作很负责。 **tā tì gōngzuò hěn fùzé**
   她对工作很负责。 **tā duì gōngzuò hěn fùzé**

3 This book is very useful for my studies.
   这本书对我学习很有用。 **zhè/zhèi běn shū duì wǒ xuéxí hěn yǒuyòng**
   这本书跟我学习很有用。 **zhè/zhèi běn shū gēn wǒ xuéxí hěn yǒuyòng**

4 Xiao Li is talking to Miss Shi (the teacher).
   小李正在对石老师谈话。 **xiǎo lǐ zhèngzài duì shí lǎoshī tánhuà**
   小李正在跟石老师谈话。 **xiǎo lǐ zhèngzài gēn shí lǎoshī tánhuà**

5 He nodded to me.
他往我点点头。 **tā wàng wǒ diǎndiǎn tóu**
他朝我点点头。 **tā cháo wǒ diǎndiǎn tóu**

6 We should learn from him.
我们应该向他学习。 **wǒmen yīnggāi xiàng tā xuéxí**
我们应该从他学习。 **wǒmen yīnggāi cóng tā xuéxí**

7 I'll write the letter for you.
我替你写信。 **wǒ tì nǐ xiě xìn**
我给你写信。 **wǒ gěi nǐ xiě xìn**

8 I'll ring you tonight.
我今晚替你打电话。 **wǒ jīn wǎn tì nǐ dǎ diànhuà**
我今晚给你打电话。 **wǒ jīn wǎn gěi nǐ dǎ diànhuà**

9 I'll write to you.
我为你写信。 **wǒ wèi nǐ xiě xìn**
我给你写信。 **wǒ gěi nǐ xiě xìn**

10 This town is as old as that town.
这个小镇与那个小镇一样古老。
zhè/zhèi gè xiǎo zhèn yǔ nà/nèi gè xiǎo zhèn yīyàng gǔlǎo
这个小镇向那个小镇一样古老。
zhè/zhèi gè xiǎo zhèn xiàng nà/nèi gè xiǎo zhèn yīyàng gǔlǎo

Exercise 24.4

Complete the Chinese sentences below with 从 **cóng**, 离 **lí** or 到 **dào** as appropriate:

1 你家 ＿＿＿ 市中心有多远？ **nǐ jiā ＿＿＿ shìzhōngxīn yǒu duō yuǎn**
How far is it from your house to the city centre?
2 我 ＿＿＿ 衣柜里拿出一条围巾。 **wǒ ＿＿＿ yīguì li ná chū yī tiáo wéijīn**
I took a scarf out of the wardrobe.
3 他 ＿＿＿ 宿舍出发。 **tā ＿＿＿ sùshè chūfā**
He set out from the dormitory.
4 ＿＿＿ 这儿 ＿＿＿ 伦敦有二百英里路。
＿＿＿ **zhèr** ＿＿＿ **lúndūn yǒu èr bǎi yīnglǐ lù**
It's two hundred miles from here to London.
5 图书馆 ＿＿＿ 这儿有三英里。 **túshūguǎn ＿＿＿ zhèr yǒu sān yīnglǐ**
The library is three miles from here.

6 ＿＿＿ 电影院 ＿＿＿ 餐馆的路很近。
＿＿＿ **diànyǐngyuàn** ＿＿＿ **cānguǎn de lù hěn jìn**
It's not far from the cinema to the restaurant.
7 邮局 ＿＿＿ 银行不远。 **yóujú** ＿＿＿ **yínháng bù yuǎn**
The post office is not far from the bank.
8 陈小姐 ＿＿＿ 中国来。 **chén xiǎojie** ＿＿＿ **zhōngguó lái**
Miss Chen comes from China.

Exercise 24.5

Complete the following Chinese sentences with 由 **yóu** or 从 **cóng**. Point out cases where both are possible:

1 这件事儿 ＿＿＿ 他负责。 **zhè/zhèi jiàn shìr** ＿＿＿ **tā fùzé**
He's responsible for this.
2 我 ＿＿＿ 去年起开始学汉语。 **wǒ** ＿＿＿ **qùnián qǐ kāishǐ xué hànyǔ**
I started learning Chinese last year.
3 教室 ＿＿＿ 学生打扫。 **jiàoshì** ＿＿＿ **xuésheng dǎsǎo**
The classroom was cleaned by students.
4 火车 ＿＿＿ 上海出发。 **huǒchē** ＿＿＿ **shànghǎi chūfā**
The train set off from Shanghai.
5 她 ＿＿＿ 昨天下午起开始发烧。 **tā** ＿＿＿ **zuótiān xiàwǔ qǐ kāishǐ fāshāo**
She started to have a fever from yesterday afternoon.
6 我 ＿＿＿ 钱包里拿出一镑钱。 **wǒ** ＿＿＿ **qiánbāo li ná chū yī bàng qián**
I took a pound out of my purse.
7 海鸥 ＿＿＿ 海面上飞过来。 **hǎi'ōu** ＿＿＿ **hǎimiàn shang fēi guòlái**
The gulls came flying across the surface of the sea.
8 圣诗班 ＿＿＿ 十个男孩和十个女孩组成。
shèngshībān ＿＿＿ **shí gè nánhái hé shí gè nǚhái zǔchéng**
The choir was made up of ten boys and ten girls.

Exercise 24.6

Complete the Chinese sentences below choosing the appropriate coverb from those in the brackets:

1 汽车 ＿＿＿ 河边开去。
qìchē ＿＿＿ **hé biān kāi qù** (向/沿 **xiàng/yán**)
The car went towards the river bank.
2 ＿＿＿ 路都是车。 ＿＿＿ **lù dōu shì chē** (沿/沿着 **yán/yán zhe**)
There are cars (parked) all along the road.
3 通知 ＿＿＿ 昨天发出。 **tōngzhī** ＿＿＿ **zuótiān fā chū** (从/于 **cóng/yú**)
The circular was issued yesterday.

4 爷爷 ——— 1949 年逝世。 **yéye** ——— **1949 nián shìshì** (于/由 **yú/yóu**)
Grandfather died in 1949.

5 那个姑娘 ——— 东走去。
nà/nèi gè gūniang ——— **dōng zǒu qù** (从/往 **cóng/wàng**)
The young woman walked towards the east.

6 图书馆 ——— 市中心不远。
túshūguǎn ——— **shìzhōngxīn bù yuǎn** (从/离 **cóng/lí**)
The library is not far from the city centre.

7 邮递员 ——— 早到晚在送信。
yóudìyuán ——— **zǎo dào wǎn zài sòng xìn** (从/由 **cóng/yóu**)
The postmen are delivering letters from morning till night.

8 请大家 ——— 九时正在此集合。
qǐng dàjiā ——— **jiǔ shí zhèng zài cǐ jíhé** (由/于 **yóu/yú**)
Would everyone please assemble here at 9 o'clock sharp!

9 汽车 ——— 车库里开出来。
qìchē ——— **chēkù li kāi chūlái** (由 /从 **yóu/cóng**)
The car emerged from the garage.

10 请 ——— 第一页开始读。 **qǐng** ——— **dì yī yè kāishǐ dú** (于/从 **yú/cóng**)
Please start reading from the first page.

Exercise 24.7

Translate the following sentences into Chinese:

1 Please come with me.
2 I'll ring you tomorrow.
3 They were very friendly to us.
4 It is not too far from here to the station.
5 I work from 9.00 to 5.00 every day.
6 There are cars all along the street.
7 Is this business all up to me?
8 Why don't you write to them?

UNIT TWENTY-FIVE
Prepositions

A Chinese disyllabic prepositions are distinct from their monosyllabic coverb (or preposition) cousins in two ways. First, these disyllabic prepositions may be used not only before nouns but also before verbs (like gerunds in English) or clauses. Second, they are often placed at the beginning of the sentence rather than directly after the subject. These two distinctive features will be clearly illustrated by the examples below of the most common disyllabic prepositions.

B 为了 **wèile** 'in order to; so that' expresses purpose and is usually followed by a verb phrase:

为了不迟到，她很早就起来/起床了。
wèile bù chídào | tā hěn zǎo jiù qǐ lái/qǐchuáng le
In order not to get there late, she got up very early.

为了买到便宜的戏票，他排了一(个)小时的队。
wèile mǎi dào piányi de xìpiào | tā pái le yī (gè) xiǎoshí de duì
In order to buy cheap theatre tickets, he queued for an hour.

为了 **wèile** also occurs in official statements to express formal objectives:

为了减少失业人数，政府努力办好教育。
wèile jiǎnshǎo shīyè rénshù | zhèngfǔ nǔlì bàn hǎo jiàoyù
In order to reduce the number of unemployed, the government strives to improve education.

It is not normally used in casual, everyday situations and one does not usually say:

*为了买东西我进城去。 **wèile mǎi dōngxi wǒ jìn chéng qù**
(*lit.* In order to buy things/go shopping, I went into town.)

*为了找我他来宿舍。 **wèile zhǎo wǒ tā lái sùshè**
(*lit.* In order to look for me, he came into the dormitory.)

Everyday purpose or intention is usually expressed by a second verb (phrase) following the first:

我进城去买东西。 **wǒ jìn chéng qù mǎi dōngxi**
I went shopping in town. (*lit* I went into town to shop.)

他来宿舍找我。 **tā lái sùshè zhǎo wǒ**
He came to the dormitory to look for me.

C   对于 **duìyú** 'as to; about', 关于 **guānyú** 'regarding; as regards' and 至于 **zhìyú** 'as for; as far as . . . is concerned', all refer to a matter or person brought up for discussion. 对于 **duìyú** draws attention, 关于 **guānyú** indicates concern, and 至于 **zhìyú** raises an additional point:

对于这件事，我一点儿也不知道。
duìyú zhè/zhèi jiàn shì | wǒ yīdiǎnr yě bù zhīdao
As to this matter I know nothing./I know nothing about this matter.

关于这个问题，我们再研究一下。
guānyú zhè/zhèi gè wèntí | wǒmen zài yánjiū yīxià
Regarding this matter, we will have more discussions./We will consider this matter further.

至于结果如何，我们明天就知道了。
zhìyú jiéguǒ rúhé | wǒmen míngtiān jiù zhīdao le
As to how the results will come out, we will know tomorrow./We will know the results by tomorrow.

Note 1: 对 **duì** (see Unit 24) can in fact be used interchangeably with 对于 **duìyú**, but in sentences where the verb specifically indicates 'attitude', 对 **duì** is preferred:

我们对她的盛情款待表示感谢。 **wǒmen duì tā de shèngqíng kuǎndài biǎoshì gǎnxiè**
We expressed thanks for her generosity/hospitality.

Note 2: 至于 **zhìyú**, unlike 关于 **guānyú** and 对于 **duìyú** which are generally followed by a noun, may also be used with a clause:

关于天文的知识	**guānyú tiānwén de zhīshi**	knowledge about astronomy
关于社会的问题	**guānyú shèhuì de wèntí**	problems about society
对于移民的条例	**duìyú yímín de tiáolì**	regulations on immigration/emigration

But:

至于这件事儿	**zhìyú zhè/zhèi jiàn shìr**	as far as this is concerned
至于他们愿意不愿意来	**zhìyú tāmen yuànyì bù yuànyì lái**	as to whether they wish to come or not (clause)

D   除了 . . . (之外/以外) **chúle . . . (zhī wài/yǐ wài)** 'apart from . . . /as well as . . .':

他除了教书(以外)还做些研究工作。
tā chúle jiāoshū (yǐ wài) hái zuò xiē yánjiū gōngzuò
As well as teaching he also does a bit of research.

除了你，大家都同意。 **chúle nǐ | dàjiā dōu tóngyì**
Everyone agrees except you.

除了英文之外，我还会说法文和德文。
chúle yīngwén zhī wài | wǒ hái huì shuō fǎwén hé déwén
As well as English, I can also speak French and German.

E   按照 **ànzhào** 'according to/in accordance with' and 根据 **gēnjù** 'according to/on the basis of':

按照学校规定，学生不得无故缺席。
ànzhào xuéxiào guīdìng | xuésheng bù dé wúgù quēxí
According to school regulations, students must not be absent from school
without good reason.

根据气象预报，明天下雪。 **gēnjù qìxiàng yùbào | míngtiān xià xuě**
According to the weather forecast, there will be snow tomorrow.

Note 1: The difference between 按照 **ànzhào** and 根据 **gēnjù** is that the former justifies action and
the latter, the basis for conclusions.

Note 2: Also, the coverb 凭(着) **píng(zhe)** also means 'on the basis of'. It is often used in the
following collocations:

凭票入场。 **píngpiào rùchǎng**
Admittance by ticket only.

你凭什么得出这个结论？ **nǐ píng shénme dé chū zhè/zhèi gè jiélùn**
On what basis did you arrive at/come to this conclusion?

他凭着毅力克服了种种困难。 **tā píng zhe yìlì kèfú le zhǒngzhǒng kùnnan**
Through his perseverance, he overcame all kinds of difficulties.

Exercise 25.1

Rephrase the Chinese sentences below using 为了 **wèile** to express the meaning
of the English:

1 他不想误了火车，决定走近路。
　 tā bù xiǎng wù le huǒchē | juédìng zǒu jìn lù
　 He didn't want to miss the train, so he took a short cut.

2 小李开了两小时的车到伦敦去看那场足球赛。

xiǎo lǐ kāi le liǎng xiǎoshí de chē dào lúndūn qù kàn nà/nèi chǎng zúqiúsài

Xiao Li drove for two hours to London to see the football match.

3 她举行了一个舞会，庆祝女儿大学毕业。

tā jǔxíng le yī gè wǔhuì | qìngzhù nǚ'ér dàxué bìyè

She held a party to celebrate her daughter's graduation.

4 他特意从法国来看这个电影。

tā tèyì cóng fǎguó lái kàn zhè/zhèi gè diànyǐng

He came from France specially to see this film.

5 护士一夜没睡，照顾那个病人。

hùshi yī yè méi shuì | zhàogù nà/nèi gè bìngrén

The nurse was up all night looking after the patient.

6 经理到北京去参加一个重要会议。

jīnglǐ dào běijīng qù cānjiā yī gè zhòngyào huìyì

The manager went to Beijing to attend an important meeting.

Exercise 25.2

Complete the following sentences using 对(于) **duì(yú)**, 关于 **guānyú** or 至于 **zhìyú**:

1 咱们 _____ (_____) 别人的意见应该表示欢迎。

zánmen _____ (_____) biérén de yìjian yīnggāi biǎoshì huānyíng

We ought to welcome other people's opinions.

2 王先生谈到 _____ _____ 中国现代文学的问题。

wáng xiansheng tándào _____ zhōngguó xiàndài wénxué de wèntí

Mr Wang talked about questions on Modern Chinese Literature.

3 我请小李来我家参加晚会，_____ _____ 他能不能来我还不知道。

wǒ qǐng xiǎo lǐ lái wǒ jiā cānjiā wǎnhuì | _____ tā néng bù néng lái wǒ hái bù zhīdao

I have invited Xiao Li to come to my party, but I don't know if he can come.

4 _____ 孩子的要求不要太严格。

_____ háizi de yāoqiú bù yào tài yángé

Don't be too hard on the children.

5 今年夏天我们去意大利度假，_____ _____ 哪天出发，现在还不能决定。

jīnnián xiàtiān wǒmen qù yìdàlì dùjià | _____ nǎ/něi tiān chūfā | xiànzài hái bù néng juédìng

This summer we are going to Italy on holiday, but we haven't decided which day we are leaving.

6 小李懂得很多 _____ _____ 电脑的知识。

xiǎo lǐ dǒng de hěn duō _____ diànnǎo de zhīshi

Xiao Li knows a great deal about computers.

7 他了解不少 ＿＿＿ ＿＿＿ 中国社会的情况。

tā liǎojiě bù shǎo ＿＿＿ zhōngguó shèhuì de qíngkuàng

He understands a lot about conditions in Chinese society.

8 ＿＿＿ (＿＿＿) 那场比赛，教练没有提出什么个人的意见。

＿＿＿(＿＿＿) nà/nèi chǎng bǐsài, jiàoliàn méiyǒu tíchū shénme gèrén de yìjian

As far as that match is concerned, the coach did not express his personal views.

Exercise 25.3

Rewrite the following Chinese sentences using '除了 **chúle**...(之外/以外) (**zhī wài/yǐ wài**)' to reflect the meaning of the English:

1 动物园里有老虎、狮子，还有熊猫。

dòngwùyuán li yǒu lǎohǔ | shīzi | hái yǒu xióngmāo

There are tigers and lions as well as pandas at the zoo.

2 班里有中国人，还有英国人和法国人。

bān li yǒu zhōngguó rén | hái yǒu yīngguó rén hé fǎguó rén

In addition to Chinese students, there are also English and French students in the class.

3 我什么都吃，只是不吃羊肉。

wǒ shénme dōu chī | zhǐshì bù chī yángròu

I eat everything apart from lamb.

4 陈小姐会弹吉它，还会弹钢琴。

chén xiǎojie huì tán jítā | hái huì tán gāngqín

Miss Chen can play the guitar as well as the piano.

Exercise 25.4

Fill in the blanks in the sentences below choosing the appropriate preposition from the two in the brackets in each case:

1 这是 ＿＿＿ 真实故事拍的电影。

zhè shì ＿＿＿ zhēnshí gùshi pāi de diànyǐng

This is a film based on a true story. (按照/根据 **ànzhào/gēnjù**)

2 ＿＿＿ 票入场。 ＿＿＿ **piào rùchǎng**

Admittance is by ticket only. (按照/凭 **ànzhào/píng**)

3 ＿＿＿ 这些研究，可以得出正确结论。

＿＿＿ zhè/zhèi xiē yánjiū | kěyǐ dé chū zhèngquè jiélùn

Based on this research we can reach an accurate conclusion. (根据/凭 **gēnjù/píng**)

4 你 _____ 什么跟我这样说话？

nǐ _____ shénme gēn wǒ zhè/zhèi yàng shuōhuà

On what grounds are you speaking to me like this? (根据/凭 **gēnjù/píng**)

5 他们 _____ 老办法去做。**tāmen _____ lǎo bànfǎ qù zuò**

They do it according to the old method. (根据/按照 **gēnjù/ànzhào**)

6 她 _____ 毅力战胜了病痛的折磨。

tā _____ yìlì zhànshèng le bìngtòng de zhémo

She overcame the pain of her illness through strength of will. (按照/凭着 **ànzhào/píng zhe**)

Exercise 25.5

Indicate whether the Chinese translations below are correct or not, and, if not, make appropriate corrections:

1 The teacher is concerned about my work.
   老师关于我的学习很关心。**lǎoshī guānyú wǒ de xuéxí hěn guānxīn**
2 I went to town to do some shopping.
   为了买东西我进城去。**wèile mǎi dōngxi wǒ jìn chéng qù**
3 He got up very early so that he wouldn't be late.
   为了不迟到，他很早就起床了。**wèile bù chídào | tā hěn zǎo jiù qǐchuáng le**
4 According to the weather forecast there will be heavy rain tomorrow.
   凭气象预报，明天下大雨。**píng qìxiàng yùbào | míngtiān xià dà yǔ**
5 As well as swimming I like playing football.
   除了游泳，我还喜欢踢足球。**chúle yóuyǒng | wǒ hái xǐhuan tī zúqiú**
6 Regarding the problem of children's bad behaviour, school teachers as well as parents should also be concerned.
   对孩子调皮的问题，除了家长之外，学校老师也应该管。
   duì háizi tiáopí de wèntí | chúle jiāzhǎng zhī wài | xuéxiào lǎoshī yě yīnggāi guǎn

Exercise 25.6

Translate the following into Chinese:

1 As regards this question, I have no opinion.
2 I am very worried about this problem.
3 I can come every day apart from Wednesday.
4 As to whether we can come, please ask my wife.
5 Apart from her, they all like Chinese food.
6 I am going into town to see a friend.
7 In order to come to a conclusion, they discussed this matter for five hours.
8 On what grounds does the government pursue this policy?

KEY TO EXERCISES

Exercise 1.1　1 一个孩子 **yī gè háizi**　2 一个孩子 **yī gè háizi**　3 两个孩子 **liǎng gè háizi**　4 三个橙子 **sān gè chéngzi**　5 一打鸡蛋 **yī dá jīdàn**　6 四个面包 **sì gè miànbāo**　7 五片面包 **wǔ piàn miànbāo**　8 一个城市 **yī gè chéngshì**　9 两个建议 **liǎng gè jiànyì**　10 六个国家 **liù gè guójiā**　11 八个/家商店 **bā gè/jiā shāngdiàn** (家 **jiā** another measure word for 'shop')　12 九个学生 **jiǔ gè xuésheng**　13 七个工程师 **qī gè gōngchéngshī**　14 一个朋友 **yī gè péngyou**　15 一个人 **yī gè rén**　16 一个杯子 **yī gè bēizi**　17 两支笔 **liǎng zhī bǐ**　18 十个杯子 **shí gè bēizi**　19 两杯茶 **liǎng bēi chá**　20 三本书 **sān běn shū**　21 四个大人 **sì gè dàrén**　22 六张纸 **liù zhāng zhǐ**　23 一个蛋糕 **yī gè dàngāo**　24 一块蛋糕 **yī kuài dàngāo**

Exercise 1.2　一 **yī** may be omitted in sentences: 1, 2, 3, 4, 5, 7; 一 **yī** cannot be omitted in sentences: 6, 8

Exercise 1.3　1 我碰见两个朋友。**wǒ pèngjiàn liǎng gè péngyou**　2 他想找一个借口。**tā xiǎng zhǎo yī gè jièkǒu**　3 孩子们要吃苹果。**háizimen yào chī píngguǒ**　4 他们想去三个国家。**támen xiǎng qù sān gè guójiā**　5 correct　6 她有中国朋友。**tā yǒu zhōngguó péngyou**　7 你要吃几片面包？**nǐ yào chī jǐ piàn miànbāo**　8 correct

Exercise 1.4　1 How many loaves of bread do you want to buy?　2 She would like to eat two pieces of cake.　3 I bumped into three Chinese people.　4 I would like to have a cup of coffee.　5 I would like to go to/visit five countries.　6 She is an engineer.　7 I have two children.　8 I only want to go to one city.　9 Who would like to buy books?　10 I have a suggestion (to make).

Exercise 1.5　1 苹果和橙子 **píngguǒ hé chéngzi**　2 大人和孩子/小孩 **dàrén hé háizi/xiǎohái** (小孩 **xiǎohái** little child)　3 三片面包、一杯咖啡和一块蛋糕 **sān piàn miànbāo| yī bēi kāfēi hé yī kuài dàngāo**　4 四本书和六支笔 **sì běn**

shū hé liù zhī bǐ   5 我想去三个国家。 **wǒ xiǎng qù sān gè guójiā**   6 我想喝（一）杯茶。 **wǒ xiǎng hē (yī)bēi chá**   7 她只想去两个/家商店。 **tā zhǐ xiǎng qù liǎng gè/jiā shāngdiàn**   8 她想买一个面包、两个蛋糕、五个苹果和一打鸡蛋。 **tā xiǎng mǎi yī gè miànbāo| liǎng gè dàngāo| wǔ gè píngguǒ hé yī dá jīdàn**   9 孩子只有一个理想。 **háizi zhǐ yǒu yī gè lǐxiǎng**   10 我碰见三个中国朋友。 **wǒ pèngjiàn sān gè zhōngguó péngyou**

Unit 2

Exercise 2.1   1 这支 **zhè/zhèi zhī**   2 这些 **zhè/zhèi xiē**   3 那个 **nà/nèi gè**   4 那些 **nà/nèi xiē**   5 那几个 **nà/nèi jǐ gè**   6 这几张 **zhè/zhèi jǐ zhāng**   7 那个 **nà/nèi gè**   8 这本 **zhè/zhèi běn**   9 那些 **nà/nèi xiē**   10 那几个 **nà/nèi jǐ gè**   11 这个 **zhè/zhèi gè**   12 这几个 **zhè/zhèi jǐ gè**   13 那个 **nà/nèi gè**   14 这些 **zhè/zhèi xiē**   15 那些 **nà/nèi xiē**   16 那块 **nà/nèi kuài**   17 那个 **nà/nèi gè**   18 这把 **zhè/zhèi bǎ**   19 那片 **nà/nèi piàn**   20 这些 **zhè/zhèi xiē**   21 那些 **nà/nèi xiē**   22 那个/家 **nà/nèi gè/jiā**   23 那几把 **nà/nèi jǐ bǎ**   24 这几幅/张 **zhè/zhèi jǐ fú/zhāng** (张 **zhāng** another measure word for 'picture')

Exercise 2.2   1 She likes dogs.   2 I'll buy this hat.   3 Have you brought an umbrella?   4 Where are the keys?   5 Have you brought the jumper?   6 Has she got any children?   7 There is a bowl on the table.   8 There is a jumper in the wardrobe.   9 The chopsticks are on the table.   10 Do you know how to usc chopsticks?

Exercise 2.3   1 Where is/are there a/some book(s)?   2 Where is/are the book(s)?   3 There is a cake in the kitchen.   4 The cat is in the room.   5 Have you brought the key(s)?   6 Have you brought an umbrella?   7 Have you eaten the bananas?   8 We would like to buy some flowers.   9 The children are at school.   10 I like (eating) apples.   11 All the four jumpers and three hats are in the wardrobe.   12 All the ten students want to go to China.   13 Do you have any chopsticks?   14 All the apples, oranges, cake and bread are in the kitchen.

Exercise 2.4   1 哪儿有商店？ **nǎr yǒu shāngdiàn**   2 橙子很好吃。 **chéngzi hěn hǎochī**   3 桌子上有几个杯子。 **zhuōzi shang yǒu jǐ gè bēizi**   4 书架上有（一）些书。 **shūjià shang yǒu (yī)xiē shū**   5 你有笔吗？/你带了笔没有？ **nǐ yǒu bǐ ma/nǐ dài le bǐ méiyǒu**   6 碗在柜子/碗柜里。 **wǎn zài guìzi/wǎnguì li** (碗柜 **wǎnguì** a more specific term for 'cupboard' *lit.* bowl cabinet)   7 钥匙在哪儿？ **yàoshi zài nǎr**   8 花瓶里有（一）些花儿。/有（一）些花儿在花瓶里。 **huāpíng li yǒu (yī)xiē huār/yǒu (yī)xiē huār zài huāpíng li**   9 男孩子们在哪儿？ **nánháizimen zài nǎr**   10 你有毛衣吗？ **nǐ yǒu máoyī ma**   11 这些照片你喜欢吗？/你喜欢这些照片吗？ **zhè/zhèi xiē zhàopiàn nǐ xǐhuan ma/nǐ xǐhuan zhè/zhèi xiē zhàopiàn ma**   12 书你找到了没有？ **shū nǐ zhǎo dào le méiyǒu**

13 这两本书很有意思。 **zhè/zhèi liǎng běn shū hěn yǒu yìsi**   14 我喜欢那三幅画儿。 **wǒ xǐhuan nà/nèi sān fú huàr**   15 那五个学生在哪儿？ **nà/nèi wǔ gè xuésheng zài nǎr**

Unit 3

Exercise 3.1   1 我喜欢他，他也喜欢我。 **wǒ xǐhuan tā | tā yě xǐhuan wǒ** 2 我们想去见他们，但是他们不想见我们。 **wǒmen xiǎng qù jiàn tāmen | dànshì tāmen bù xiǎng jiàn wǒmen**   3 你不认识她，但是她认识你。 **nǐ bù rènshi tā | dànshì tā rènshi nǐ**   4 爸爸、妈妈，你们要喝咖啡吗？ **bàba | māma | nǐmen yào hē kāfēi ma**   5 她在哪儿？我想跟她谈谈。 **tā zài nǎr | wǒ xiǎng gēn tā tántán**   6 我们有两条狗，它们都住在他的房间里。 **wǒmen yǒu liǎng tiáo gǒu | tāmen dōu zhù zài tā de fángjiān li**   7 我不喜欢那些花儿。你喜欢吗？ **wǒ bù xǐhuan nà/nèi xiē huār | nǐ xǐhuan ma**   8 你想看那个电影吗？咱们去看吧。 **nǐ xiǎng kàn nà/nèi gè diànyǐng ma | zánmen qù kàn ba**

Exercise 3.2   1 我的 **wǒ de**   2 你(的) **nǐ (de)**   3 我 **wǒ**   4 我哥哥的 **wǒ gēge de**   5 她的 **tā de**   6 我们邻居的 **wǒmen línjū de**   7 他们(的) **tāmen (de)**   8 她(的) **tā (de)**, 我(的) **wǒ (de)**   9 爸爸/父亲的 **bàba/fùqīn de**   10 我们的 **wǒmen de**   11 自己 **zìjǐ**   12 自己的 **zìjǐ de**

Exercise 3.3   1 我哥哥的 **wǒ gēge de**, 我自己的 **wǒ zìjǐ de**   2 他的 **tā de**, 我的 **wǒ de**   3 他家的 **tā jiā de**   4 我的 **wǒ de**, 你的 **nǐ de**   5 我 **wǒ**   6 他 **tā**   7 你的 **nǐ de**, 我的 **wǒ de**   8 你的 **nǐ de**, 她的 **tā de**   9 爸爸/父亲的 **bàba/fùqīn de**, (她)自己的 **(tā) zìjǐ de**   10 你家的 **nǐ jiā de**   11 我们邻居的那些 **wǒmen línjū de nà/nèi xiē**   12 (他)自己的那件 **(tā) zìjǐ de nà/nèi jiàn**

Exercise 3.4   1 您 **nín**   2 您几位 **nín jǐ wèi**   3 您几位 **nín jǐ wèi**   4 您 **nín**   5 您几位 **nín jǐ wèi**   6 您 **nín**

Exercise 3.5   1 我们 **wǒmen**   2 咱们 **zánmen**   3 我们 **wǒmen**   4 咱们 **zánmen**   5 咱们 **zánmen**   6 我们 **wǒmen**

Unit 4

Exercise 4.1   1a 谁去市场买鸡蛋？ **shéi/shuí qù shìchǎng mǎi jīdàn** b 妈妈去哪儿买鸡蛋？ **māma qù nǎr mǎi jīdàn** c 妈妈去市场买什么？ **māma qù shìchǎng mǎi shénme** d 妈妈去市场做什么？ **māma qù shìchǎng zuò shénme**   2a 爸爸在哪儿写推荐信？ **bàba zài nǎr xiě tuījiànxìn** b 爸爸在办公室做什么？ **bàba zài bàngōngshì zuò shénme** c 爸爸在办公室写什么？ **bàba zài bàngōngshì xiě shénme** d 谁在办公室写推荐信？ **shéi/shuí zài bàngōngshì xiě tuījiànxìn**   3a 姐姐在哪儿喂猫？ **jiějie zài nǎr wèi māo** b 姐姐在厨房里做

什么？ **jiějie zài chúfáng li zuò shénme** c 谁在厨房里喂猫？ **shéi/shuí zài chúfáng li wèi māo** 4a 哥哥在外面做什么？ **gēge zài wàimian zuò shénme** b 哥哥在外面修什么？ **gēge zài wàimian xiū shénme** c 哥哥在哪儿修车？ **gēge zài nǎr xiū chē** d 谁在外面修车？ **shéi/shuí zài wàimian xiú chē** 5a 弟弟去游泳池做什么？ **dìdi qù yóuyǒngchí zuò shénme** b 谁去游泳池学游泳？ **shéi/shuí qù yóuyǒngchí xué yóuyǒng** c 弟弟去哪儿学游泳？ **dìdi qù nǎr xue yóuyǒng** 6a 弟弟想请谁帮他的忙？ **dìdi xiǎng qǐng shéi/shuí bāng tā de máng** b 弟弟想请姐姐做什么？ **dìdi xiǎng qǐng jiějie zuò shénme** c 谁想请姐姐帮忙？ **shéi/shuí xiǎng qǐng jiějie bāngmáng** 7a 谁的孩子在街上骑自行车？ **shéi/shuí de háizi zài jiē shang qí zìxíngchē** b 谁在街上骑自行车？ **shéi/shuí zài jiē shang qí zìxíngchē** c 邻居的孩子在街上做什么？ **línjū de háizi zài jiē shang zuò shénme** d 邻居的孩子在街上骑什么？ **línjū de háizi zài jiē shang qí shénme** e 邻居的孩子在哪儿骑自行车？ **línjū de háizi zài nǎr qí zìxíngchē** 8a 谁明年想跟爷爷去中国旅行？ **shéi/shuí míngnián xiǎng gēn yéye qù zhōngguó lǚxíng** b 妹妹明年想做什么？ **mèimei míngnián xiǎng zuò shénme** c 妹妹明年想跟谁去中国旅行？ **mèimei míngnián xiǎng gēn shéi/shuí qù zhōngguó lǚxíng** d 妹妹明年想跟爷爷去哪儿旅行？ **mèimei míngnián xiǎng gēn yéye qù nǎr lǚxíng** e 妹妹明年想跟爷爷去中国做什么？ **mèimei míngnián xiǎng gēn yéye qù zhōngguó zuò shénme**

Exercise 4.2 1 哪儿有自行车租？ **nǎr yǒu zìxíngchē zū** 2 哪儿有咖啡喝？ **nǎr yǒu kāfēi hē** 3 哪儿有花儿买/卖？ **nǎr yǒu huār mǎi/mài** 4 哪儿有啤酒喝？ **nǎr yǒu píjiǔ hē** 5 哪儿有东西吃？ **nǎr yǒu dōngxi chī** 6 哪儿有电影看？ **nǎr yǒu diànyǐng kàn** 7 哪儿有报纸买/卖？ **nǎr yǒu bàozhǐ mǎi/mài** 8 哪儿有书借？ **nǎr yǒu shū jiè** 9 哪儿有新鲜蔬菜买/卖？ **nǎr yǒu xīnxiān shūcài mǎi/mài** 10 哪儿有好(汽)车租？ **nǎr yǒu hǎo (qì)chē zū**

Exercise 4.3 1 谁想喝茶？ **shéi/shuí xiǎng hē chá** 2 谁想吃蛋糕？ **shéi/shuí xiǎng chī dàngāo** 3 这个杯子是谁的？/这是谁的杯子？ **zhè/zhèi gè bēizi shì shéi/shuí de/zhè shì shéi/shuí de bēizi** 4 你想吃什么？ **nǐ xiǎng chī shénme** 5 你喜欢哪幅画儿？ **nǐ xǐhuan nǎ/něi fú huàr** 6 谁会说中文？ **shéi/shuí huì shuō zhōngwén** 7 哪个孩子是你的？ **nǎ/něi gè háizi shì nǐ de** 8 张先生是谁的老师？ **zhāng xiānsheng shì shéi/shuí de lǎoshī** 9 你要买哪些橙子？ **nǐ yào mǎ nǎ/něi xiē chéngzi** 10 你喜欢什么蔬菜？ **nǐ xǐhuan shénme shūcài** 11 谁会修车？ **shéi/shuí huì xiū chē** 12 谁能帮我的忙？/谁能帮助我？ **shéi/shuí néng bāng wǒ de máng/shéi/shuí néng bāngzhù wǒ** 13 你想见谁？ **nǐ xiǎng jiàn shéi/shuí** 14 你带了哪两本书？ **nǐ dài le nǎ/něi liǎng běn shū** 15 你去了什么地方？/你去了哪儿？ **nǐ qù le shénme dìfang/nǐ qù le nǎr** 16 你去哪些国家？ **nǐ qù nǎ/něi xiē guójiā** 17 我的钱包在哪儿？ **wǒ de qiánbāo zài nǎr** 18 你去哪儿喝咖啡？ **nǐ qù nǎr hē kāfēi** 19 你和/跟谁去中国？/你是和/跟谁去中国？ **nǐ hé/gēn shéi/shuí qù zhōngguó/nǐ shì hé/gēn shéi/shuí qù zhōngguó** 20 你在哪儿认识她？/你是在哪儿认识她的？ **nǐ zài nǎr rènshi tā/nǐ shì zài nǎr rènshi tā de**

Unit 5

Exercise 5.1   1 89   2 16   3 10,000   4 600,000,000   5 7,000,000
6 13,526   7 180,000   8 6,934   9 3,652   10 780,000,469   11 64,504
12 4,004.005

Exercise 5.2   1 八万零二百零五 **bā wàn líng èr bǎi líng wǔ**   2 六百三十二
万九千八百一十四 **liù bǎi sān shí èr wàn jiǔ qiān bā bǎi yī shí sì** (一十四 **yī shí sì**
for fourteen is only used in counting when following a figure in the hundreds)
3 六亿 **liù yì**   4 一千零八十 **yī qiān líng bā shí**   5 三十六分之七 **sān shí liù
fēn zhī qī**   6 四分之一 **sì fēn zhī yī**   7 百分之三 **bǎi fēn zhī sān**   8 百分之九
十七 **bǎi fēn zhī jiǔ shí qī**   9 四点一三一六 **sì diǎn yī sān yī liù**   10 五百八十六
点二三 **wǔ bǎi bā shí liù diǎn èr sān**   11 七千零五 **qī qiān líng wǔ**   12 六百
零一点零零七 **liù bǎi líng yī diǎn líng líng qī**

Exercise 5.3   1 半天 **bàn tiān**   2 两(个)星期/两个礼拜/两周 **liǎng (gè) xīngqī/
liǎng gè lǐbài/liǎng zhōu** (周 **zhōu** is also used to mean 'week')   3 三年半 **sān
nián bàn**   4 六个月 **liù gè yuè**   5 二楼 **èr lóu**   6 半个橙子 **bàn gè
chéngzi**   7 半瓶酒 **bàn píng jiǔ**   8 五个半梨 **wǔ gè bàn lí**   9 第五周 **dì wǔ
zhōu**   10 第四个孩子 **dì sì gè háizi**   11 第十二场比赛 **dì shí èr chǎng bǐsài**
12 三年级 **sān niánjí**   13 第二天 **dì èr tiān**   14 七个半小时/钟头 **qī gè bàn
xiǎoshí/zhōngtóu**

Exercise 5.4   1 两 **liǎng**   2 两 **liǎng**   3 二 **èr**   4 二 **èr**   5 二 **èr**   6 两
liǎng   7 二 **èr**   8 两 **liǎng**   9 二 **èr**   10 两 **liǎng**

Exercise 5.5   1 一、两周/一、两个星期/一、两个礼拜 **yī | liǎng zhōu/yī | liǎng
gè xīngqī/yī | liǎng gè lǐbài**   2 两百年 **liǎng bǎi nián**   3 六十来岁/大约六十岁/
六十岁左右/上下 **liù shí lái suì/dàyuē liù shí suì/liù shí suì zuǒyòu/shàngxià**
4 三、四十辆自行车 **sān | sì shí liàng zìxíngchē**   5 十多天 **shí duō tiān**   6 两百
来个商店 **liǎng bǎi lái gè shāngdiàn**   7 百分之十 **bǎi fēn zhī shí**   8 二十左右/
上下/大约二十 **èr shí zuǒyòu/shàngxià/dàyuē èr shí**   9 十五米左右/上下/大约
十五米 **shí wǔ mǐ zuǒyòu/shàngxià/dàyuē shí wǔ mǐ**   10 一个月左右/上下/大约
一个月 **yī gè yuè zuǒyòu/shàngxià/dàyuē yī gè yuè**   11 一万多个学生 **yī wàn
duō gè xuésheng**   12 两、三个孩子 **liǎng | sān gè háizi**   13 大约五十个朋友
和邻居 **dàyuē wǔ shí gè péngyou hé línjū**   14 大约七十英里/七十英里左右/
上下 **dàyuē qī shí yīnglǐ/qī shí yīnglǐ zuǒyòu/shàngxià**   15 八公斤多
bā gōngjīn duō   16 十多个城市 **shí duō gè chéngshì**

Exercise 5.6   1 碗柜/柜子里有三个橙子、两个梨、一个面包和一瓶酒。 **wǎnguì/
guìzi li yǒu sān gè chéngzi | liǎng gè lí | yī gè miànbāo hé yī píng jiǔ**
2 桌子上有一个碗、一个杯子和一双筷子。 **zhuōzi shang yǒu yī gè wǎn | yī gè
bēizi hé yī shuāng kuàizi**   3 冰箱里有半打鸡蛋、一公斤白菜和一些冰激凌。
bīngxiāng li yǒu bàn dá jīdàn | yī gōngjīn báicài hé yīxiē bīngjilíng

4 衣柜/柜子里有两件毛衣和十二条裙子。 **yīguì/guìzi li yǒu liǎng jiàn máoyī hé shí èr tiáo qúnzi** (衣柜 **yīguì** is a more specific term for 'wardrobe' (*lit.* clothes cabinet)   5 李明请了三、四十个朋友和同学。 **lǐ míng qǐng le sān | sì shí gè péngyou hé tóngxué**   6 我男朋友带来了一束花儿和几瓶啤酒。 **wǒ nán péngyou dài lái le yī shù huār hé jǐ píng píjiǔ**   7 我写了大约五封推荐信。 **wǒ xiě le dàyuē wǔ fēng tuījiànxìn**   8 我女朋友去过十多个国家。 **wǒ nǚ péngyou qù guo shí duō gè guójiā**   9 我碰见了二十多个同学。 **wǒ péngjiàn le èr shí duō gè tóngxué**   10 我儿子今年看了十来个电影。 **wǒ érzi jīnnián kàn le shí lái gè diànyǐng**   11 那件毛衣多少钱? **nà/nèi jiàn máoyī duōshao qián**   12 他有几个妹妹? **tā yǒu jǐ gè mèimei**   13 北京有多少人? **běijīng yǒu duōshao rén**   14 你爸爸/父亲认识多少中国人? **nǐ bàba/fùqīn rènshi duōshao zhōngguó rén**   15 你要/想买几公斤白菜? **nǐ yào/xiǎng mǎi jǐ gōngjīn báicài**

Unit 6

Exercise 6.1   1 一匹马 **yī pǐ mǎ** a/one horse   2 两架飞机 **liǎng jià fēijī** two planes   3 三个国家 **sān gè guójiā** three countries   4 四、五把椅子 **sì | wǔ bǎ yǐzi** four or five chairs   5 几张桌子 **jǐ zhāng zhuōzi** a few/how many tables   6 六家商店 **liù jiā shāngdiàn** six shops   7 七所学校 **qī suǒ xuéxiào** seven schools   8 八座山 **bā zuò shān** eight mountains   9 九本书 **jiǔ běn shū** nine books   10 十块蛋糕 **shí kuài dàngāo** ten pieces of cake

Exercise 6.2   1 张 **zhāng**   2 床 **chuáng**   3 所 **suǒ**   4 副 **fù**   5 部 **bù**   6 个 **gè**   7 座 **zuò**   8 对 **duì**

Exercise 6.3   1 一天 **yī tiān**   2 一碗饭 **yī wǎn fàn**   3 一年 **yī nián**   4 这副眼镜 **zhè/zhèi fù yǎnjìng**   5 一双鞋(子) **yī shuāng xié(zi)**   6 一(个)星期/一个礼拜/一周 **yī (gè) xīngqī/yī gè lǐbài/yī zhōu**   7 一个耳环 **yī gè ěrhuán**   8 一只袜子 **yī zhī wàzi**   9 一块/片面包 **yī kuài/piàn miànbāo**   10 那把剪刀 **nà/něi bǎ jiǎndāo**   11 一块/条肥皂 **yī kuài/tiáo féizào**   12 一条裤子 **yī tiáo kùzi**   13 一个月 **yī gè yuè**   14 两磅苹果 **liǎng bàng píngguǒ**   15 三英里(路) **sān yīnglǐ (lù)**   16 七升汽油 **qī shēng qìyóu**   17 哪支毛笔 **nǎ/něi zhī máobǐ**   18 一条/只/艘船 **yī tiáo/zhī/sōu chuán** (艘 **sōu** is another measure word for 'ship')   19 两首歌 **liǎng shǒu gē**   20 一张/幅地图 **yī zhāng/fú dìtú**

Exercise 6.4   1 一群羊 **yī qún yáng**   2 一杯啤酒 **yī bēi píjiǔ**   3 一群人 **yī qún rén**   4 一把(雨)伞 **yī bǎ (yǔ)sǎn**   5 一把刀 **yī bǎ dāo**   6 那只鸟 **nà/nèi zhī niǎo**   7 那两束花(儿) **nà/nèi liǎng shù huā(r)**   8 一支乐曲 **yī zhī yuèqǔ**   9 这张报纸 **zhè/zhèi zhāng bàozhǐ**   10 哪三支铅笔 **nǎ/něi san zhī qiānbǐ**   11 一个机会 **yī gè jīhuì**   12 一滴水 **yī dī shuǐ**   13 一杯茶 **yī bēi chá**   14 哪朵花(儿) **nǎ/něi duǒ huā(r)**   15 一条绳子 **yī tiáo shéngzi**   16 一张床 **yī zhāng chuáng**   17 一条裤子 **yī tiáo kùzi**   18 一把剪刀 **yī bǎ jiǎndāo**   19 这条狗 **zhè/zhèi tiáo gǒu**   20 这三支(香)烟 **zhè/zhèi sān zhī (xiāng)yān**

Exercise 6.5   1 这间/个 **zhè/zhèi jiān/gè** 四张 **sì zhāng**, 五把 **wǔ bǎ**   2 两条 **liǎng tiáo**, 三只 **sān zhī**   3 四辆 **sì liàng**   4 一顶 **yī dǐng**   5 四杯 **sì bēi**   6 那个 **nà/nèi gè** 几个/条 **jǐ gè/tiáo**   7 一些 **yī xiē**   8 一家 **yī jiā** 一碗 **yī wǎn**   9 一张 **yī zhāng**   10 那两只 **nà/nèi liǎng zhī**

Unit 7

Exercise 7.1   1 correct   2 不少孩子 **bù shǎo háizi**   3 不少朋友 **bù shǎo péngyou**   4 correct   5 很多面包 **hěn duō miànbāo**   6 correct   7 correct   8 correct   9 很多人 **hěn duō rén**   10 一些工程师 **yīxiē gōngchéngshī**   11 correct   12 correct   13 correct   14 correct   15 家里连一粒米也没有。**jiā li lián yī lì mǐ yě méi yǒu**   16 correct

Exercise 7.2   1 很多 **hěn duō**/不少 **bù shǎo**   2 一点(儿) **yīdiǎnr**   3 很多 **hěn duō**/不少 **bù shǎo**   4 一个 **yī gè**   5 很多 **hěn duō**/不少 **bù shǎo**   6 很多 **hěn duō**/不少 **bù shǎo**   7 一点(儿) **yīdiǎnr**/一些 **yīxiē**   8 一点(儿) **yīdiǎnr**   9 很多 **hěn duō**/不少 **bù shǎo**   10 不少 **bù shǎo**

Exercise 7.3   1 我身上(连)一分钱也没有。**wǒ shēn shang (lián) yī fēn qián yě méi yǒu**   2 我家里(连)一本词典也没有。**wǒ jiā li (lián) yī běn cídiǎn yě méi yǒu**   3 冰箱里一点儿水果也没有。**bīngxiāng li yīdiǎnr shuǐguǒ yě méi yǒu**   4 她什么也没(有)说。**tā shénme yě méi(yǒu) shuō**   5 他什么(东西)也没(有)吃。**tā shénme (dōngxi) yě méi(yǒu) chī**   6 妈妈什么肉也没(有)买。**māma shénme ròu yě méi(yǒu) mǎi**   7 我们哪儿也没(有)去。**wǒmen nǎr yě méi(yǒu) qù**   8 我昨天谁也没(有)碰见。**wǒ zuótiān shéi/shuí yě méi(yǒu) pèngjiàn**

Exercise   7.4   1 一点(儿) **yīdiǎn(r)**   2 一点(儿) **yīdiǎn(r)**   3 一点(儿) **yīdiǎn(r)**   4 一些/一点(儿) **yīxiē/yīdiǎnr**   5 一点(儿) **yīdiǎn(r)**   6 一点(儿) **yīdiǎn(r)**   7 一点(儿) **yīdiǎn(r)**   8 一点(儿) **yīdiǎn(r)**

Unit 8

Exercise 8.1   1 three o'clock   2 twelve o'clock   3 twenty past two   4 five to eight/seven fifty-five   5 ten to eight   6 a quarter past eleven   7 half past nine   8 one minute past ten   9 five past twelve   10 a quarter to seven/six forty-five

Exercise 8.2   1 我上午八点半去学校。**wǒ shàngwǔ bā diǎn bàn qù xuéxiào**   2 我上午八点五十五分/九点差五分去游泳。**wǒ shàngwǔ bā diǎn wǔ shí wǔ fēn/jiǔ diǎn chà wǔ fēn qù yóuyǒng**   3 我朋友下午五点三刻/五点四十五分下班。**wǒ péngyou xiàwǔ wǔ diǎn sān kè/wǔ diǎn sì shí wǔ fēn xiàbān**   4 我们大约九点(钟)吃晚饭。**wǒmen dàyuē jiǔ diǎn (zhōng) chī wǎnfàn**   5 我六号碰

见你叔叔。 **wǒ liù hào pèngjiàn nǐ shūshu**   6 我爸爸十一号去中国。 **wǒ bàba shí yī hào qù zhōngguó**   7 我妹妹晚上十二点左右睡觉。 **wǒ mèimei wǎnshang shí èr diǎn zuǒyòu shuìjiào**   8 我下个月二十一号给他写信。 **wǒ xià gè yuè ér shí yī hào gěi tā xiě xìn**   9 我下星期四来这儿开座谈会。 **wǒ xià xīngqī sì lái zhèr kāi zuòtánhuì**   10 我一九九九年毕业。 **wǒ yī jiǔ jiǔ jiǔ nián bìyè**   11 我明年/今年九月到欧洲去。 **wǒ míngnián/jīnnián jiǔ yuè dào ōuzhōu qù**   12 我同学明年十二月回国。 **wǒ tóngxué míngnián shí èr yuè huí guó**

Note: 大约 **dàyuē**, 左右 **zuǒyòu** and 上下 **shàngxià** may be used interchangeably in this exercise.

Exercise 8.3   1 她几点(钟)吃晚饭？ **tā jǐ diǎn (zhōng) chī wǎnfàn**   2 你礼拜五晚上几点(钟)来我家？ **nǐ lǐbài wǔ wǎnshang jǐ diǎn (zhōng) lái wǒ jiā**   3 你们八月几号去度假？ **nǐmen bā yuè jǐ hào qù dùjià**   4 你哪年第一次见到她？ **nǐ nǎ/něi nián dì yī cì jiàn dào tā**   5 你妈妈几点(钟)回家？ **nǐ māma jǐ diǎn (zhōng) huí jiā**   6 新经理下星期几来这儿上班？ **xīn jīnglǐ xià xīngqī jǐ lái zhèr shàngbān**   7 你们什么时候来找我？ **nǐmen shénme shíhou lái zhǎo wǒ**   8 他们什么时候/哪年毕业？ **tāmen shénme shíhou/nǎ/něi nián bìyè**   9 你姐姐上星期几下午在学开车？ **nǐ jiějie shàng xīngqī jǐ xiàwǔ zài xué kāichē**   10 你去年几月/什么时候买这幅画？ **nǐ qùnián jǐ yuè/shénme shíhou mǎi zhè/zhèi fú huà**   11 座谈会上午几点(钟)开始？ **zuòtánhuì shàngwǔ jǐ diǎn (zhōng) kāishǐ**   12 你明天什么时候在家里休息？ **nǐ míngtiān shénme shíhou zǎi jiā li xiūxi**

Exercise 8.4   1 你明天什么时候去学校(上课)？ **nǐ míngtiān shénme shíhou qù xuéxiào (shàngkè)**   2 我下个月来这儿开座谈会。 **wǒ xià gè yuè lái zhèr kāi zuòtánhuì**   3 你什么时候去欧洲旅行？ **nǐ shénme shíhou qù ōuzhōu lǚxíng**   4 你明天几点(钟)上班？ **nǐ míngtiān jǐ diǎn (zhōng) shàngbān**   5 你下午几点(钟)去游泳池游泳？ **ni xiàwǔ jǐ diǎn (zhōng) qù yóuyǒngchí yóuyǒng**   6 你哪天到那儿去踢足球？ **nǐ nǎ/něi tiān dào nàr qù tī zúqiú**   7 你几月/哪个月去海边度假？ **nǐ jǐ yuè/nǎ/něi gè yuè qù hǎi biān dùjià**   8 你什么时候去火车站买票？ **nǐ shénme shíhou qù huǒchēzhàn mǎi piào**   9 你上午几点(钟)去市场(买东西)？ **nǐ shàngwǔ jǐ diǎn (zhōng) qù shìchǎng (mǎi dōngxi)**   10 你几时/什么时候去图书馆借书？ **nǐ jǐ shí/shénme shíhou qù túshūguǎn jiè shū**

Unit 9

Exercise 9.1   1 你在路上花了多长时间？ **nǐ zài lù shang huā le duō cháng shíjiān**   2 你在教室里看了多久/多长时间的书？ **nǐ zài jiàoshì li kàn le duō jiǔ/duō cháng shíjiān de shū**   3 足球比赛开始多久/多长时间了？ **zúqiú bǐsài kāishǐ duō jiǔ/duō cháng shíjiān le**   4 你和姐姐在花园里坐了多久/多长时间？ **nǐ hé jiějie zài huāyuán li zuò le duō jiǔ/duō cháng shíjiān**   5 妈妈在厨房里忙了多久/多长时间？ **māma zài chúfáng li máng le duō jiǔ/duō cháng shíjiān**   6 妹妹帮了你几天/多少天/多长时间的忙？ **mèimei bāng le nǐ jǐ tiān/**

duōshao tiān/duō cháng shíjiān de máng   7 你开了几年/多少年车，骑了几年/多少年自行车？ **nǐ kāi le jǐ nián/duōshao nián chē | qí le jǐ nián/duōshao nián zìxíngchē**   8 足球场有多长/多少米长？ **zúqiúchǎng yǒu duō cháng/duōshao mǐ cháng**   9 你哥哥有多高？ **nǐ gēge yǒu duō gāo**   10 巴黎离伦敦有多远？ **bālí lí lúndūn yǒu duō yuǎn**

Exercise 9.2   1 Shall we go to his place to visit him next Monday?   2 How do you get to the bus station?   3 What is the traffic like in London?   4 How can I get to the cinema (from here)?   5 How about going to the pub for a beer tomorrow evening?   6 What is the weather like in Beijing?   7 What are the goods like in that shop?   8 Let's go on holiday next month./Why don't we go on holiday next month?

Exercise 9.3   1 你吃了多少？ **nǐ chī le duōshao**   2 你怎(么)样/怎么去伦敦？ **nǐ zěn(me) yàng/zěnme qù lúndūn**   3 他为什么离开？ **tā wèi shénme líkāi**   4 你准备待(呆)多久/多长时间？ **nǐ zhǔnbèi dāi duō jiǔ/duō cháng shíjiān**   5 你怎么做这个蛋糕？ **nǐ zěnme zuò zhè/zhèi gè dàngāo**   6 你的新房子(是)怎么样(的)？ **nǐ de xīn fángzi (shì) zěnme yàng (de)**   7 你有多少钱？ **nǐ yǒu duōshao qián**   8 (那个)电影怎么样？ **(nà/nèi) gè diànyǐng zěnme yàng**   9 咱们(去)喝(一)杯酒，怎么样？ **zánmen (qù) hē (yī) bēi jiǔ | zěnme yàng**   10 你为什么学中文？ **nǐ wèi shénme xué zhōngwén**   11 我怎么认识小李？ **wǒ zěnme rènshi xiǎo lǐ**   12 你认为那位中文老师怎么样？ **nǐ rènwéi nà/nèi wèi/zhōngwén lǎoshī zěnme yàng**   13 你怎么样去上班？ **nǐ zěnme yàng qù shàngbān**   14 你等了她多久/多长时间了？ **nǐ děng le tā duō jiǔ/duō cháng shíjiān le**   15 她睡了几(个)小时/几个钟头？ **tā shuì le jǐ (gè) xiǎoshí/jǐ gè zhōngtóu**   16 你们开了几天/多少天(的)车？ **nǐmen kāi le jǐ tiān/duōshao tiān (de) chē** 你们开车开了几天/多少天？ **nǐmen kāichē kāi le jǐ tiān/duōshao tiān**   17 你等了多久/多长时间(的)车？ **nǐ děng le duō jiǔ/duō cháng shíjiān (de) chē** 你等车等了多久/多长时间？ **nǐ děng chē děng le duō jiǔ/duō cháng shíjiān**   18 你走了多远(的)(路)/多少路？ **nǐ zǒu le duō yuǎn (de) (lù)/duōshao lù**

Exercise 9.4   1 多远 **duō yuǎn**   2 多高 **duō gāo**   3 多少 **duōshao**   4 多远 **duō yuǎn**   5 多重 **duō zhòng**   6 多大 **duō dà**   7 多少 **duōshao**   8 多大 **duō dà**   9 多少 **duōshao**   10 多久/多长时间 **duō jiǔ/duō cháng shíjiān**   11 多久/多长时间 **duō jiǔ/duō cháng shíjiān**   12 多少/多长 **duōshao/duō cháng**   13 多久/多长时间 **duō jiǔ/duō cháng shíjiān**   14 多少 **duōshao**

Unit 10

Exercise 10.1   1 一个很大的游泳池 **yī gè hěn dà de yóuyǒngchí**   2 新楼房 **xīn lóufáng**   3 白猫 **bái māo**   4 一只/个大碗 **yī zhī/gè dà wǎn**   5 一个美丽的花园 **yī gè měilì de huāyuán**   6 一个小孩(子) **yī gè xiǎo hái(zi)**   7 一个有趣的电影 **yī gè yǒuqù de diànyǐng**   8 一场精彩的比赛 **yī chǎng jīngcǎi de bǐsài**

9 新鲜(的)蔬菜 **xīnxiān (de) shūcài**   10 很多钱 **hěn duō qián**   11 一辆旧车 **yī liàng jiù chē**   12 十分重的行李 **shífēn zhòng de xíngli**   13 干净的衣服 **gānjìng de yīfu**   14 一间整齐的屋子/房间 **yī jiān zhěngqí de wùzi/fángjiān**   15 很狭窄的街道 **hěn xiázhǎi de jiēdào**   16 古老的城市 **gǔlǎo de chéngshì**   17 一个非常好的音乐会 **yī gè fēicháng hǎo de yīnyuèhuì**   18 脏鞋子 **zāng xiézi**

Exercise 10.2   1 今天天气很好。 **jīntiān tiānqì hěn hǎo**   2 她很有钱。 **tā hěn yǒu qián**   3 这个沙发不很舒服。 **zhè/zhèi gè shāfā bù hěn shūfu**   4 那个教室非常干净。 **nà/nèi gè jiàoshì fēicháng gānjìng**   5 我弟弟不太高。 **wǒ dìdi bù tài gāo**   6 这场比赛不十分精彩。 **zhè/zhèi chǎng bǐsài bù shífēn jīngcǎi**   7 地上都是红红绿绿的玩具。 **dì shang dōu shì hónghónglǜlǜ de wánjù**   8 王先生是个非常有趣的人。 **wáng xiānsheng shì gè fēicháng yǒuqù de rén**

Exercise 10.3   1 北京是(一)个十分/非常古老的城市。 **běijīng shì (yī) gè shífēn/fēicháng gǔlǎo de chéngshì**   2 那本旧书不太贵。 **nà/nèi běn jiù shū bù tài guì**   3 (这个)图书馆非常大。 **(zhè/zhèi gè) túshūguǎn fēicháng dà**   4 我没有新衣服。/我(连)一件新衣服也没有。 **wǒ méi yǒu xīn yīfu/wǒ (lián) yī jiàn xīn yīfu yě méi yǒu**   5 那些鲜花很美丽/漂亮。 **nà/nèi xiē xiān huā hěn měilì/piàoliang** (鲜花 **xiānhuā** has become a set expression for 'fresh flowers', *not*: 新鲜的花儿 **xīnxiān de huār**)   6 那双鞋(子)太大。 **nà/nèi shuāng xié(zi) tài dà**   7 这儿的天气真好。 **zhèr de tiānqì zhēn hǎo**   8 那条街(道)不够干净。 **nà/nèi tiáo jiē(dào) bù gòu gānjìng**   9 我不喜欢不新鲜的牛奶。 **wǒ bù xǐhuan bù xīnxiān de niúnǎi**   10 那杯咖啡太甜。**nà/nèi bēi kāfēi tài tián**

Exercise 10.4   1 路旁坐着一个高高大大的小伙子。 **lù páng zuò zhe yī gè gāogāodàdà de xiǎohuǒzi**   2 小王长着弯弯的眉毛，高高的鼻子，小小的嘴巴和一双大大的眼睛，留着一头整整齐齐的短发。 **xiǎo wáng zhǎng zhe wānwān de méimao | gaogao de bízi | xiǎoxiǎo de zuǐba hé yī shuāng dàdà de yǎnjing | liú zhe yī tóu zhěngzhěngqíqí de duǎn fà**   3 这是一间干干净净的房间。白白的床单，蓝蓝的窗帘，红红的炉火，给你一种舒舒适适的感觉。 **zhè shì yī jiān gāngānjìngjìng de fángjiān | báibái de chuángdān | lánlán de chuānglián | hónghóng de lúhuǒ | gěi nǐ yī zhǒng shūshūshìshì de gǎnjué**   4 她那朴朴素素的衣着，大大方方的举止，甜甜美美的声音给人留下了很深刻的印象。 **tā nà/nèi pǔpǔsùsù de yīzhuó | dàdàfāngfāng de jǔzhǐ | tiántiánměiměi de shēngyīn gěi rén liú xià le hěn shēnkè de yìnxiàng**

Unit 11

Exercise 11.1   1 她是我的邻居。 **tā shì wǒ de línjū**   2 我的妹妹很漂亮。 **wǒ de mèimei hěn piàoliang**   3 昨天(是)星期二。 **zuótiān (shì) xīngqī èr**   4 我的车是红的。 **wǒ de chē shì hóng de**   5 这条鱼是活的。 **zhè/zhèi tiáo yú shì huó de**   6 我们的房间很干净。 **wǒmen de fángjiān hěn gānjìng**   7 那个

故事很有趣。 **nà/nèi gè gùshi hěn yǒuqù** 8 这些蔬菜很新鲜。 **zhè/zhèi xiē shūcài hěn xīnxiān** 9 这条裙子不太脏。 **zhè/zhèi tiáo qúnzi bù tài zāng** 10 音乐会非常精彩。 **yīnyuèhuì fēicháng jīngcǎi** 11 这些衣服都是旧的。 **zhè/zhèi xiē yīfu dōu shì jiù de** 12 那副眼镜是谁的？ **nà/nèi fù yǎnjìng shì shéi/shuí de**

Exercise 11.2 1 小王没有狗。 **xiǎo wáng méu yǒu gǒu** 2 花园里没有很多花儿。 **huāyuán li méi yǒu hěn duō huār** 3 他们都不是英国人。 **tāmen dōu bù shì yīngguó rén** 4 这幢房子不是他的。 **zhè/zhèi zhuàng fángzi bù shì tā de** 5 那杯咖啡不是我朋友的。 **nà/nèi bēi kāfēi bù shì wǒ péngyou de** 6 楼下没有人。 **lóuxià méi yǒu rén** 7 她不是经理。 **tā bù shì jīnglǐ** 8 她没有两件行李。 **tā méi yǒu liǎng jiàn xíngli** 9 我的同学不都是中国人。 **wǒ de tóngxué bù dōu shì zhōngguó rén** 10 图书馆后面不是电影院。**túshūguǎn hòumian bù shì diànyǐngyuàn**

Exercise 11.3 1 抽屉里有信纸。 **chōuti li yǒu xìnzhǐ** 2 那幅画儿很美。 **nà/nèi fú huàr hěn měi** 3 这条蛇是活的。 **zhè/zhèi tiáo shé shì huó de** 4 我没有手套。 **wǒ méi yǒu shǒutào** 5 他不是经理。 **tā bù shì jīnglǐ** 6 树下没有兔子。 **shù xià méi yǒu tùzi** 7 那条裤子不是我的。 **nà/nèi tiáo kùzi bù shì wǒ de** 8 书架上都是书。 **shūjià shang dōu shì shū**

Exercise 11.4 1 柜子/衣柜里有两件红毛衣。 **guìzi/yīguì li yǒu liǎng jiàn hóng máoyī** 2 厨房里有一个大炉子。 **chúfáng li yǒu yī gè dà lúzi** 3 书架上有很多书。 **shūjià shang yǒu hěn duō shū** 4 教室里有很多学生。 **jiàoshì li yǒu hěn duō xuésheng** 5 游泳池里都是人。 **yóuyǒngchí li dōu shì rén** 6 房间/屋子里一把椅子也没有。 **fángjiān/wùzi li yī bǎ yǐzi yě méi yǒu** 7 抽屉里什么也没有。 **chōuti li shénme yě méi yǒu** 8 花园里没有花儿。 **huāyuán li méi yǒu huār** 9 办公室里没有电话。 **bàngōngshì li méi yǒu diànhuà** 10 山脚下有一群羊。 **shānjiǎo xià yǒu yī qún yáng** 11 饭店对面是电影院。 **fàndiàn duìmiàn shì diànyǐngyuàn** 12 锅里有很多饭。 **guō li yǒu hěn duō fàn** 13 瓶子里只有一点儿牛奶。 **píngzi li zhǐ yǒu yīdiǎnr niúnǎi** 14 地板上都是玩具。 **dìbǎn shang dōu shì wánjù** 15 (那栋)房子里没有人。 **(nà/nèi dòng) fángzi li méi yǒu rén**

Exercise 11.5 1 这是(一张)车票，不是(一张)电影票。 **zhè shì (yī zhāng) chēpiào | bù shì (yī zhāng) diànyǐngpiào** 2 那是一对鸳鸯，不是一对普通的鸭子。 **nà shì yī duì yuānyāng | bù shì yī duì pǔtōng de yāzi** 3 那些是土豆/马铃薯，不是番薯。**nà/nèi xiē shì tǔdòu/mǎlíngshǔ | bù shì fānshǔ** 4 这些是蜜蜂，不是苍蝇。 **zhè/zhèi xiē shì mìfēng | bù shì cāngying** 5 这是汽油，不是菜油。 **zhè shì qìyóu | bù shì càiyóu** 6 那是张经理，不是李工程师。 **nà shì zhāng jīnglǐ | bù shì lǐ gōngchéngshī** 7 外面只有一辆自行车，没有汽车。 **wàimian zhǐ yǒu yī liàng zìxíngchē | méi yǒu qìchē** 8 盒子里有珠子，但是没有耳环。 **hézi li yǒu zhūzi | dànshì méi yǒu ěrhuán** 9 墙上只有一幅地图，没

有画儿。 **qiáng shang zhǐ yǒu yī fú dìtú | méi yǒu huàr**   10 我有一包(香)烟，但是没有火柴。 **wǒ yǒu yī bāo (xiāng)yān | dànshì méi yǒu huǒchái**   11 厨房里有一个炉子，没有冰箱。 **chúfáng li yǒu yī gè lúzi | méi yǒu bīngxiāng**   12 我只有一把刀，没有剪刀。 **wǒ zhǐ yǒu yī bǎ dāo | méi yǒu jiǎndāo**   13 这些都不是她的。 **zhè/zhèi xiē dōu bù shì tā de**   14 那些不都好。 **nà/nèi xiē bù dōu hǎo**   15 那些都不好。 **nà/nèi xiē dōu bù hǎo**

Unit 12

Exercise 12.1   1 飞机比火车快。 **fēijī bǐ huǒchē kuài** Planes are faster than trains.   2 法国跟美国不一样大。 **fǎguó gēn měiguó bù yīyàng dà** France and America are not the same size.   3 春天比冬天暖和。 **chūntiān bǐ dōngtiān nuǎnhuo** Spring is warmer than winter.   4 猫比老虎小得多。 **māo bǐ lǎohǔ xiǎo de duō** Cats are much smaller than tigers.   5 阿尔卑斯山没有喜马拉雅山那么高。 **ā'ěrbēisī shān méiyǒu xīmǎlāyǎ shān nàme gāo** The Alps aren't as high as the Himalayas.   6 中国的人口比俄国的人口多。 **zhōngguó de rénkǒu bǐ éguó de rénkǒu duō** China's population is bigger than Russia's.   7 金字塔和长城一样有名。 **jīnzìtǎ hè chángchéng yīyàng yǒumíng** The Pyramids and the Great Wall are equally famous.   8 小李没有老张那么勤奋。 **xiǎo lǐ méiyǒu lǎo zhāng nàme qínfèn** Xiao Li is not as diligent as Lao Zhang.   9 炒饭比炒面好吃得多。 **chǎofàn bǐ chǎomiàn hǎochī de duō** Fried rice is much nicer than fried noodles.   10 你的行李比我的行李重两公斤。 **nǐ de xíngli bǐ wǒ de xíngli zhòng liǎng gōngjīn** Your luggage is 2 kilos heavier than mine.

Exercise 12.2   1 鲸鱼比鲨鱼大。 **jīngyú bǐ shāyú dà** Whales are bigger than sharks.   2 摄象机比照相机贵。 **shèxiàngjī bǐ zhàoxiàngjī guì** Video cameras are more expensive than cameras.   3 苹果比桃子硬。 **píngguǒ bǐ táozi yìng** Apples are harder than peaches.   4 那个城市比这个城市美丽。 **nà/nèi gè chéngshì bǐ zhè/zhèi gè chéngshì měilì** That city is more beautiful than this one.   5 英国的夏天比春天热。 **yīngguó de xiàtiān bǐ chūntiān rè** Summer in Britain is hotter than spring.   6 德语比法语难。 **déyǔ bǐ fǎyǔ nán** German is more difficult than French.   7 我比你重。 **wǒ bǐ nǐ zhòng** I am heavier than you.   8 长江比黄河长。 **chángjiāng bǐ huánghé cháng** The Yangtze River is longer than the Yellow River.   9 你的肩膀比他的宽。 **nǐ de jiānbǎng bǐ tā de kuān** Your shoulders are broader than his.   10 那首歌比这首歌好听。 **nà/nèi shǒu gē bǐ zhè/zhèi shǒu gē hǎotīng** That song is nicer than this one.

Exercise 12.3   1 胖得多 **pàng de duō**   2 长得多 **cháng de duō**   3 便宜一点儿/一些 **piányi yīdiǎnr/yīxiē**   4 瘦一点儿/一些 **shòu yīdiǎnr/yīxiē**   5 小两岁 **xiǎo liǎng suì**   6 贵两镑 **guì liǎng bàng**   7 有趣得多 **yǒuqù de duō**   8 漂亮一点儿/一些 **piàoliang yīdiǎnr/yīxiē**   9 新鲜得多 **xīnxiān de duō**   10 干净一点儿/一些 **gānjìng yīdiǎnr/yīxiē**

Exercise 12.4 1 最 **zuì** 2 更 **gèng** 3 还要 **hái (yào)** 4 最 **zuì** 5 最 **zuì**
6 最 **zuì** 7 更 **gèng** 8 更 **gèng** 9 还要 **hái (yào)** 10 还要 **hái (yào)**

Exercise 12.5 1 他比其他人来得早。 **tā bǐ qítā rén lái de zǎo** 他来得比其他
人早。 **tā lái de bǐ qítā rén zǎo** 2 她走得比他慢。 **tā zǒu de bǐ tā màn** 她比他
走得慢。 **tā bǐ tā zǒu de màn** 3 昨天他睡得比我晚。 **zuótiān tā shuì de bǐ wǒ
wǎn** 昨天他比我睡得晚。 **zuótiān tā bǐ wǒ shuì de wǎn** 4 我妻子开车开得比
我好。 **wǒ qīzi kāichē kāi de bǐ wǒ hǎo** 我妻子开车比我开得好。 **wǒ qīzi kāichē
bǐ wǒ kāi de hǎo** 5 我的一个同学唱歌唱得比我好。 **wǒ de yī gè tóngxué chàng
gē chàng de bǐ wǒ hǎo** 我的一个同学唱歌比我唱得好。 **wǒ de yī gè tóngxué
chàng gē bǐ wǒ chàng de hǎo** 6 我丈夫打网球打得比我好。 **wǒ zhàngfu dǎ
wǎngqiú dǎ de bǐ wǒ hǎo** 我丈夫打网球比我打得好。 **wǒ zhàngfu dǎ wǎngqiú
bǐ wǒ dǎ de hǎo** 7 我哥哥比我高一英寸。 **wǒ gēge bǐ wǒ gāo yī yīngcùn**
8 妹妹比姐姐轻半公斤。 **mèimei bǐ jiějie qīng bàn gōngjīn** 9 松鼠有老鼠那
么大吗？ **sōngshǔ yǒu lǎoshǔ nàme dà ma** 10 这幢房子没有那幢那么漂亮。
zhè/zhèi zhuàng fángzi méiyǒu nà/nèi zhuàng nàme piàoliang

Exercise 12.6 1 我越来越饿。 **wǒ yuè lái yuè è** 2 厨师越来越胖。 **chúshī
yuè lái yuè pàng** 3 那匹马在比赛中越跑越慢/跑得越来越慢。 **nà/nèi pǐ mǎ zài
bǐsài zhōng yuè pǎo yuè màn/pǎo de yuè lái yuè màn** 4 足球比赛越来越
精彩。 **zúqiú bǐsài yuè lái yuè jīngcǎi** 5 路越来越宽。 **lù yuè lái yuè kuān**
6 祖父的病越来越严重。 **zǔfù de bìng yuè lái yuè yánzhòng** 7 他越喝越醉。
tā yuè hē yuè zuì 8 越快越好。 **yuè kuài yuè hǎo** 9 他越唱我越不高兴。
tā yuè chàng wǒ yuè bù gāoxìng 10 (菜)越辣我越喜欢。 **(cài) yuè là wǒ yuè
xǐhuan**

Unit 13

Exercise 13.1 1 上 **shang** 2 里 **li** 3 旁(边) **páng(biān)** 4 外 **wài** 5 (底)下
(dǐ)xia 6 附近 **fùjìn** 7 那儿 **nàr** 8 四周 **sìzhōu** 9 东面 **dōngmiàn**/东边
dōngbian 10 左边/面 **zuǒbian/miàn,** 右边/面 **yòubian/miàn** 11 旁边
pángbiān 12 中间 **zhōngjiān** 13 里面/(边)/(头) **lǐ(mian)/(bian)/(tou)** 14 左面/
边 **zuǒmiàn/bian** 15 中间 **zhōngjiān** 16 右面/边 **yòumiàn/bian** 17 后面/
边/头 **hòumian/bian/tou** 18 周围 **zhōuwéi**

Exercise 13.2 1 在大学(里) **zài dàxué (li)** 2 在车站 **zài chēzhàn** 3 在柜子
里(面)/(边)/(头) **zài guìzi lǐ(mian)/(bian)/(tou)** 4 在城市北面/北边/北部
zài chéngshì běimiàn/běibian/běibù 5 在盒子/箱子里 **zài hézi/xiāngzi li**
6 在床上(面)/(边) **zài chuáng shàng(mian)/(bian)** 7 在屋子中间 **zài wūzi
zhōngjiān** 8 在山脚下 **zài shānjiǎo xià** 9 在车上 **zài chē shang** 10 在树
(底)下 **zài shù (dǐ)xia** 11 在妈妈旁边 **zài māma pángbiān** 12 在游泳池
上边/面/头 **zài yóuyǒngchí shàngbian/mian/tou** 13 在图书馆前面/边/头 **zài**

túshūguǎn qiánmian/bian/tou   14 在房子后面/边/头 **zài fángzi hòumian/bian/ tou**   15 在河边/旁/旁边 **zài hé biān/páng/pángbiān**   16 在桌(子)上(面)/(边) **zài zhuō(zi) shàng(mian)/(bian)**   17 在公园附近 **zài gōngyuán fùjìn**   18 在孩子 周围 **zài háizi zhōuwéi**   19 在祖父家里/那儿 **zài zǔfù jiā li/nàr**   20 在西面/边 **zài xīmiàn/bian**

Exercise 13.3   1 报纸在桌子上(面)/(边)。 **bàozhǐ zài zhuōzi shàng(mian)/ (bian)**   2 他们在屋子里开会。 **tāmen zài wūzi li kāihuì**   3 泰晤士河是英国有 名的河。 **tàiwùshì hé shì yīngguó yǒumíng de hé**   4 医生在病人的床边/旁边站 了一会儿，没有说话。 **yīshēng zài bìngrén de chuáng bian/pángbiān zhàn le yīhuìr | méiyǒu shuō huà**   5 correct   6 correct   7 你的钥匙在门上。 **nǐ de yàoshi zài mén shang**   8 叔叔在伦敦工作。 **shūshu zài lúndūn gōngzuò**   9 她在门前站着。 **tā zài mén qián zhàn zhe**   10 correct   11 金鱼在水池里游 着。 **jīnyú zài shuǐchí li yóu zhe**   12 电影院在鞋店左面/左边。 **diànyǐngyuàn zài xiédiàn zuǒmiàn/zuǒbian**   13 报纸上有不少广告。**bàozhǐ shang yǒu bù shǎo guǎnggào**   14 天上没有云。 **tiān shang méi yǒu yún**

Exercise 13.4   1 楼上 **lóushang**; 中间 **zhōngjiān**   2 东面 **dōngmiàn**; 左边 **zuǒbian**   3 楼下 **lóuxià**; 下面 **xiàmian**

Exercise 13.5   1 牛肉在锅里煮着。 **niú ròu zài guō li zhǔ zhe**   2 我的一个 朋友在一家医院工作。 **wǒ de yī gè péngyou zài yī jiā yīyuàn gōngzuò** 我的一个 朋友在一家医院里工作。 **wǒ de yī gè péngyou zài yī jiā yīyuàn li gōngzuò**   3 我们住在巴黎。 **wǒmen zhù zài bālí**/我们在巴黎住。 **wǒmen zài bālí zhù** (*not*: *我们在巴黎住着。 **wǒmen zài bālí zhù zhe**)   4 她在博物馆等你。 **tā zài bówùguǎn děng nǐ**/她在博物馆里等你。 **tā zài bówùguǎn li děng nǐ**   5 有一群羊 在山脚下吃草。 **yǒu yī qún yáng zài shānjiǎo xià chī cǎo**   6 我叔叔在海边 晒太阳。 **wǒ shūshu zài hǎi biān shài tàiyáng**

Unit 14

Exercise 14.1   1 我明天去北京。 **wǒ míngtiān qù běijīng** 明天我去北京。 **míngtiān wǒ qù běijīng**   2 我去北京两天。 **wǒ qù běijīng liǎng tiān**   3 我去年 去了北京。 **wǒ qùnián qù le běijīng** 去年我去了北京。 **qùnián wǒ qù le běijīng**   4 我两天后去北京。 **wǒ liǎng tiān hòu qù běijīng** 两天后我去北京。 **liǎng tiān hòu wǒ qù běijīng**   5 我结婚前去北京。 **wǒ jiéhūn qián qù běijīng** 结婚前我去北京。 **jiéhūn qián wǒ qù běijīng**   6 明年我要去北京两次。 **míngnián wǒ yào qù běijīng liǎng cì** 我明年要去北京两次。 **wǒ míngnián yào qù běijīng liǎng cì** 明年我要去两次北京。 **míngnián wǒ yào qù liǎng cì běijīng** 我明年要去两次北京。 **wǒ míngnián yào qù liǎng cì běijīng**   7 我半年没去 北京了。 **wǒ bàn nián méi qù běijīng le** 我没去北京半年了。 **wǒ méi qù běijīng bàn nián le**   8 我每年夏天去北京半个月。 **wǒ měi nián xiàtiān qù běijīng bàn gè yuè** 每年夏天我去北京半个月。 **měi nián xiàtiān wǒ qù běijīng bàn gè yuè**

Exercise 14.2   1 他前年去了上海。 **tā qiánnián qù le shànghǎi** 前年他去了上海。 **qiánnián tā qù le shànghǎi**   2 妈妈上个月离开(了)英国。 **māma shàng gè yuè líkāi (le) yīngguó** 上个月妈妈离开(了)英国。 **shàng gè yuè māma líkāi (le) yīngguó**   3 哥哥星期二去游泳了。 **gēge xīngqī èr qù yóuyǒng le** 星期二哥哥去游泳了。 **xīngqī èr gēge qù yóuyǒng le**   4 爷爷每天(都)看两、三个小时(的)小说。 **yéye měi tiān (dōu) kàn liǎng | sān gè xiǎoshí (de) xiǎoshuō** 每天爷爷(都)看两、三个小时(的)小说。 **měi tiān yéye (dōu) kàn liǎng | sān gè xiǎoshí (de) xiǎoshuō** 5 我现在在学习汉语。 **wǒ xiànzài zài xuéxí hànyǔ** 现在我在学习汉语。 **xiànzài wǒ zài xuéxí hànyǔ**   6 我们全家下个周末去海滨。 **wǒmen quán jiā xià gè zhōumò qù hǎibīn** 下个周末我们全家去海滨。 **xià gè zhōumò wǒmen quán jiā qù hǎibīn**   7 我们每个星期四晚上(都)去跳舞。 **wǒmen měi gè xīngqī sì wǎnshang (dōu) qù tiàowǔ** 每个星期四晚上我们(都)去跳舞。 **měi gè xīngqī sì wǎnshang wǒmen (dōu) qù tiàowǔ**   8 小张下(个)星期一去银行。 **xiǎo zhāng xià (gè) xīngqī yī qù yínháng** 下(个)星期一小张去银行。 **xià (gè) xīngqī yī xiǎo zhāng qù yínháng**   9 请在这儿等我五分钟。 **qǐng zài zhèr děng wǒ wǔ fēn zhōng**   10 我去年去探望我父母两次。 **wǒ qùnián qù tànwàng wǒ fùmǔ liǎng cì** 去年我去探望我父母两次。 **qùnián wǒ qù tànwàng wǒ fùmǔ liǎng cì** 我去年去探望(了)两次我(的)父母。 **wǒ qùnián qù tànwàng (le) liǎng cì wǒ (de) fùmǔ** 去年我去探望(了)两次我(的)父母。 **qùnián wǒ qù tànwàng (le) liǎng cì wǒ (de) fùmǔ**

Exercise 14.3   1 correct   2 他在海里游了一会儿泳。 **tā zài hǎi li yóu le yīhuìr yǒng**   3 我马上上班。 **wǒ mǎshàng shàngbān**   4 correct   5 我们永远记得他。 **wǒmen yǒngyuǎn jìde tā**   6 correct   7 我已经写了信了。 **wǒ yǐjing xiě le xìn le**   8 队长刚刚看见小李。 **duìzhǎng gānggāng kànjiàn xiǎo lǐ**   9 correct   10 correct   11 她来了这儿两次。 **tā lái le zhèr liǎng cì**   12 爷爷和奶奶今天散了半个钟头步。 **yéye hé nǎinai jīntiān sàn le bàn gè zhōngtóu bù**/爷爷和奶奶今天散步散了半个钟头。 **yéye hé nǎinai jīntiān sànbù sàn le bàn gè zhōngtóu**

Exercise 14.4   1 I swam for two hours this morning.   2 My English friend stayed in China for two months.   3 They have been learning Chinese for two years now.   4 The meeting has been going on for forty minutes./The meeting started forty minutes ago.   5 My coursemates and I are going to play football tomorrow afternoon.   6 (My) younger sister was writing letters the whole evening.   7 Mr Wang and his wife are going to China on holiday next year.   8 He graduated last June.   9 My younger brother bought a pair of beautiful sports shoes.   10 My father often goes to work by bicycle.   11 I stayed at his place for half an hour on three occasions.   12 She danced for three hours that evening.

Exercise 14.5   1 你在中国的时候尝/吃过馒头没有？ **nǐ zài zhōngguó de shíhou cháng/chī guo mántou méiyǒu**   2 你能在外面等一会儿吗？ **nǐ néng zài wàimian děng yīhuìr ma**   3 咱们在公园里坐一会儿吧。 **zánmen zài**

gōngyuán li zuò yīhuìr ba   4 你能帮/替我看(管)一会儿孩子吗？ **nǐ néng bāng/ tì wǒ kān(guǎn) yīhuìr háizi ma**   5 我们去采了一(个)小时草莓。 **wǒmen qù cǎi le yī (gè) xiǎoshí cǎoméi**   6 他看了一下那张照片。 **tā kàn le yīxià nà/nèi zhāng zhàopiàn**/他看了看那张照片。 **ta kàn le kàn nà/nèi zhāng zhàopiàn** 7 请(你)先看一下今天的报纸。 **qǐng (nǐ) xiān kàn yīxià jīntiān de bàozhǐ**/ 请(你)先看一看今天的报纸。 **qǐng (nǐ) xiān kàn yī kàn jīntiān de bàozhǐ** 8 他整整一年没喝过酒了。 **tā zhěngzhěng yī nián méi hē guo jiǔ le**   9 我认识 他三年了。 **wǒ rènshi tā sān nián le**   10 我已经洗过/了澡了。 **wǒ yǐjing xǐ guo/le zǎo le**

Unit 15

Exercise 15.1   1 在 **zài**   2 着 **zhe**   3 过 **guo**   4 着 **zhe**   5 着 **zhe**   6 了 **le**   7 过 **guo**   8 在 **zài**   9 了 **le**   10 过 **guo**   11 在 **zài**   12 在 **zài**   13 在 **zài**   14 了/过 **le/guo**   15 了 **le**

Exercise 15.2   1 他(正)在擦窗(户)。 **tā (zhèng)zài cā chuāng(hu)**   2 他们 到/来过这儿。 **tāmen dào/lái guo zhèr**   3 我(正)在浇花。 **wǒ (zhèng)zài jiāo huā**   4 我的朋友(正)在喝啤酒。 **wǒ de péngyou (zhèng)zài hē píjiǔ**   5 (那位) 教师站着讲课。 **(nà/nèi wèi) jiàoshī zhàn zhe jiǎngkè**   6 他跳起舞来。 **tā tiào qǐ wǔ lái**   7 他(正)在开车。 **tā (zhèng)zài kāichē**   8 她买了一双鞋。 **tā mǎi le yī shuāng xié**   9 爷爷(正)在看电视。 **yéye (zhèng)zài kàn diànshì**   10 妈妈 戴着一顶漂亮的帽子。 **māma dài zhe yī dǐng piàoliang de màozi**

Exercise 15.3   1 起来 **qǐlái**   2 下来 **xiàlái**   3 下去 **xiàqù**   4 起来 **qǐlái** 5 下来 **xiàlái**   6 下去 **xiàqù**   7 起来 **qǐlái**   8 起来 **qǐlái**   9 起来 **qǐlái** 10 下来 **xiàlái**

Exercise 15.4   1 讲下去 **jiǎng xiàqù**   2 学习起来 **xuéxí qǐlái**   3 写起信来 **xiě qǐ xìn lái**   4 学下去 **xué xiàqù**   5 correct   6 吵起架来 **chǎo qǐ jià lái** 7 游起泳来 **yóu qǐ yǒng lái**   8 correct   9 聪明起来 **cóngming qǐlái** 10 correct

Unit 16

Exercise 16.1   1 我想休息一会儿。 **wǒ xiǎng xiūxi yīhuìr**   2 你要早点儿 起床。 **nǐ yào zǎo diǎnr qǐchuáng**   3 他想去中国旅游。 **tā xiǎng qù zhōngguó lǚyóu**   4 你想喝点儿什么？ **nǐ xiǎng hē diǎnr shénme**   5 你要好好儿学习。 **nǐ yào hǎohāor xuéxí**   6 妈妈想买一件外套。 **māma xiǎng mǎi yī jiàn wàitào**

Exercise 16.2   1 能 **néng**   2 会 **huì**   3 该 **gāi**   4 能 **néng**   5 可以 **kěyǐ** 6 会 **huì**; 肯 **kěn**   7 必须 **bìxū**   8 必 **bì**

Exercise 16.3 1 不愿意 **bù yuànyì** 2 不敢 **bù gǎn** 3 可以 **kěyǐ** 4 不肯 **bù kěn** 5 不想 **bù xiǎng** 6 要 **yào**/想 **xiǎng** 7 敢 **gǎn** 8 得 **děi** 9 不必 **bù bì** 10 该 **gāi** 11 必须 **bìxū** 12 不该 **bù gāi** 13 可以 **kěyǐ** 14 会 **huì** 15 能 **néng** 16 可以 **kěyǐ** 17 不能 **bù néng** 18 会 **huì** 19 会 **huì** 20 会 **huì**; 不能 **bù néng** 21 会 **huì**; 能 **néng** 22 不能 **bù néng** 23 能 **néng** 24 能 **néng** 25 会 **huì** 26 会 **huì** 27 能 **néng** 28 不应该 **bù yīnggāi**

Exercise 16.4 1 你会开车吗？ **nǐ huì kāichē ma** 2 周末会下雨吗？ **zhōumò huì xià yǔ ma** 3 你想去探望/看望你父母吗？ **nǐ xiǎng qù tànwàng/kànwàng nǐ fùmǔ ma** 4 你必须/该去复习功课了。 **nǐ bìxū/gāi qù fùxí gōngkè le** 5 这个星期我们能去海滩吗？ **zhè/zhèi gè xīngqī wǒmen néng qù hǎitān ma** 6 我必须/得记住音乐会的时间。 **wǒ bìxū/děi jìzhù yīnyuèhuì de shíjiān** 7 你们不应该打架。 **nǐmen bù yīnggāi dǎjià** 8 我三月份/明年三月能/可以休假吗？ **wǒ sān yuèfèn/míngnián sān yuè néng/kěyǐ xiūjià ma** 9 你愿意帮助他吗？ **nǐ yuànyì bāngzhù tā ma** 10 她不敢乘/坐飞机。 **tā bù gǎn chéng/zuò fēijī**

Unit 17

Exercise 17.1 1 不 **bù** 2 没(有) **méi(yǒu)** 3 没(有) **méi(yǒu)** 4 没(有) **méi(yǒu)** 5 没(有) **méi(yǒu)** 6 不 **bù** 7 不 **bù** 8 不 **bù** 9 没(有) **méi(yǒu)** 10 没(有) **méi(yǒu)** 11 没(有) **méi(yǒu)** 12 不 **bù** 13 不 **bù** 14 没(有) **méi(yǒu)** 15 不 **bù**

Exercise 17.2 1 孩子们都不喜欢吃蔬菜。 **háizimen dōu bù xǐhuan chī shūcài** None of the children like eating vegetables. 2 他们也没有去看京剧。 **tāmen yě méiyǒu qù kàn jīngjù** They didn't go to watch the Beijing Opera either. 3 他吃饭前常常不洗手。 **tǎ chīfàn qián chángcháng bù xǐ shǒu** He doesn't often wash his hands before meals. 4 我从来不抽烟。 **wǒ cónglái bù chōuyān** I have never smoked. 5 她刚才没喝茶。 **tā gāngcái méi hē chá** She didn't drink any tea just now. 6 他今天没看电视。 **tā jīntiān méi kàn diànshì** He didn't watch TV today. 7 她那天没吃蛋糕。 **tā nà/nèi tiān méi chī dàngāo** She didn't touch the cake that day. 8 妹妹从来没坐过飞机。 **mèimei cónglái méi zuò guo fēijī** (My) younger sister has never flown in a plane before.

Exercise 17.3 1 我认为那个答案不对。 **wǒ rènwéi nà/nèi gè dá'àn bù duì** 2 我认为这不值得多想。 **wǒ rènwéi zhè bù zhíde duō xiǎng** 3 我从来没有喜欢过她。 **wǒ cónglái méiyǒu xǐhuan guo tā** 4 他没穿大衣。 **tā méi chuān dàyī**

Exercise 17.4 1 他不可以在那幢房子的墙上写标语。 **tā bù kěyǐ zài nà/nèi zhuàng fángzi de qiáng shang xiě biāoyǔ** 2 你不会包饺子吗？ **nǐ bù huì bāo jiǎozi ma** 3 经理不愿意加陈先生的工资。 **jīnglǐ bù yuànyì jiā chén xiānsheng de gōngzī** 4 我这个星期/礼拜能不来吗？ **wǒ zhè/zhèi gè xīngqī/lǐbài néng bù**

lái ma   5 她来英国前(从来)没见过松鼠。 **tā lái yīngguó qián (cónglái) méi jiàn guo sōngshǔ**   6 妹妹不敢去邻居那儿借椅子。 **mèimei bù gǎn qù línjū nàr jiè yǐzi**   7 裤子太短，弟弟不肯/愿意穿。 **kùzi tài duǎn | dìdi bù kěn/yuànyì chuān**   8 水果一点儿也不新鲜，谁也/大家都不想吃。 **shuǐguǒ yīdiǎnr yě bù xīnxiān | shuí/shéi yě/dàjiā dōu bù xiǎng chī**   9 昨天下大雨，我们没(有)去操场踢足球。 **zuótiān xià dà yǔ | wǒmen méi(yǒu) qù cāochǎng tī zúqiú**   10 你不该告诉他们这件事。 **nǐ bù gāi gàosu tāmen zhè/zhèi jiàn shì**   11 这些花儿不香，蜜蜂不来采蜜。 **zhè/zhèi xiē huār bù xiāng | mìfēng bù lái cǎi mì**   12 草莓没有桃子好吃。 **cǎoméi méiyǒu táozi hǎochī**

Unit 18

Exercise 18.1   1 他们是农民吗？ **tāmen shì nóngmín ma** 他们是不是农民？ **tāmen shì bù shì nóngmín** 是。 **shì** 不是。 **bù shì**   2 他想打乒乓球吗？ **tā xiǎng dǎ pīngpāngqiú ma** 他想不想打乒乓球？ **tā xiǎng bù xiǎng dǎ pīngpāngqiú** 想。 **xiǎng** 不想。 **bù xiǎng**   3 他去过动物园吗？ **tā qù guo dòngwùyuán ma** 他去过动物园没有？ **tā qù guo dòngwùyuán méiyǒu** 去过。 **qù guo** 没有。/没(有)去过。 **méiyǒu/méi(yǒu) qù guo**   4 那条街干净吗？ **nà/nèi tiáo jiē gānjìng ma**/那条街干(净)不干净？ **nà/nèi tiáo jiē gān(jìng) bù gānjìng** 干净。 **gānjìng** 不干净。 **bù gānjìng**   5 她明天会来吗？ **tā míngtiān huì lái ma**/她明天会不会来？ **tā míngtiān huì bù huì lái** 会。 **huì** 不会。 **bù huì**   6 他有图书证吗？ **tā yǒu túshūzhèng ma**/他有没有图书证？ **tā yǒu méi yǒu túshūzhèng** 有。 **yǒu** 没有。 **méiyǒu**   7 她带了钥匙吗？ **tā dài le yàoshi ma**/她带了钥匙没有？ **tā dài le yàoshi méiyǒu**/她带没带钥匙？ **tā dài méi dài yàoshi**/她有没有带钥匙？ **tā yǒu méiyǒu dài yàoshi** 带了。 **dài le** 没有。/没(有)带。 **méiyǒu/méi(yǒu) dài**   8 火旺吗？ **huǒ wàng ma**/火旺不旺？ **huǒ wàng bù wàng** 很旺。 **hěn wàng** 不旺。 **bù wàng**   9 你的朋友会哼那个曲了吗？ **nǐ de péngyou huì hēng nà/nèi gè qǔzi ma**/你的朋友会不会哼那个曲了？ **nǐ de péngyou huì bù huì hēng nà/nèi gè qǔzi** 会。 **huì** 不会。 **bù huì**   10 他的弟弟喜欢穿牛仔裤吗？ **tā de dìdi xǐhuan chuān niúzǎikù ma**/他的弟弟喜(欢)不喜欢穿牛仔裤？ **tā de dìdi xǐ(huan) bù xǐhuan chuān niúzǎikù** 喜欢。 **xǐhuan** 不喜欢。 **bù xǐhuan**

Exercise 18.2   1 你洗了衬衫没有？ **nǐ xǐ le chènshān méiyǒu** Did you wash the shirt?   2 你昨天读了报没有？ **nǐ zuótiān dú le bào méiyǒu** Did you read the newspaper yesterday?   3 上个月你看了电影没有？ **shàng gè yuè nǐ kàn le diànyǐng méiyǒu** Did you watch a film last month?   4 昨晚你写了信没有？ **zuó wǎn nǐ xiě le xìn méiyǒu** Did you write letters last night?   5 你买了票没有？ **nǐ mǎi le piào méiyǒu** Have you bought the ticket?   6 她碰见了张先生没有？ **tā pèngjiàn le zhāng xiānsheng méiyǒu** Did she bump into Mr Zhang?   7 你们前天上了酒吧间没有？ **nǐmen qiántiān shàng le jiǔbājiān méiyǒu** Did you go to the pub the day before yesterday?   8 你们那儿上星期下了雪没有？ **nǐmen nàr shàng xīngqī xià le xuě méiyǒu** Did you have any snow in your area last week?

9 他家去年夏天去了海边度假没有？ **tā jiā qùnián xiàtiān qù le hǎi biān dùjià méiyǒu** Did his family go to the seaside on holiday last summer? 10 这件事小黄告诉了你没有？ **zhè/zhèi jiàn shì xiǎo huáng gàosu le nǐ méiyǒu** Did Xiao Huang tell you about this?/Has Xiao Huang told you about this?

Exercise 18.3 1 你爬过山吗/没有？ **nǐ pá guo shān ma/méiyǒu** 2 你碰见过你的邻居吗/没有？ **nǐ pèngjiàn guo nǐ de línjū ma/méiyǒu** 3 你责备过你自己吗/没有？ **nǐ zébèi guo nǐ zìjǐ ma/méiyǒu** 4 你看过足球比赛吗/没有？ **nǐ kàn guo zúqiú bǐsài ma/méiyǒu** 5 你骑过马吗/没有？ **nǐ qí guo mǎ ma/méiyǒu** 6 你去过海边吗/没有？ **nǐ qù guo hǎi biān ma/méiyǒu** 7 你尝/吃过饺子吗/没有？ **nǐ cháng/chī guo jiǎozi ma/méiyǒu** 8 你见过鲸鱼吗/没有？ **nǐ jiàn guo jīngyú ma/méiyǒu** 9 你养过狗吗/没有？ **nǐ yǎng guo gǒu ma/méiyǒu** 10 你去/进过酒吧间吗/没有？ **nǐ qù/jìn guo jiǔbājiān ma/méiyǒu**

All the sentences may also be translated as: 1 你有没有爬过山？ **nǐ yǒu méiyǒu pá guo shān** 2 你有没有碰见过你的邻居？ **nǐ yǒu méiyǒu pèngjiàn guo nǐ de línjū** etc.

Exercise 18.4 1 图书馆安静吗/安(静)不安静？ **túshūguǎn ānjìng ma/ān(jìng) bù ānjìng** 2 北京热吗/热不热？ **běijīng rè ma/rè bù rè** 3 你的朋友高兴吗/高(兴)不高兴？ **nǐ de péngyou gāoxìng ma/gāo(xìng) bù gāoxìng** 4 菜好吃吗/好(吃)不好吃？ **cài hǎochī ma/hǎo(chī) bù hǎochī** 5 那个电视节目有趣吗/有没有趣？ **nà gè diànshì jiémù yǒuqù ma/yǒu méiyǒu qù** 6 足球比赛精彩吗/精(彩)不精彩？ **zúqiú bǐsài jīngcǎi ma/jīng(cǎi) bù jīngcǎi** 7 这把椅子舒服吗/舒(服)不舒服？ **zhè/zhèi bǎ yǐzi shūfu ma/shū(fu) bù shūfu** 8 花儿香吗/香不香？ **huār xiāng ma/xiāng bù xiāng** 9 蛋糕甜吗/甜不甜？ **dàngāo tián ma/tián bù tián** 10 桌子干净吗/干(净)不干净？ **zhuōzi gānjìng ma/gān(jìng) bù gānjìng** 11 房间整齐吗/整(齐)不整齐？ **fángjiān zhěngqí ma/zhěng(qí) bù zhěngqí** 12 经理慷慨吗/慷慨不慷慨？ **jīnglǐ kāngkǎi ma/kāngkǎi bù kāngkǎi**

Exercise 18.5 1 他喝醉了呢？ **tā hē zuì le ne** 2 裤子洗了。衬衫呢？ **kùzi xǐ le | chènshān ne** 3 明天晚上下雨呢？ **míngtiān wǎnshang xià yǔ ne** 4 我没(有)时间呢？ **wǒ méi(yǒu) shíjiān ne** 5 咖啡很好喝/不错。蛋糕呢？ **kāfēi hěn hǎohē/bù cuò | dàngāo ne** 6 我很忙。你呢？ **wǒ hěn máng | nǐ ne** 7 她去了哪儿呢？ **tā qù le nǎr ne** 8 这是谁的电脑呢？ **zhè shì shuí/shéi de diànnǎo ne** 9 我的钥匙呢？ **wǒ de yàoshi ne** 10 小猫(在哪儿)呢？ **xiǎo māo (zài nǎr) ne**

Unit 19

Exercise 19.1 1 请你关上窗(户)，好吗？ **qǐng nǐ guān shàng chuāng(hù) | hǎo ma** 2 请你们说中文，行/可以吗？ **qǐng nǐmen shuō zhōngwén | xíng/kěyǐ ma** 3 我用一下电话，行/可以吗？ **wǒ yòng yīxià diànhuà | xíng/kěyǐ ma**

4 咱们去看电影，好吗？ **zánmen qù kàn diànyǐng| hǎo ma** 5 我借一支笔，可以/行吗？ **wǒ jiè yī zhī bǐ | kěyǐ/xíng ma** 6 我明天睡懒觉，可以/行吗？ **wǒ míngtiān shuì lǎn jiào | kěyǐ/xíng ma** 7 我坐在这儿，行/可以吗？ **wǒ zuò zài zhèr | xíng/kěyǐ ma** 8 我提个建议，好/行/可以吗？ **wǒ tí gè jiànyì | hǎo/xíng/kěyǐ ma** 9 你给我们讲个故事，好吗？ **nǐ gěi wǒmen jiǎng gè gùshi | hǎo ma** 10 我们今晚去跳舞，好/行吗？ **wǒmen jīn wǎn qù tiàowǔ | hǎo/xíng ma**

Exercise 19.2 1(i) 是不是小李骑自行车去运动场？ **shì bù shì xiǎo lǐ qí zìxíngchē qù yùndòngchǎng** (ii) 小李是不是去运动场？ **xiǎo lǐ shì bù shì qù yùndòngchǎng** (iii) 小李是不是骑自行车去运动场？ **xiǎo lǐ shì bù shì qí zìxíngchē qù yùndòngchǎng** 2(i) 是不是王小姐去的邮局？ **shì bù shì wáng xiǎojie qù de yóujú** (ii) 王小姐是不是刚才去的邮局？ **wáng xiǎojie shì bù shì gāngcái qù de yóujú** (iii) 王小姐是不是去的邮局？ **wáng xiǎojie shì bù shì qù de yóujú**

Exercise 19.3 1 你是老师还是学生？ **nǐ shì lǎoshī háishi xuésheng** 2 他喜欢看小说还是(喜欢)看电视？ **tā xǐhuan kàn xiǎoshuō háishi (xǐhuan) kàn diànshì** 3 他是昨天还是前天去的中国？ **tā shì zuótiān háishi qiántiān qù de zhōngguó** 4 你是坐火车还是坐汽车去上班？ **nǐ shì zuò huǒchē háishi zuò qìchē qù shàngbān** 5 你是去电影院还是去饭馆？ **nǐ shì qù diànyǐngyuàn háishi qù fànguǎn** 6 这是医院还是大学？ **zhè/zhèi shì yīyuàn háishi dàxué** 7 她那天是穿的裙子还是(穿的)裤子？ **tā nà/nèi tiān shì chuān de qúnzi háishi (chuān de) kùzi** 8 你前天是碰见的老王还是小张？ **nǐ qiántiān shì pèngjiàn de lǎo wáng háishi xiǎo zhāng**

Exercise 19.4 1 这本书是你写的吧？ **zhè/zhèi běn shū shì nǐ xiě de ba** This book was written by you, wasn't it?/You wrote this book, didn't you? 是的。 **shì de** 不是的。 **bù shì de** 2 伦敦离北京很远吧？ **lúndūn lí běijīng hěn yuǎn ba** London is a long way from Beijing, isn't it? 是的。 **shì de** 3 火车已经开走了吧？ **huǒchē yǐjing kāi zǒu le ba** The train has already gone, hasn't it? 是的。 **shì de** 还没有。 **hái méiyǒu** Not yet. 4 那条裙子太长了吧？ **nà/nèi tiáo qúnzi tài cháng le ba** That skirt is too long, isn't it? 对/是的。 **duì/shì de** 不对/不是的。 **bù duì/bù shì de** 5 你每天都剃/刮胡子吧？ **nǐ měi tiān dōu tì/guā húzi ba** You shave every day, don't you? 是的。 **shì de** 不是的。 **bù shì de** 6 你爸爸、妈妈下个月去度假吧？ **nǐ bàba | māma xià gè yuè qù dùjià ba** Your parents are going away on holiday next month, aren't they? 对/是的。 **duì/shì de** 不对/不是的。 **bù duì/bù shì de** 7 你不喜欢喝中国茶吧？ **nǐ bù xǐhuan hē zhōngguó chá ba** You don't like Chinese tea, do you? 对/是的。 **duì/shì de** 不对/不是的。 **bù duì/bù shì de** 8 你妻子不吃牛肉吧？ **nǐ qīzi bù chī niúròu ba** Your wife doesn't eat beef, does she? 对/是的。 **duì/shì de** 不对/不是的。 **bù duì/bù shì de**

Note: 是的 **shì de** is interchangeable with 是 **shì** or 对 **duì** and 不是的 **bù shì de** with 不是 **bù shì** or 不对 **bù duì** in all answers.

Exercise 19.5 1 你是不是下个月去中国？ **nǐ shì bù shì xià gè yuè qù zhōngguó** 2 你是不是去年去的中国？ **nǐ shì bù shì qùnián qù de zhōngguó** 3 你是坐飞机去还是坐船去？ **nǐ shì zuò fēijī qù háishi zuò chuán qù** 4 你是开车去的还是骑自行车去的？ **nǐ shì kāichē qù de háishi qí zìxíngchē qù de** 5 你是在哪儿学的中文？ **nǐ shì zài nǎr xué de zhōngwén** 6 你是在哪儿学中文？ **nǐ shì zài nǎr xué zhōngwén** 7 昨晚是谁洗的碗？ **zuó wǎn shì shéi/shuí xǐ de wǎn** 8 今晚是谁洗碗？ **jīn wǎn shì shéi/shuí xǐ wǎn**

Unit 20

Exercise 20.1 1 进来！ **jìn lái** 2 站起来！ **zhàn qǐlái** 3 出去！ **chū qù** 4 坐下！ **zuò xià** 5 起来！ **qǐ lái** 6 快！ **kuài** 7 早点回来！ **zǎo diǎn huí lái** 8 关门！ **guān mén** 9 严肃(一)点儿！ **yánsù (yī)diǎnr** 10 不要/别关灯！ **bù yào/bié guān dēng**

Exercise 20.2 1 多吃(一)点儿吧！ **duō chī (yī)diǎnr ba** 2 咱们这儿下车吧。 **zánmen zhèr xià chē ba** 3 让他去吧。 **ràng tā qù ba** 4 快(一)点儿吧！ **kuài (yī)diǎnr ba** 5 请在这儿排队！ **qǐng zài zhèr páiduì** 6 请开灯！ **qǐng kāi dēng** 7 请进(来)！ **qǐng jìn (lái)** 8 咱们休息一会儿吧！ **zánmen xiūxi yīhuìr ba** 9 请听！是谁？ **qǐng tīng | shì shéi/shuí** 10 请开门。 **qǐng kāi mén**

Exercise 20.3 1 不要/别关窗！ **bù yào/bié guān chuāng** 2 不要/别关灯！ **bù yào/bié guān dēng** 3 不要/别晾衣服！ **bù yào/bié liàng yīfu** 4 不要/别上车！ **bù yào/bié shàng chē** 5 不要/别过来！ **bù yào/bié guò lái** 6 不要/别穿这双鞋！ **bù yào/bié chuān zhè/zhèi shuāng xié** 7 不要/别开车！ **bù yào/bié kāichē** 8 不要/别让他走！ **bù yào/bié ràng tā zǒu** 9 不要/别叫她回来！ **bù yào/bié jiào tā huí lái** 10 请大家不要/别带伞！ **qǐng dàjiā bù yào/bié dài sǎn**

Exercise 20.4 1(i) 咱们进去吧！ **zánmen jìn qù ba** (ii) 好吧。你进去吧！ **hǎo ba | nǐ jìn qù ba** 2(i) 你去割草，好吗？ **nǐ qù gē cǎo | hǎo ma** (ii) 请现在就去割草！ **qǐng xiànzài jiù qù gē cǎo** 3(i) 咱们下车吧！ **zánmen xià chē ba** (ii) 快，咱们在这儿下车！ **kuài | zánmen zài zhèr xià chē** 4(i) 咱们(去)喝一杯吧！ **zánmen (qù) hē yī bēi ba** (ii) 好吧，你(去)喝一杯吧！ **hǎo ba | nǐ (qù) hē yī bēi ba**

Exercise 20.5 1 啊 **a** 2 哇 **wa** 3 啊 **a** 4 啦 **la** 5 哇 **wa** 6 呀/啊 **ya/a** 7 哇 **wa** 8 哪 **na** 9 呀 **ya** 10 啊 **a** 11 呀 **ya** 12 哇/啊 **wa/a**

Unit 21

Exercise 21.1 1 回去 **huí qù** 2 过来 **guò lái** 3 上去 **shàng qù** 4 下来 **xià lái** 5 拿来 **ná lái** 6 出去 **chū qù** 7 回来 **huí lái** 8 拿去 **ná qù** 9 起来 **qǐ lái** 10 进去 **jìn qù** 11 过去 **guò qù** 12 出来 **chū lái** 13 回家来 **huí jiā lái** 14 开过桥去 **kāi guò qiáo qù** 15 爬上树去 **pá shàng shù qù** 16 下山

来 **xià shān lái**   17 带到教室来 **dài dào jiàoshì lái**   18 走出房子去 **zǒu chū fángzi qù**   19 跑回办公室去 **pǎo huí bàngōngshì qù**   20 带回医院去 **dài huí yīyuàn qù**   21 跳进游泳池去 **tiào jìn yóuyǒngchí qù**   22 走进邮局去 **zǒu jìn yóujú qù**   23 穿过马路去 **chuān guò mǎlù qù**   24 走出房间/屋子来 **zǒu chū fángjiān/wūzi lái**

Exercise 21.2   1 出去 **chūqù**   2 下来 **xiàlái**   3 下来 **xiàlái**   4 进来 **jìnlái**   5 过去 **guòqù**   6 出...去 **chū...qù**   7 回...去 **huí...qù**   8 回...去 **huí...qù**   9 上...来 **shàng...lái**   10 过...去 **guò...qù**   11 进...去 **jìn...qù**   12 进...去 **jìn...qù**

Exercise 21.3   1 老师走进图书馆去了。 **lǎoshī zǒu jìn túshūguǎn qù le** The teacher has gone into the library.   2 飞机飞过山去了。 **fēijī fēi guò shān qù le** The plane has flown over the hill.   3 我爬上山坡去。 **wǒ pá shàng shānpō qù** I climbed up the hillside.   4 孩子们跑过马路去了。 **háizimen pǎo guò mǎlù qù le** The children went across the road.   5 他们走出教堂去了。 **tāmen zǒu chū jiàotáng qù le** They went out of the church.   6 医生回医院去了。 **yīshēng huí yīyuàn qù le** The doctor has gone back to the hospital.   7 青蛙跳下水去了。 **qīngwā tiào xià shuǐ qù le** The frog jumped into the water.   8 车开过桥来了。 **chē kāi guò qiáo lái le** The car came over the bridge.   9 小鸡钻出蛋壳来了。 **xiǎo jī zuān chū dànké lái le** The chicken broke out of the shell.   10 小猫爬上树去了。 **xiǎo māo pá shàng shù qù le** The kitten climbed up the tree.   11 鸟儿飞出笼子去了。 **niǎor fēi chū lóngzi qù le** The bird flew out of the cage.   12 学生走进教室来了。 **xuésheng zǒu jìn jiàoshì lái le** The students came into the classroom.   13 老鼠钻回洞去了。 **lǎoshǔ zuān huí dòng qù le** The rat scurried back to its hole.   14 渡船开过河去了。 **dùchuán kāi guò hé qù le** The ferry went across the river (to the other side).

Exercise 21.4   1 衣服都装进箱子里去了。 **yīfu dōu zhuāng jìn xiāngzi li qù le**   2 钱都存在银行里了。 **qián dōu cún zài yínháng li le**   3 垃圾都倒进垃圾桶里去了。 **lājī dōu dào jìn lājītǒng li qù le**   4 你的行李都放在行李架上了。 **nǐ de xíngli dōu fàng zài xínglijià shang le**   5 洗好的衣服都晾在晾衣绳上(边)了。 **xǐ hǎo de yīfu dōu liàng zài liàngyīshéng shang(bian) le**   6 煮好的菜都搁在冰箱里了。 **zhǔ hǎo de cài dōu ge zài bīngxiāng li le**   7 首饰都放在保险箱里。 **shǒushi dōu fàng zài bǎoxiǎnxiāng li**   8 他们搬进城(里)来了。 **tāmen bān jìn chéng (li) lái le**   9 汽车一直开到海边。 **qìchē yīzhí kāi dào hǎi biān**   10 气球一直升到天上去了。 **qìqiú yīzhí shēng dào tiān shang qù le**   11 乌鸦飞到屋顶上去了。 **wūyā fēi dào wūdǐng shang qù le**   12 我的帽子让风给吹到湖里去了。 **wǒ de màozi ràng fēng gěi chuī dào hú li qù le**

Unit 22

Exercise 22.1   1 得很快 **de hěn kuài**   2 干净 **gānjìng**   3 懂 **dǒng**   4 得最好 **de zuì hǎo**   5 熟 **shú/shóu**   6 得很流利 **de hěn liúlì**   7 好 **hǎo**   8 会

huì   9 到 **dào**   10 干 **gān**   11 得很晚 **de hěn wǎn**   12 到/见 **dào/jiàn**
13 得真高 **de zhēn gāo**   14 得很清楚 **de hěn qīngchǔ**   15 得很对 **de hěn duì**   16 住 **zhù**

Exercise 22.2   1 我嗓子疼得饭也吃不下了。 **wǒ sǎngzi téng de fàn yě chī bù xià le** My throat was so sore I could not eat.   2 他游泳游得气也喘不过来了。 **tā yóuyǒng yóu de qì yě chuǎn bù guòlái le** He swam so much he could not get his breath.   3 她跑路跑得腿都酸了。 **tā pǎo lù pǎo de tuǐ dōu suān le** She ran so much/fast that her legs ached.   4 老师说话说得嗓子都哑了。 **lǎoshī shuōhuà shuō de sǎngzi dōu yǎ le** The teacher spoke so much his/her throat became sore/hoarse.   5 我眼睛花得什么也看不清楚了。 **wǒ yǎnjing huā de shénme yě kàn bù qīngchu le** My eyes were so blurred I could not see anything.   6 我高兴得话也说不出来了。 **wǒ gāoxìng de huà yě shuō bù chūlái le** I was so happy I was speechless.   7 哥哥醉得谁也不认识了。 **gēge zuì de shuí yě bù rènshi le** (My) elder brother was so drunk he couldn't recognize anyone.   8 学生写字写得手也酸了。 **xuésheng xiě zì xiě de shǒu yě suān le** The students wrote so much their hands ached.   9 妹妹哭得眼睛都红了。 **mèimei kū de yǎnjing dōu hóng le** (My) younger sister cried so much her eyes were red.   10 她开玩笑开得大家都笑起来了。 **tā kāi wánxiào kāi de dàjiā dōu xiào qǐlái le** Her jokes made everyone begin to laugh. (*lit.* She joked so that everyone began to laugh.)

Exercise 22.3   1 对 **duì**   2 到 **dào**   3 醉了 **zuì le**   4 得很漂亮 **de hěn piàoliang**   5 饱 **bǎo**   6 好 **hǎo**   7 倒 **dǎo**   8 破 **pò**   9 干净 **gānjìng**   10 明白 **míngbai**   11 得很早 **de hěn zǎo**   12 得很晚 **de hěn wǎn**

Exercise 22.4   1 他们跳得很美/很好。 **tāmen tiào de hěn měi/hěn hǎo**   2 救生员游得非常快。 **jiùshēngyuán yóu de fēicháng kuài**   3 学生念/读得很慢。 **xuésheng niàn/dú de hěn màn**   4 孩子吃了很多。 **háizi chī le hěn duō**   5 大家都睡得很熟。 **dàjiā dōu shuì de hěn shú/shóu**   6 演员唱得很糟糕。 **yǎnyuán chàng de hěn zāogāo**   7 我们跑得太累了。 **wǒmen pǎo de tài lèi le**   8 运动员跳得真高。 **yùndòngyuán tiào de zhēn gāo**   9 哥哥喝得不多。 **gēge hē de bù duō**   10 我的同学说得不流利。 **wǒ de tóngxué shuō de bù liúlì**

Unit 23

Exercise 23.1   1 动 **dòng**   2 过去 **guòqù**   3 起来 **qǐlái**   4 着 **zháo**   5 下 **xià**   6 了/掉 **liǎo/diào**   7 起 **qǐ**   8 到/着 **dào/zháo**   9 及 **jí**   10 完/了 **wán/liǎo**

Exercise 23.2   1 吃得饱 **chī de bǎo**   2 站不起来 **zhàn bu qǐlái**   3 喝不下/了 **hē bu xià/liǎo**   4 洗不干净 **xǐ bu gānjìng**   5 坐得舒服 **zuò de shūfu**   6 够不着 **gòu bu zháo**   7 看不清楚 **kàn bu qīngchǔ**   8 记得住 **jì de zhù**   9 合得来 **hé de lái**   10 活得下去 **huó de xiàqù**

Exercise 23.3 1 关不上 **guān bu shàng** 2 晒得干 **shài de gān** 3 坐得下 **zuò de xià** 4 走不动 **zǒu bu dòng** 5 赶得上 **gǎn de shàng** 6 行不通 **xíng bu tòng** 7 合得来合不来 **hé de lái hé bu lái** 8 记得起 **jì de qǐ** 9 禁不住 **jīn bu zhù** 10 听得懂 **tīng de dǒng**

Exercise 23.4 1 我还睡不了。 **wǒ hái shuì bu liǎo** 2 我睡不着。 **wǒ shuì bu zháo** 3 我今天买不了了。 **wǒ jīntiān mǎi bu liǎo le** 4 我买不起。 **wǒ mǎi bu qǐ** 5 我不能告诉你。 **wǒ bù néng gàosu nǐ** 6 我告诉不了你。 **wǒ gàosu bu liǎo nǐ** 7 这件事儿我做不到。 **zhè/zhèi jiàn shìr wǒ zuò bu dào** 8 这件事儿我不能做。 **zhè/zhèi jiàn shìr wǒ bù néng zuò** 9 我说不下去了。 **wǒ shuō bu xiàqù le** 10 我不能说下去了。 **wǒ bù néng shuō xiàqù le**

Unit 24

Exercise 24.1 1 对 **duì** 2 和/跟 **hé/gēn** 3 和/跟 **hé/gēn** 4 向/朝/往 **xiàng/cháo/wàng** 5 对 **duì** 6 向/朝/往 **xiàng/cháo/wàng** 7 向/朝 **xiàng/cháo** 8 和/跟 **hé/gēn**

Exercise 24.2 1 为 **wèi** 2 替 **tì**; 给 **gěi** 3 给 **gěi** 4 替 **tì** 5 为 **wèi** 6 为 **wèi** 7 替 **tì** 8 为 **wèi**

Exercise 24.3 1 我们朝哪个方向走？ **wǒmen cháo nǎ/něi gè fāngxiàng zǒu** 2 她对工作很负责。 **tā duì gōngzuò hěn fùzé** 3 这本书对我学习很有用。 **zhè/zhèi běn shū duì wǒ xuéxí hěn yǒuyòng** 4 小李正在跟石老师谈话。 **xiǎo lǐ zhèngzài gēn shí lǎoshī tánhuà** 5 他朝我点点头。 **tā cháo wǒ diǎndiǎn tóu** 6 我们应该向他学习。 **wǒmen yīnggāi xiàng tā xuéxí** 7 我替你写信。 **wǒ tì nǐ xiě xìn** 8 我今晚给你打电话。 **wǒ jīn wǎn gěi nǐ dǎ diànhuà** 9 我给你写信。 **wǒ gěi nǐ xiě xìn** 10 这个小镇与那个小镇一样古老。 **zhè/zhèi gè xiǎo zhèn yǔ nà/nèi gè xiǎo zhèn yīyàng gǔlǎo**

Exercise 24.4 1 离 **lí** 2 从 **cóng** 3 从 **cóng** 4 从 **cóng**; 到 **dào** 5 离 **lí** 6 从 **cóng**; 到 **dào** 7 离 **lí** 8 从 **cóng**

Exercise 24.5 1 由 **yóu** 2 从 **cóng** 3 由 **yóu** 4 由 **yóu**/从 **cóng** 5 从 **cóng** 6 从 **cóng** 7 从 **cóng** 8 由 **yóu**

Exercise 24.6 1 向 **xiàng** 2 沿 **yán** 3 于 **yú** 4 于 **yú** 5 往 **wàng** 6 离 **lí** 7 从 **cóng** 8 于 **yú** 9 从 **cóng** 10 从 **cóng**

Exercise 24.7 1 请跟我来。 **qǐng gēn wǒ lái** 2 我明天给你打电话。 **wǒ míngtiān gěi nǐ dǎ diànhuà** 3 他们对我们很友好。 **tāmen duì wǒmen hěn yǒuhǎo** 4 这儿离车站不很远。 **zhèr lí chēzhàn bù hěn yuǎn** 5 我每天从九点工作到五点。**wǒ měi tiān cóng jiǔ diǎn gōngzuò dào wǔ diǎn** 6 沿街

都是汽车。 **yán jiē dōu shì qìchē** 7 这件事儿全由我负责吗？ **zhè/zhèi jiàn shìr quán yóu wǒ fùzé ma** 8 你为什么不给他们写信？ **nǐ wèi shénme bù gěi tāmen xiě xìn**

Unit 25

Exercise 25.1 1 为了不误火车，他决定走近路。 **wèile bù wù huǒchē | tā juédìng zǒu jìn lù** 2 为了看那场足球赛，小李开了两小时的车到伦敦去。 **wèile kàn nà/nèi chǎng zúqiúsài | xiǎo lǐ kāi le liǎng xiǎoshí de chē dào lúndūn qù** 3 为了庆祝女儿大学毕业她举行了一个舞会。 **wèile qìngzhù nǚ'ér dàxué bìyè tā jǔxíng le yī gè wǔhuì** 4 为了看这个电影他特意从法国来。 **wèile kàn zhè/zhèi gè diànyǐng tā tèyì cóng fǎguó lái** 5 为了照顾那个病人，护士一夜没睡。 **wèile zhàogù nà/nèi gè bìngrén | hùshi yī yè méi shuì** 6 为了参加一个重要会议经理到北京去。 **wèile cānjiā yī gè zhòngyào huìyì jīnglǐ dào běijīng qù**

Exercise 25.2 1 对 **duì** 2 关于 **guānyú** 3 至于 **zhìyú** 4 对 **duì** 5 至于 **zhìyú** 6 关于 **guānyú** 7 关于 **guānyú** 8 对(于) **duì(yù)**

Exercise 25.3 1 动物园里除了老虎、狮子之外/以外，还有熊猫。**dòngwùyuán li chúle lǎohǔ | shīzi zhī wài/yǐ wài | hái yǒu xióngmǎo** 2 班里除了中国人之外/以外，还有英国人和法国人。 **bān li chúle zhōngguó rén zhī wài/yǐ wài | hái yǒu yīngguó rén hé fǎguó rén** 3 我除了羊肉之外/以外，什么都吃。 **wǒ chúle yángròu zhī wài/yǐ wài | shénme dōu chī** 4 陈小姐除了会弹吉它之外/以外，还会弹钢琴。 **chén xiǎojie chúle huì tán jítā zhī wài/yǐ wài | hái huì tán gāngqín**

Exercise 25.4 1 根据 **gēnjù** 2 凭 **píng** 3 根据 **gēnjù** 4 凭 **píng** 5 按照 **ànzhào** 6 凭着 **píng zhe**

Exercise 25.5 1 老师对(于)我的学习很关心。 **lǎoshī duì(yú) wǒ de xuéxí hěn guānxīn** 2 我进城去买东西。 **wǒ jìn chéng qù mǎi dōngxi** 3 correct 4 根据气象预报，明天下大雨。 **gēnjù qìxiàng yùbào | míngtiān xià dà yǔ** 5 correct 6 对(于)孩子调皮的问题，除了家长之外/以外，学校老师也应该管。 **duì(yú) háizi tiǎopí de wèntí | chúle jiāzhǎng zhī wài/yǐ wài | xuéxiào lǎoshī yě yīnggāi guǎn**

Exercise 25.6 1 至于这个问题，我没有意见。 **zhìyú zhè/zhèi gè wèntí | wǒ méi yǒu yìjian** 2 对于这个问题，我十分担心。 **duìyú zhè/zhèi gè wèntí | wǒ shífēn dānxīn** 3 除了星期三之外/以外，我每天都能来。 **chúle xīngqī sān zhī wài/yǐ wài | wǒ měi tiān dōu néng lái** 4 至于我们能不能来，请你问我太太/夫人。 **zhìyú wǒmen néng bù néng lái | qǐng nǐ wèn wǒ tàitai/fūrén** 5 除了她之外/以外，大家都喜欢吃中国菜。 **chúle tā zhī wài/yǐ wài | dàjiā dōu**

xǐhuan chī zhōngguó cài   6 我进城去看一个朋友。 **wǒ jìn chéng qù kàn yī gè péngyou** 7 为了下结论，这个问题他们讨论了五个小时/钟头。 **wèile xià jiélùn | zhè/zhèi gè wèntí tāmen tǎolùn le wǔ gè xiǎoshí/zhōngtóu**   8 政府根据什么执行这种政策？ **zhèngfǔ gēnjù shénme zhíxíng zhè/zhèi zhǒng zhèngcè**